Military Uniforms
in Colour

WRITTEN AND ILLUSTRATED BY

Preben Kannik

ENGLISH EDITION EDITED BY

William Y. Carman

BLANDFORD PRESS
LONDON

First English Edition published in 1968
by Blandford Press Ltd, 1968 High Holborn,
London W.C.1.
English text © 1968 Blandford Press
Copyright for the World © Politikens Forlag, 1967.

Originally published in Danish
as *Alverdens Uniformer I Farver*
by Politikens Forlag.
Translated into English by
John Hewish.

SBN 71370482 9

Text filmset by Keyspools Ltd, Golborne, Lancs.
Colour printed in Denmark by F. E. Bording A/s.
Text printed and bound in Great Britain
by Fletcher & Son Ltd, Norwich.

CONTENTS

The uniforms are illustrated in chronological order, grouped according to the wars listed below. The numbers are those of the first uniform in the group, in both the illustrations and the text.

Contents

PREFACE

MILITARY UNIFORMS OF THE WORLD IN COLOUR is the first real manual of its kind ever published in the English language, as well as the most comprehensive guide to uniforms available in the world today at a popular price. It illustrates and describes more than five hundred uniforms worn past and present by the navies, armies and air forces of the world. They are dealt with war by war, in chronological order, from the germ of military uniforming in the bodyguards and household guards of the fifteenth and sixteenth centuries, *via* those of the European and colonial wars of the seventeenth, eighteenth and nineteenth, fought by troops in bright colours, to the field-grey and khaki of the two World Wars. The blue berets and steel helmets of the United Nations peace keeping forces with the traditional uniforms of guards and ceremonial units, logically bring up the rear of this cavalcade of uniforms.

The text forms an invaluable supplement to the illustrations, giving as it does full information as to the design, cut, colour-combination, ornamentation, marks of rank and other distinctive features. Functional aspects of dress and equipment are also explained. But its interest transcends the individual uniform described: read as a whole it forms an invaluable account of the development of uniforms through the ages, not only as worn by national armies but also in relation to the various branches of the service comprising them.

There is a glossary of military terms and a comprehensive index which facilitates quick reference to the uniforms which are grouped under countries or states.

Acknowledgements

The production of a work of this order has involved comprehensive research by the author and illustrator, into uniforms and uniform components, not to mention illustrations, regulations, books and newspapers both in and out of museums on a world-wide basis. It would clearly be impossible to mention here all the scholars and writers whose work has been consulted, or all the collections studied during its preparation. Thanks are however due to the German scholars, the late Herbert Knötel and Herbert Sieg; also to Paul Goudime-Levkovitch of Russia and C. C. P. Lawson of England whose assistance was vital. Likewise to W. Y. Carman of England, Frederick P. Todd of America and J. Hefter of Mexico, for their never-failing assistance. A special word of thanks is due to the staff of the *Tøjhusmuseet* in Copenhagen, whose valuable collections have been available during the preparation of the book.

The Editors

INTRODUCTION

Military uniforming as at present understood, that is, as a fixed form of dress officially prescribed and which indicates that its wearer belongs to a particular unit, branch or force, is of relatively recent date in the historical context.

Uniforms proper came in with the formation of standing armies after the Thirty Years War. It is hardly possible to give the credit for inventing uniforms to a particular country, even less to a particular individual. The idea appeared more or less simultaneously in several countries. From earliest times military clothing had a tendency towards uniformity, without being uniform in the true sense. There were various reasons for this: as with the Roman legions, uniformity could result from quantity-produced and state-supplied equipment. The need to distinguish friend from foe also played a part.

Military dress is strongly influenced by tradition: this is a factor that holds good for all periods and cultures. Even today, as in earlier periods, uniforms bear a firm impress of the familiar. Long after the original function of a piece of equipment is forgotten it is retained as a traditional or symbolic ornament in military dress. The need to distinguish friend from foe is counteracted by the tendency in uniforms to follow the dominant fashion— usually set by the dominant power.

General fashion also influences uniforms, and they should be considered against the background of, or combined with, current civilian fashion of the period. The difference between uniform and civilian dress has been less than one might think at first.

To identify friend from foe it was necessary as early as the Middle Ages to use some form of identification. So, early in the fifteenth century, we find the English troops wearing red crosses on chest and back, the French and Swiss white crosses, and the Imperial German troops red St. Andrew's or Burgundian crosses. These were later replaced by sashes, worn round the waist or over the shoulder. The colours of these sashes, or field emblems as they were called, were laid down by the commander, who often chose his personal armorial colour.

Frederick II of Denmark laid down in his Articles of War in 1563 that 'each man (in the royal army) must wear a token in his hat, on his clothing or over his armour, in the form of a red and yellow band.' The colours were taken from the ancestral arms of the Oldenburg royal house. When Christian IV entered the Thirty Years War he chose blue and orange sashes, with a white hat feather. Later, in 1625, he reverted to the Oldenburg colours, which remained in use for this purpose. They are found today, for instance, in the small gilt sword-knot called the *port-épée* suspended from an officer's sabre-hilt. The sash frequently changed colour in Sweden. Gustavus Adolphus II's army wore blue sashes during the Thirty Years War, but Charles X adopted blue and yellow, the combination still in use. Among other Thirty Years War sashes, red was worn by Imperial and Spanish troops, white by French, orange by the Netherlands, and green by Saxony.

Besides the permanent emblems, it was often necessary to use special signs, such as a wisp of straw or sprig of leaves worn prominently on the hat or helmet, especially for a major battle. Even when uniforms were in general use, it was often necessary to retain such signs, especially when the armies were formed of contingents from several nations.

Of course uniforms evolved only in stages, and their introduction caused various problems. Originally the uniform or set of equipment was part of the soldier's pay, and its various elements actually became his own property after use.

For the civilian, uniforming was primarily an arrangement to reassure him that the soldier fighting on his behalf had sufficient clothing and equipment. So, to begin with, there were special regulations specifying the items that the latter must possess. Usually it was the task of the head or commander of the regiment to administer the stores department—not always to the advantage of the troops. Every guinea saved on the stores account went into his own pocket. When the regiment was disbanded or amalgamated with another, both used and new equipment had to be transferred or dispatched to other regiments, consequently a certain centralisation of stores administration developed.

When uniform was in its infancy, the regimental commander naturally had considerable influence on dress. But with the greater power of the civil administration, and the evolution of centralized government, the sway of the regimental commanders was curtailed, and very precise instructions were issued concerning the appearance and wearing of the outfit.

Attempts were made at first to give each regiment its own uniform, but later it proved more practical to dress each branch, or even the whole army, in uniforms of a single basic colour. The regiments could then be identified by collars, lapels, cuffs, buttons and trimming in different colours, so that each regiment had its own colour-combination. The style was generally the same for a whole army, though certain units, such as the hussars, often had a special uniform.

By the beginning of the nineteenth century the larger part of an army, usually the infantry, wore identical uniforms, the individual regiments being identifiable only by the number or mark on buttons or cap. This tendency continued through the century in most armies, though it was counteracted by a certain dogged retention of the traditional. At the commencement of the twentieth century, most armies wore uniforms of a common style throughout, varying in colour only according to the branch. Guards and cavalry usually still wore special—and specially decorative—uniforms.

In the days of muzzle-loaders and black powder, the

colour of uniform was immaterial because of the short range of the weapons, but breech-loaders and, especially, smokeless powder led to the choice of uniforms of sombre shade. The soldier's movements had to be as inconspicuous as possible, so that a uniform matching his background was a necessity. In the Great War period this was the principle in all armies. Meanwhile the single standard uniform came in generally. From now on, all soldiers in a given army wore uniform of the same cut and colour, and the identification marks were reduced to inconspicuous numbers, marks, narrow coloured borders and the like.

The steady development of arms has required the utmost degree of protection from the uniform, with unimpaired mobility. Today's battledress is further from normal civilian dress than uniform has ever been. Consequently, in many countries, special military uniforms are being adopted for wear on leave, guard-duty etc.

It was not possible to include all the uniforms worn throughout history in this work. The principle behind the selection has been to include a characteristic uniform from each country involved in the various conflicts dealt with, to give, with the help of the written text, a general impression of the uniforms of the period. Although, however, the aim was to show typical examples, certain more singular and bizarre specimens are also included.

UNIFORMS IN GREAT BRITAIN

The origins of uniforms are lost in the early days of antiquity. Although it might seem logical to assume that uniforms originated in the garb of a personal bodyguard or with a company of armed retainers bearing a common link with their commander, evidence indicates a national connection at an early date.

The carrying of a standard for a rallying point served to produce a homogeneous body of fighting men in the ancient world but the gradual disappearance of man under armour and the use of surcoats brought about a necessity to recognize friend from foe. In the Crusades white surcoats were worn and although this barrier may have checked the sun's rays from the armour, it was difficult to know the soldiers of one nation from another. The common uniting Cross was worn in different colours by different nations. Thus the red Cross of St. George became the mark of the English soldier, not only in the Holy Land but also back at home. The Scots had the Saltire of St. Andrew and during the fourteenth century these crosses were worn on the jacks of the opposing English and Scottish forces.

The rise of heraldry brought distinction to the individual but not at once to the fighting man. The wars of the Middle Ages saw the use of badges on the retainers' garments, like the White Feather worn by the men of the Black Prince. Examples of special clothing were not only personal but indicated places of origin like the green and white coats of the Welsh archers of the Black Prince and the red and white garments for the citizens of London. For the various contingents raised in cities, towns and shires, a 'jackette' was supplied at local expense. Canterbury troops were dressed in yellow in the sixteenth century, the troops of Norfolk had coats of red guarded with white, which colours the levy from Lancashire also wore. Service in Ireland was considered a greater trial because of the wet weather and coats of 'sadd green colour or russett' were worn. However, on the continent the English soldier was more and more wearing a red coat and this soon became his distinguishing mark.

By the time of the English Civil War the regiments belonging to the king were clothed in a uniform fashion. Both the King's and the Queen's Life Guard of Foot wore red coats as did another raised to protect the king against his Parliament. But there were others dressed in blue, white, yellow, etc. and the Parliamentary army also had a variety of coats. Thus there was little to distinguish friend from foe in the heat of battle. The sash worn by English officers was red or crimson and of course worn by the king's troops. Some Parliamentarian officers also wore this colour but the Earl of Essex had the unusual colour of orange or tawny for his standards and this hue was used for the scarves of the Roundheads on some occasions. In the heat of battle such distinguishing sashes could be lost or wilfully misplaced so that the true cause of a person would be unknown. In some measure the use of the field sign (a piece of white or a green sprig) and the field word (like 'God and the King' and 'Lord of Hosts' used respectively by Royalist and Parliamentary troops) helped, but even these were not foolproof measures. When the New Model Army was formed in 1645 Cromwell gave red coats to all the soldiers, a colour which his son, Richard as Protector, continued to use later in the Interregnum.

The troops of King Charles the II in exile continued to wear the red coat on the battlefields of Europe and this was the colour worn by the returning troops at the Restoration. The king's troops—horse guards, foot guards and even artillery—wore red coats with the royal blue facings. Red and blue were the 'fields' of the coat of arms for England and France combined, long used by kings of England. The Queen Catherine of Braganza brought sea-green facings to the regiments bearing her name and the Duke of York had yellow as his distinction.

A blue uniform was worn by the Royal Regiment of Horse Guards, a colour which became more popular when William of Orange came to be king of England. The Dutch troops wore blue coats and newly raised regiments took this colour also, but when the war with James II ceased, red coats came again into favour, and continued so in the reign of the Georges. The artillery man now took a blue coat and later in the century light cavalry changed to dark blue coats. The advent of rifle corps brought green coats, but the main distinction was in the facing colour, i.e. the lining of the coat which showed in the turned-up cuffs, the turned-down collar and the turned-back lapels when they came in use. Colonels of regiments who paid for their men's uniforms frequently chose facings which had a connection with their coat-of-arms, but later facing colours were chosen more arbitrarily. In fact, the reforms of 1881 brought the idea of white facings for English regiments, yellow for Scottish and green for Irish, etc., but these dull distinctions were eroded and many traditional facings came back into use.

The heyday of the red coat was nearly over for the outbreak of the First World War saw khaki as the general uniform, and in the post-war period the red coat was not re-introduced for infantry of the line. Officers were permitted their full dress uniforms at levees and other special occasions right up to the outbreak of the Second World War. Later military bands were permitted full dress uniforms, presumably for the purpose of recruiting, but the infantry man never made a complete return to the red coat, although it was occasionally to be seen at tattoos and tournaments.

The introduction of a blue uniform, firstly as a Coronation dress and then as No. 1 'blues' was a poor substitute for the old full dress. The addition of embellishments and special features after the Second World War produced a slight return to the old traditional dress, but it is abroad in many of the now separated parts of the Empire that the full dress may still be seen.

The Scottish troops, however, cling to much of their

national dress—the kilt, the sporran, the hose and gaiters, the ancient Scottish sidearms, and at least a couple of the Scottish headdresses—and one occasionally sees a mounted section of the Royal Scots Greys in full dress. The Royal Company of Archers still act as the Royal Bodyguards in Scotland and hold periodical competitions dressed in their picturesque uniforms.

In the case of the Royal Navy and the Royal Air Force, their more modern uniforms are worn without much loss of tradition, although in the case of officers the Royal Navy has lost its cocked hat and the long tailed dress coat with elaborate epaulettes while the Royal Air Force has lost its unusual plumed headdress based on a flying helmet.

In a different category are the Sovereign's own troops. Both the Household Cavalry and the Foot Guards were restored to their full dress after the recent World Wars, and are to be seen carrying out guard duties and ceremonial parades in both London and Windsor. The brilliant idea of the late King George VI which resulted in the formation of the King's Troop of the Royal Horse Artillery in full dress, was most successful, and the occasions on which they appear firing salutes, etc. are popular with the public. Two of the most ancient guards of the Sovereign—Her Majesty's Body Guard of the Honourable Corps of Gentlemen-at-Arms and Her Majesty's Body Guard of the Yeomen of the Guard still appear in their ceremonial roles wearing their ancient and traditional uniforms.

W. Y. Carman

A NOTE ON NOMENCLATURE

In such a work as this, covering as it does many armies all around the world and over a long period of time, it is not surprising that the reader may find some terms difficult to understand or even what he may consider an inconsistent use of basic terms. It is not possible to be consistent, for each nation has its own particular development and word for the basic soldier.

Even the name for the common British infantry man—the private—cannot be applied to all nations and times. The private, a term used in the British army and the early days of the United States, is not always applicable to the lowest ranks in the infantry. At the beginning of the seventeenth century, the terms used included musketeer, caliver man and pikeman and later in the century came the grenadier. In the next century came the light infantry man and the rifleman as well as the fusilier, more or less an honour title. The militia man and the volunteer indicate terms of service rather than the contract of the regular soldier. It has been suggested that this 'private contract' gave the soldier his name although the origin is given elsewhere as from the Latin 'privatus'—a deprived man.

Abroad the term 'private' is replaced by many other words. The word 'soldier' (based on a fighting man who was paid) was popular. Germany had 'soldat', Italy had 'soldato' and France 'soldat' as well as 'homme'. But the specialist use of weapons gave the basic soldier a special name. The fusil or flintlock gave the French infantry man in the eighteenth century the title of fusilier whereas the German soldier continued the use of 'musketeer' long after it disappeared in the British army. The German huntsmen were armed with rifles when that weapon was used extensively in the German regiments the men were called 'jägers' meaning hunters. The French used the word 'chasseur' but the British found 'rifleman' sufficient.

In France during the seventeenth century there had

been 'pikeniers' and 'mousquetaires' as in England, but when the pikeman disappeared early in the next century a variety of terms came in use—the 'fusilier' as mentioned already, the 'chasseur', the 'carabineer' and the 'voltigeur'. In the United States the term 'enlisted man' had a venerable antiquity but specialist names like 'sharpshooter' and 'parachutist' followed the practice of other nations.

Promotion also brings problems. In the sixteenth century the non-commissioned officers consisted of sergeants and corporals but today each nation has a wide variety of N.C.O.s carrying out a variety of tasks and ranging from temporary local unpaid lance-corporal up to regimental sergeant-major. Foreign nations frequently have their own structure, the ranks of which will not equate with the British terms. The Nazi forces had at least six different groups of ranks which caused difficulties even among themselves, as to precedence. Thus in some cases it has been found less confusing to leave the rank in the original language rather than give a misleading equivalent.

Apart from the infantryman, the basic cavalry man also had variations. In the early days of standing armies, the common man was the trooper who rode in a troop of horse. Abroad he could be a 'reiter' (rider) or 'cavalier' (cavalry man). While the use of armour continued 'cuirassier' was a common term abroad but not in Great Britain. Our regiments of Horse who had worn the cuirass were converted into Dragoon Guards, an economic saving and the ceremonial cuirass was revived early in the nineteenth century for use in Household Cavalry but not with the title of 'cuirassier'.

To move infantry quickly from place to place they were given light horses and they acquired the title of dragoons, said to have come from the flaming match of the firearms. The dragoon eventually became a fully fledged cavalry man and developed his own offshoot— the light cavalry man, who on the continent was called a hussar. Some of these light dragoon regiments were converted early in the nineteenth century to hussars but the first troops to be officially named hussars were the 11th Hussars formed for the Prince Consort in 1840. Even the regiments converted to lancers after Napoleon's defeat were still officially known as light dragoons until the Crimean war. Men of these new arms were known as hussars and lancers. On the continent the term hussar was widely used but 'jäger-zu-pferde' or 'chasseur à cheval' indicated a type of light cavalry who used a carbine with effect from horseback. To add to the confusion the Bavarian cavalry used a French term 'chevaulégers' to indicate their light cavalry.

There are other arms of service which have their own special terms. The artillery has different words in different countries. In England the Train of Artillery was specially raised in times of conflict. The gunner of early days was a trained man who took charge and fired his gun. He was aided by mattrosses who were not far short of labourers and who also helped with defence. The bombardier was originally in charge of a bombard and corporals and lance-corporals were also on the establishment, the term of lance-bombardier not coming into use until after the First World War. Abroad the gunner might be named a 'cannonier', and 'artillerist' or even a 'constable'.

Originally in England the engineer was a specialist officer and the lowly rank and file were sappers and miners. The term 'sapper' may be confusing abroad for the 'sappeur' in the French army was not much more than a carpenter, known as a pioneer in the British forces. An interesting member of continental troops was the cantinière, the vivandière or marketendrin, a woman who accompanied the troops carrying a canteen with spirits, or refreshments. She was never a part of the British Army.

W. Y. Carman

1. The Vatican (The Papal States): The Swiss Guards. Guardsman, 1506.
2. England: The Yeomen of the Guard. Yeoman, 1520.
3. Spain: The Noble Guard. Guardsman, 1646.
4. France: Musketeers of the King. Musketeer, 1665.

5

6

7

8

5. France: The Carignan-Sallières Regiment. Ensign, 1665.
6. France: Amiral de France Regiment. Officer, 1670.
7. France: The Dauphin's Regiment of Dragoons. Officer, 1675.
8. France: Swiss Regiment 'Greder'. Musketeer, 1673.

The Dutch Wars
1652-1678

9. England: Foot Guards. Musketeer, 1660.
10. England: King's Troop of Horse Guards. Officer, 1670.
11. England: Coldstream Guards. Officer, Tangier, 1669.
12. England: Dragoon, 1672.

13. Netherlands: Artillery Officer, 1668.
14. Hesse: The Landgraf's Leibwache. Musketeer, 1660.
15. Saxony: Graf von Promnitz Cuirassiers. Trooper, 1660.
16. Bavaria: Steinau Infantry. Officer, 1670.

17. Austria: Saxe-Coburg Regiment. Musketeer, 1690.
18. Austria: Artillery. Gunner, 1671.
19. Brandenburg (Prussia): Electress Dorothea of Brandenburg's Regiment.
    Musketeer, 1681.
20. Savoy: Regiment 'Guardie'. Musketeer, 1664.

21
22
23
24

21. Denmark: Queen's Life Regiment. Pikeman, 1675.
22. Denmark: Prince George's Regiment. Staff officer, 1675.
23. Denmark: Life Regiment of Cavalry. Trooper, 1675.
24. Denmark: 1st Fyn National Regiment. Musketeer, 1676.

25. Sweden: East Gotland Infantry Regiment. Musketeer, 1675.
26. Sweden: Skaraborg Infantry Regiment. Ensign, 1675.
27. Sweden: Hälsinge Infantry Regiment. Musketeer, 1675.
28. Sweden: National Cavalry. Trooper, 1676.

29. Spain: Dragoon. 1690.
30. Austria: Infantry Regiment, 'Deutschmeister'. Fifer, 1700.
31. Hanover: Infantry Regiment, 'von Podewils'. N.C.O., 1687.
32. Bavaria: Puech Infantry Regiment. Musketeer, 1682.

The War of the Palatinate

1688–1697

33. Savoy: Artillery. Gunner, 1698.
34. Netherlands: Life Guard of Foot. Musketeer, 1691.
35. France: Gardes françaises Regiment. Grenadier, 1697.
36. England: Queen's Troop of Horse Grenadiers. Grenadier, 1688.

37
38
39
40

37. Denmark: The Grenadier Corps. Grenadier, 1709.
38. Sweden: The Drabant Corps. Drabant, 1700.
39. Russia: 'Nichegorodski' Infantry Regiment. Musketeer, 1711.
40. Russia: Dragoons. Officer, 1701.

The Great Northern War

1700–1721

41. Sweden: Life Guards. Musketeer, 1709.
42. Saxony: Life Guard of Horse. Officer, 1700.
43. Poland: Light Horse. Trooper, 1702.
44. Brandenburg (Prussia): Infantry Regiment, 'von Schlabrendorff'. Musketeer, 1700.

45. Austria: 'Bayreuth' Dragoons. Grenadier officer, 1713.
46. Austria: 'Hasslingen' Infantry Regiment. Musketeer, 1713.
47. Netherlands: 'Van Frieheim' Infantry Regiment. Grenadier, 1701.
48. Great Britain: The Princess of Wales's Own Regiment of Foot (later the Queen's).
    Grenadier, 1715.

49. France: 'De Bourbon' Regiment. Drummer, 1713.
50. France: 'Royal Cravattes' Cavalry Regiment. Trooper, 1701.
51. Spain: Numancia Dragoon Regiment. Private, 1707.
52. Bavaria: Leib Regiment. Musketeer, 1701.

53
54
55
56

53. Savoy: Marine Regiment. Musketeer with Colonel's Colour, 1701.
54. Denmark: Prince Carl's Regiment. Musketeer, 1701.
55. Hanover: Von Bülow's Dragoons. Officer, 1706.
56. German Empire: Salzburg Regiment. Musketeer, 1705.

57
58
59
60

57. Poland-Saxony: Guard Cuirassiers. Officer, 1734.
58. Poland-Saxony: Foot Guards. Bagpiper, 1732.
59. Poland-Saxony: Guard Musketeers. Officer, 1735.
60. Russia: Infantry of the Line. Grenadier, 1740.

The War of the Austrian Succession
1740–1748

61. Austria: Emmanuel of Portugal Cuirassiers. Captain, 1740.
62. Austria: Nádasdy Hussars. Man, 1743.
63. Austria: Kokényesdi Hungarian Infantry Regiment. Private, 1742.
64. Austria: Vasquez de Binas Italian Infantry Regiment. Grenadier drummer, 1740

65. Prussia: Fürst Moritz Infantry Regiment. Grenadier, 1741.
66. Prussia: The Artillery. Bombardier, 1740.
67. France: Royal-Comtois Infantry Regiment. Musketeer, 1740.
68. France: De Beauffremont Dragoons. Man, 1740.

69. Bavaria: Leib Regiment. Grenadier, 1740.
70. Palatinate: Graf von Hatzfeld's Carabiniers. Officer, 1748.
71. Saxony: Queen's Regiment. Drummer, 1745.
72. Saxony: Artillery. Gunner, 1740.

73. Russia: Preobraschenski Guards. Grenadier officer, 1740.
74. Spain: 'Soboya' Infantry Regiment. Ensign, 1748.
75. Sardinia: 'Sardinia' Regiment. Musketeer, 1744.
76. Naples: General, 1740.

77. Hanover: Horse Grenadiers. Trooper, 1742.
78. Great Britain: Major General Howard's Regiment of Foot (The Buffs). Private, 1742.
79. Schwartzburg: Infantry Regiment, 'von Diepenbroik'. Officer, 1740.
80. Netherlands: Foot Guards. Pioneer, 1750.

81. Great Britain: The King's Own Regiment of Foot (later 4th Foot'. Officer, 1743.
82. Hessen-Kassel: Prince Maximilian's Regiment. Grenadier, 1750.
83–84. Great Britain: The Black Watch (later 42nd Foot). Bagpiper and corporal,
    1745.

85. Prussia: Von Ruesch Hussar Regiment. Hussar, 1757.
86. Prussia: Margraf Friedrich von Bayreuth Dragoons. Officer, 1757.
87. Prussia: Von Seydlitz Cuirassiers. Trooper, 1762.
88. Prussia: Erbprinz von Hessen-Kassel Fusilier Regiment nr. 48. Drummer, 1759.

The Seven Years War

1756–1763

89. Austria: Erzherzog Josef (Archduke Joseph) Dragoons. Man, 1763.
90. Austria: Bethlen Hussars. Officer, 1760.
91. Austria: Graf Franz Gyulai Hungarian Infantry Regiment. Musketeer, 1759.
92. Austria: Gradisca Slavonian Frontier Regiment. Man, 1759.

The Seven Years War
1756-1763

93. Saxony: Prince Xaver Infantry Regiment. Musketeer, 1756.
94. Saxony: Brühl Dragoon Regiment. Dragoon, 1756.
95. Sweden: North Scania Cavalry Regiment. Trooper, 1757.
96. Sweden: Södermanland Infantry Regiment. Grenadier, 1757.

97. Russia: Infantry of the Line. Grenadier, 1756.
98. Russia: Artillery. Gunner, 1757.
99. Russia: Moldavian Hussars. Hussar, 1756.
100. Russia: Pandour Regiment. Grenadier N.C.O., 1756.

The Seven Years War
1756–1763

101. Hanover: Von Scheither Infantry Regiment. Grenadier, 1756.
102. Hanover: Von Müller Dragoons. Grenadier officer, 1761.
103. Great Britain: 11th Dragoons. Man of light squadron, 1757.
104. Great Britain: 20th Regiment of Foot. Grenadier, 1759.

105. France: Royal Lorraine Infantry Regiment. Grenadier, 1756.
106. France: Royal Regiment of Cavalry. Trumpeter, 1756.
107. France: Berchény Hussars. Hussar, 1756.
108. France: Maison du Roi Chevau-légers. Trooper, 1760.

109

110

111

112

109. Bavaria: Electoral Guards. Guardsman, 1760.
110. Württemberg: Infantry Regiment 'von Roeder'. Grenadier, 1757.
111. Brunswick-Wolfenbüttel: Leib Regiment. Drummer, 1760.
112. Baden: District Regiment Baden-Baden. Grenadier, 1760.

113. German Empire: Frankish district. Ferentheil Infantry. Grenadier, 1760.
114. Saxe-Gotha: Garde du Corps. Trooper, 1760.
115. Schaumburg-Lippe: Carabinier Squadron. Trooper, 1756.
116. German Empire: Upper Rhine District. Artillery Fireworker, 1760.

117. Great Britain: Royal Navy. Commander, 1756.
118. Great Britain: Light Infantry in North America. Man, 1758.
119. France: 'Volontaire de Bussy' in India. Grenadier, 1756.
120. France: Royal Navy. Commander, 1763.

121. Poland: Royal Hussars. Captain, 1770.
122. Poland: Confederation Cavalry. Man, 1769.
123. Russia: Chevalier Guard. Man, 1772.
124. Russia: General Field-Marshal. 1768.

125. U.S.A.: Washington's Guard. Man, 1776.
126. U.S.A.: 1st Georgia Regiment. Private, 1777.
127. U.S.A.: 3rd Continental Artillery. Officer, 1776.
128. U.S.A.: 2nd Canadian Regiment. Corporal of light company, 1778.

129

130

131

132

129. Great Britain: 37th Regiment of Foot. Grenadier officer, 1776.
130. Great Britain: 64th Regiment of Foot. Private, 1777.
131. Great Britain: 5th Regiment of Foot. Man of light company, 1778.
132. Great Britain: 42nd Royal Highland Regiment of Foot. Private, 1783.

133. Hessen-Hanau: Erbprinz Regiment. Grenadier, 1776.
134. Brunswick: Prinz Ludwig Dragoons. Dragoon, 1777.
135. Brunswick: Regiment 'von Riedesel'. Man of light company, 1776.
136. Hessen-Kassel: Rifle Corps. Rifleman, 1780.

137. U.S.A.: New Jersey Infantry. Private, 1780.
138. U.S.A.: 2nd Continental Light Dragoons. Drummer, 1780.
139. U.S.A.: Marine Corps. Marine, 1780.
140. U.S.A.: 4th Massachusetts Regiment. Man of light company, 1781.

The American War of Independence

1776–1783

141. France: 'Touraine' Infantry Regiment. Officer, 1780.
142. France: 'Gâtineau' Infantry Regiment. Grenadier, 1780.
143. Great Britain: Queen's Rangers. Hussar, 1781.
144. France: Lauzun's Legion. Hussar officer, 1780.

145. Russia: Life Cuirassier Regiment. Cuirassier, 1788.
146. Sweden: East Gotland Cavalry Regiment. Officer, 1788.
147. Russia: Line Infantry. Musketeer, 1788.
148. Sweden: Kronobergs Regiment. Musketeer, 1788.

149

150

151

152

149. France: Swiss Guards. Grenadier, 1792.
150. France: National Guards. Grenadier, 1792.
151. France: Artillery. Gunner, 1792.
152. France: 39th Infantry Regiment. Fusilier, 1792.

153

154

155

156

153. Austria: Infantry Regiment nr. 42. Fusilier, 1792.
154. Prussia: Infantry Regiment 'Teufel von Birkensee'. Sharpshooter, 1792.
155. Hessen-Darmstadt: Chevauleger Regiment. Officer, 1798.
156. Hessen-Kassel: Light Infantry Battalion. Man, 1793.

157

158

159

160

157. France: General, 1797.
158. France: Hussards de la Liberté. Hussar, 1793.
159. France: 5th Chasseurs-à-cheval. Trumpeter, 1797.
160. France: Light Infantry. Officer, 1793.

The French Revolution

1792–1804

161. Prussia: Hussar Regiment nr. 11. Officer, 1792.
162. Prussia: Fusilier Battalion 'Stuttenheim'. Fusilier, 1798.
163. Austria: Lower Austrian State Corps. Private, 1797.
164. Austria: 'Degelmann' Lancers. Man, 1796.

165
166
167
168

165. Great Britain: Coldstream Guards. Man of light company, 1794.
166. Great Britain: 14th (Bedfordshire) Regiment of Foot. Private, 1794.
167. Netherlands: 12th National Regiment. Private, 1791.
168. Portugal: Infantry officer, 1798.

169
170
171
172

169. Baden: Leib Regiment. Grenadier corporal, 1793.
170. Bavaria: 2nd Fusilier Regiment. Drum-major, 1793.
171. Kur-Mainz: Hussar Corps. Hussar, 1790.
172. German Empire, Swabian District: 'Württemberg' Dragoons. Man, 1793.

173

174

175   176

173. Sardinia: Light Infantry. Officer, 1792.
174. Spain: Swiss Regiment 'Schwaller'. Private, 1795.
175. Russia: 14th Rifle Battalion. Rifleman, 1797.
176. Russia: Duke of Bourbon's Grenadier Regiment from Condé's Army. N.C.O.
      1797.

177. France: 4th Light Demi-Brigade. Rifleman, 1799.
178. France: Dromedary Corps. Camelrider, 1799.
179. France: Coptic Legion. Man, 1799.
180. Great Britain: 50th (West Kent) Regiment of Foot. Officer, 1801.

The French Revolution
1792–1804

181. The Cisalpine Republic: Lombardy-Cisalpine Legion. Infantry officer, 1797.
182. France: Polish Danube Legion. Artillery man, 1799.
183. The Batavian Republic: Light Infantry. Carabinier, 1801.
184. The Helvetic Republic: Light Cavalry. Trooper, 1800.

The French Revolution
1792–1804

185

186

187

188

185. Russia: Pereaslavski Dragoons. N.C.O., 1803.
186. Prussia: Infantry Regiment 'Unruh'. Grenadier, 1801.
187. Austria: Light Infantry Battalion nr. 9. Officer, 1800.
188. Great Britain: 8th or King's Regiment of Foot. Grenadier, 1801.

189

190

191

192

189. France: Imperial Guard. Grenadiers-à-pied. Grenadier, 1804.
190. France: Imperial Guard. 2nd Conscrit-Chasseurs. Sapper, 1810.
191. France: Imperial Guard. Pupilles or King of Rome's Guard. Boy, 1811.
192. France: Imperial Guard. Corporal of Engineers, 1810.

193. France: Imperial Guard. Chasseurs-à-cheval. Man, 1804.
194. France: Imperial Guard. Dragoons. Trooper, 1809.
195. France: Imperial Guard. Horse Grenadiers. Corporal, 1815.
196. France: Imperial Guard. 1st Chevau-légers Lanciers. Lancer, 1810.

197. France: 9th Line Infantry. Drum-major, 1809.
198. France: 5th Light Infantry Cuirassiers. Sharpshooter, 1808.
199. France: 9th Cuirassiers. Trooper, 1805.
200. France: 3rd Hussars. Hussar, 1808.

The Napoleonic Wars
1804–1815

201. France: Foreign Troops, Croatian Regiment. Infantry man, 1813.
202. France: Marshal Soult's Staff. Captain, 1808.
203. France: 15th Light Infantry. Cantinière, 1809.
204. France: Imperial Navy. Sailor, 1808.

205. Bavaria: 9th Line Infantry 'Ysenburg-Büddingen'. Man, 1807.
206. Bavaria: King's Chevaulegers Regiment nr. 4. Officer, 1809.
207. Württemberg: Infantry Regiment 'Franquemont'. Musketeer, 1809.
208. Württemberg: Life Guard of Horse. Man of Leibjäger Squadron, 1810.

209. Berg: Infantry. Regimental Pioneer, 1812.
210. Berg: Artillery. Gunner, 1810.
211. Baden: Regiment 'Markgraf Ludwig'. Musketeer, 1804.
212. Baden: Hussar Regiment. N.C.O., 1812.

213
214
215
216

213. Saxony: Leib-Kurassiers. Trooper, 1812.
214. Saxony: Infantry Regiment 'Rechten'. Grenadier N.C.O., 1810.
215. Hesse-Darmstadt: Guards Brigade. Musketeer, 1806.
216. Würzberg: Dragoon Regiment. Dragoon, 1807.

217. Westphalia: 4th Infantry Regiment. Rifleman, 1808.
218. Westphalia: Garde-Chevauleger. Trumpeter, 1808.
219. Schwarzburg-Rudolstadt: Infantry. Officer, 1812.
220. Schaumburg-Lippe: Infantry. Drummer, 1814.

221. Anhalt: Jager zu Pferde (Light Cavalry) Trumpeter, 1813.
222. Lippe-Detmold: Fusilier-Battalion 'Lippe'. N.C.O., 1807.
223. Reuss: Infantry. Officer, 1812.
224. Waldeck: Infantry. Musketeer, 1812.

225. Nassau: 2nd Infantry Regiment. Grenadier, 1810.
226. Saxe-Weimar: Light Infantry Battalion. Officer, 1812.
227. Oldenburg: Infantry. Grenadier drummer, 1808.
228. Frankfurt: Infantry. Grenadier, 1806.

229. Duchy of Warsaw: 1st Infantry Regiment. Sergeant-Major with regimental colour, 1810.
230. Duchy of Warsaw: 12th Lancers. Captain, 1812.
231. Holland: Colonial Marines. Marine, 1806.
232. Holland: 7th Line Infantry Regiment. Drum-major, 1808.

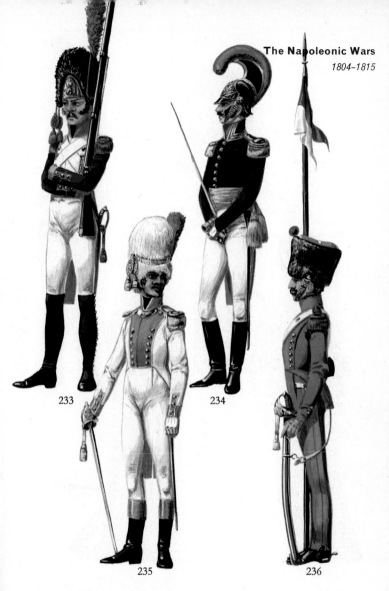

233. Italy: Infantry of the Line. Grenadier, 1805.
234. Sardinia: Infantry Regiment 'Savoyen'. Officer, 1814.
235. Naples: 7th Line Regiment 'Africa'. Grenadier captain, 1812.
236. Naples: 4th Light Cavalry Regiment. Trooper, 1815.

237. Spain: The Prince's Cavalry Regiment. Trooper, 1808.
238. Spain: 'Princesa' Infantry Regiment. Grenadier, 1808.
239. Spain: Catalonian Light Regiment. Private, 1807.
240. Spain: The 'Death' Regiment. Private, 1808.

241   242

243   244

241. Austria: Infantry Regiment 'Graf Erbach', nr. 42. Captain, 1811.
242. Austria: Dragoon Regiment 'Baron Knesewick', nr. 3. Dragoon, 1815.
243. Austria: 'Saxe-Coburg-Saalfeld' Lancers. Lancer, 1815.
244. Austria: Regimental Surgeon, 1811.

245. Prussia: 1st West Prussian Infantry Regiment, nr. 6. Grenadier, 1810.
246. Prussia: 11th Reserve Regiment. Man, 1813.
247. Prussia: Neumark Dragoon Regiment, nr. 6. Captain, 1808.
248. Prussia: 1st East Prussia Infantry Regiment, nr. 1. Rifle Volunteer, 1814

249. Russia: Line Infantry. Musketeer, 1809.
250. Russia: The Chevalier Guard. Captain, 1811.
251. Russia: 'Actirski' Hussar Regiment. Hussar, 1813.
252. Russia: Ural Cossacks. Cossack, 1812.

253

254

255

256

253. Great Britain: 93rd Highlanders. Private, 1810.
254. Great Britain: 95th or Rifle Regiment. Rifleman, 1807.
255. Great Britain: 3rd (or the King's Own) Regiment of Dragoons. Trooper, 18
256. Great Britain: 15th Light Dragoons, or King's Hussars. Officer, 1813.

257. Great Britain: The King's German Legion. Infantry man, 1812.
258. Great Britain: The Brunswick Black Corps. Infantry man, 1809.
259. Great Britain: Royal Navy. Able-seaman, H.M.S. *Tribune*, 1805.
260. Great Britain: 2nd Greek Light Infantry. Private, 1813.

261. Sweden: Kalmar Regiment. Private, 1814.
262. Sweden: Smålands Light Dragoons. Trooper, 1808.
263. Denmark-Norway: Norwegian Life Regiment. Grenadier lieutenant, 1807.
264. Denmark-Norway: Fyn Light Dragoons. Trooper, 1813.

265. U.S.A.: New York Rifle Corps. Rifleman, 1812.
266. U.S.A.: 16th Infantry Regiment. Enlisted man, 1812.
267. Portugal: 1st Rifle Battalion (Caçadores). Rifleman, 1808.
268. Netherlands: Belgian Militia. Infantry lieutenant, 1815.

269. Argentine: 'Patricios' Regiment. Private, 1807.
270. Argentine: 'Infernales' Cavalry Regiment. Trooper, 1807.
271. Brazil: Rio de Janeiro Militia. Infantry man, 1822.
272. Brazil: Diamantina Civic Guard. Private, 1824.

273. Mexico: Insurgent Army. Officer, 1814.
274. Mexico: General Iturbide's Independence Army. Light cavalryman, 1820.
275. Venezuela: General Bolivar's Bodyguard. Man, 1820.
276. Chile: Infantry of the Line. Private, 1820.

The Belgian and Polish Uprisings
1830–1831

277. Netherlands: Horse Artillery. Senior N.C.O., 1830.
278. Belgium: Partisans of Capiaumont. Senior N.C.O., 1831.
279. Russia: 12th Infantry Regiment 'Nishnij-Novgorod'. Private, 1830.
280. Poland: 10th Infantry Regiment. Captain, 1831.

281. France: Infantry of the Line. Grenadier, 1833.
282. Great Britain: 96th Regiment of Foot. Private, 1836.
283. Prussia: Guard Grenadier Regiment 'Kaiser Alexander'. Private, 1828.
284. Austria: Infantry Regiment 'Graf Kinsky' nr. 47. Musketeer, 1837.

The Greek Civil War
1831–1832

The Spanish Carlist Uprising
1834–1839

285

286

287

288

285. Greece: Infantry of the Line. Fusilier, 1832.
286. Bavaria: Chevaulegers-Regiment 'Konig'. Light cavalryman, 1833.
287. Spain: Carlist Infantry. Private, 1835.
288. Spain: Royal Guard Horse Artillery. Gunner, 1834.

289. U.S.A.: 1st Dragoons. Trooper, 1847.
290. U.S.A.: Infantry of the Line. Enlisted man, 1847.
291. Mexico: 1st Regular Infantry Regiment. Private, 1846.
292. Mexico: 7th Regular Cavalry Regiment. Senior sergeant, 1846.

293. Switzerland: Vaud Canton. Carabinier, 1847.
294. Prussia: 2nd Silesian Infantry Regiment nr. 12. N.C.O., 1848.
295. Hungary: Honvéd Infantry. N.C.O., 1848.
296. Schleswig-Holstein: Artillery. Train-constable, 1849.

297

298

299

300

297. Denmark: 1st Line Infantry Battalion. Private, 1848.
298. Denmark: 2nd Rifle Corps. Bugler, 1848.
299. Denmark: 5th Line Infantry Battalion. Private, 1849.
300. Sweden: West Gotland Infantry Regiment. Private, 1848.

301

302

303

304

301. Great Britain: 17th Lancers. Lancer, 1854.
302. Russia: Infantry of the Line. Private, 1854.
303. Great Britain: 89th Regiment of Foot. Man of grenadier company, 1854.
304. Turkey: Artillery. Gunner, 1854.

305. Russia: Caucasian Rifle Battalion. Lance-corporal, 1854.
306. France: 3rd Zouave Regiment. Zouave, 1854.
307. Sardinia: 1st Grenadier Regiment. Corporal, 1855.
308. France: Infantry of the Line. Cantinière, 1854.

309. France: Imperial Guard, Chasseurs-à-cheval. Trooper, 1858.
310. Austria: Jaczygier Volunteer Hussars. Lieutenant, 1859.
311. France: Imperial Guard. Grenadier à Pied. Grenadier, 1859.
312. Austria: Infantry Regiment 'Grosshergoz von Hessen', nr. 14. Private, 1859.

313

314

315

316

313. Tuscany: Infantry of the Line. Private, 1859.
314. Modena: Dragoon Regiment. Cavalryman, 1859.
315. Parma: Field Artillery. Officer, 1859.
316. Papal States: Infantry of the Line. Sapper, 1859.

317
318
319
320

317. Naples: The Guard of Honour. Officer, 1860.
318. Naples: Infantry Carabiniers. Officer, 1860.
319. Naples: Swiss Artillery. Gunner, 1860.
320. Naples: 5th Rifle Battalion. Rifleman, 1860.

321. Sardinia: Bersaglieri. Private, 1860.
322. Sardinia: Field Artillery. Officer, 1860.
323. Sicily: Garibaldist, 1860.
324. Sardinia: Engineer Corps. Sapper, 1860.

325. The Union: Infantry. Enlisted man, 1861.
326. The Union: Cavalry. Sergeant, 1861.
327. The Union: Field Artillery. Captain, 1861.
328. The Union: 11th Indiana Volunteers (Wallace's Zouaves). Man, 1861.

329. The Confederate States: Infantry. Enlisted man, 1862.
330. The Confederate States: Louisiana Tigers. Zouave, 1862.
331. The Confederate States: South Carolina Volunteers. Hampton's Legion. Trooper, 1861.
332. The Confederate States: Horse Artillery. Lieutenant, 1862.

333.

334.

335.

336.

333. Mexico: Belgian Expeditionary Corps, Rifle battalion. Cantinière, 1864.
334. Mexico: Austrian Volunteer Brigade, Rifle battalion. 1st Lieutenant, 1864.
335. Mexico: Turkish Auxiliary Battalion. Lieutenant, 1864.
336. Mexico: Imperial Palace Guard. Sergeant, 1865.

337. Prussia: Westphalian Field Artillery, Regiment nr. 7. Gunner, 1864.
338. Austria: Feld-Jäger-Bataillon nr. 9. Rifleman, 1864.
339. Denmark: 11th Infantry Regiment. Lance-corporal, 1864.
340. Denmark: 6th Dragoon Regiment. Dragoon, 1864.

341
342
343
344

341. Prussia: 3rd Garde-Regiment zu Fuss. 1st Lieutenant, 1866.
342. Prussia: 2nd Brandenburg Lancers, nr. 11. Trumpeter, 1866.
343. Mecklinburg-Schwerin: 4th Infantry Battalion. Sergeant, 1866.
344. Hamburg: Contingent Cavalry. Dragoon, 1866.

345. Austria: Field Artillery. Lieutenant, 1866.
346. Saxony: 4 Infanterie-(Leib)-Brigade. Private, 1866.
347. Hanover: 6th Infantry Regiment. Private, 1866.
348. Bavaria: 2nd Cuirassiers. Trooper, 1866.

349

350

351

352

349. Prussia: Madgeburg Cuirassier Regiment, nr. 7. Trooper, 1870.
350. Prussia: 1st Silesian Rifle Battalion, nr. 5. Rifleman, 1870.
351. Bavaria: 2nd Lancers. Lancer, 1870.
352. Bavaria: 5th Infantry Regiment. Private, 1870.

353. France: Chasseurs à pied. Lance-corporal, 1870.
354. France: Cuirassiers. Trooper, 1870.
355. France: Imperial Guard. Grenadier à pied. Grenadier, 1870.
356. France: Field Artillery. Gunner, 1870.

The Franco-Prussian War
1870–1871

357

358

359

360

357. France: 2nd Hussars. Corporal, 1870.
358. France: Chasseurs d'Afrique. Trooper, 1870.
359. France: Garde Mobile. Battalion commander, 1870.
360. France: Naval Battalion. Lance-corporal, 1870.

361

362

363

364

361. Baden: 2nd Dragoon Regiment. Dragoon, 1870.
362. Brunswick: Hussar Regiment, nr. 17. Lieutenant, 1871.
363. Württemberg: 4th Infantry Regiment. Private, 1870.
364. Hessen-Darmstadt: Pioneer Company. Pioneer, 1870.

Colonial Troops

1870–1960

365

366

367

368

365. French North Africa: Spahi, 1898.
366. Italian Somaliland: Askari, 1900.
367. German South-West Africa: Protectorate Troops. Trooper, 1899.
368. The Congo: Army Force. 1st Lieutenant, 1890.

369

370

371

372

369. British India: 15th Ludhiana Sikhs. Sepoy, 1888.
370. British India: 27th Light Cavalry. Native officer, 1906.
371. French Indo-China: Annamite Sharpshooters. Lance-corporal, 1889.
372. Dutch East Indies: Colonial Army. Infantry man, 1900.

373. Australia: New South Wales Lancers. Trooper, 1900.
374. New Zealand: Canterbury Volunteer Cavalry. Trooper, 1875.
375. The Fiji Islands: Artillery. Sergeant, 1957.
376. Samoa (U.S.A.): Governor's Bodyguard. Private, 1943.

377

378

379

380

377. Canada: Infantry Officer, 1870.
378. Canada: Governor-General's Bodyguard. Trooper, 1898.
379. British West Indies: West India Regiment. Lance-corporal, 1926.
380. Danish West Indies: Police Corps on St. Thomas. Man, 1916.

The Boer Wars

1880–1881 and 1899–1902

381

382

383

384

381. Great Britain: 58th (Rutlandshire) Foot. Private, 1880.
382. The Boer Republic: Boer Army. Sharpshooter, 1880–1902.
383. Great Britain: The Gordon Highlanders. Private, 1900.
384. Great Britain: City Imperial Volunteers. Volunteer, 1900.

385

386

387

388

385. Japan: Guard Infantry. Private, 1904.
386. Russia: Infantry of the Line. Private, 1904.
387. Japan: Imperial Navy. Commander, 1905.
388. Russia: Imperial Navy. Commander, 1905.

389

390

391

392

389. Bulgaria: Field Artillery. Captain, 1913.
390. Serbia: Cavalry. Trooper, 1913.
391. Greece: Infantry. Private, 1913.
392. Greece: The Royal Guard. Evzone, 1913.

393. Rumania: 3rd Rifle Battalion. Rifleman, 1913.
394. Albania: Officer, 1913.
395. Montenegro: Corporal of the Reserve. 1913.
396. Turkey: Brigadier-General. 1913.

397

398

399

400

397. Germany: (Mecklenburg-Strelitz): Grenadier Regiment, nr. 89. Grenadier
     1914.
398. Austria-Hungary: Infantry Regiment. 'King of Denmark', nr. 75. Private, 1914
399. Russia: Preobraschenski Guards. Guardsman, 1914.
400. France: 5th Line Regiment. Infantry man, 1914.

Troops of the Great Powers at the Outbreak of the First World War

1914

401

402

403

404

401. Great Britain: The Buffs (East Kent Regiment). Private, 1914.
402. Italy: Grenadiers of Sardinia. Grenadier, 1914.
403. U.S.A.: Infantry. Enlisted man, 1914.
404. China: Infantry of the Line. Private, 1914.

405

406

407

408

405. Germany (Prussia): Lancer Regiment, 'Hennigs von Treffenfeld', nr. 16. Lancer 1914.
406. Germany: 10th Württemberg Infantry Regiment, nr. 180. Private, 1914.
407. Germany (Prussia): 1st Guard Field Artillery Regiment. Captain, 1914.
408. Germany: Machine-gun Section, nr. 11. Man, 1914.

The First World War

1914–1918

409

410

411

412

409. France: 145th Regiment of the Line. Soldier, 1914.
410. France: 13th Cuirassiers. Lieutenant, 1914.
411. Belgium: The Carabiniers. Private, 1914.
412. Great Britain: The Royal Fusiliers. Private, 1914.

The First World War
1914–1918

413

414

415

416

413. Russia: 180th Windau Infantry Regiment. Private, 1914.
414. Russia: Chóper Regiment, Kuban Cossacks. Captain, 1914.
415. Russia: Guard Horse Artillery. Gunner, 1914.
416. Serbia: 20th Infantry Regiment. Private, 1914.

417

418

419

420

417. Austria-Hungary: Tiroler Kaiserjäger Regiment, nr. 4. 1st Lieutenant, 1914.
418. Austria-Hungary: Dragoon Regiment, nr. 15. Dragoon, 1914.
419. Austria-Hungary: Infantry Regiment, nr. 102. Private, 1914.
420. Turkey: General, 1914.

The First World War
1914–1918

421. Montenegro: Infantry. Private, 1915.
422. Bulgaria: Infantry Regiment, nr. 40. Private, 1915.
423. Italy: 94th Infantry Regiment. Soldier, 1915.
424. Rumania: 44th Infantry Regiment. Private, 1916.

425. Germany: Imperial Navy. U-boat sailor, 1915.
426. Great Britain: Royal Navy. Petty Officer, 1st Class, 1915.
427. Germany: Air Battalion, nr. 2. Lieutenant, 1916.
428. Great Britain: Royal Flying Corps. Sergeant, 1915.

429. Germany: Infantry. Private, 1917.
430. France: Infantry. Private, 1917.
431. Austria-Hungary: Infantry. Private, 1917.
432. Great Britain: Infantry. Private, 1917.

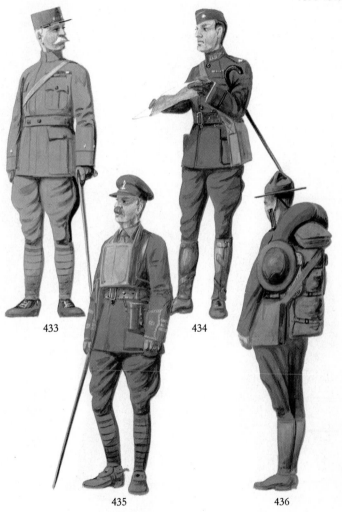

433. France: General of Brigade, 1917.
434. U.S.A.: Infantry. Lieutenant-Colonel, 1918.
435. Great Britain: Cavalry. Major, 1917.
436. U.S.A.: Infantry. Enlisted man, 1918.

The Wars of Liberation in Eastern Europe

1918–1922

437. Poland: The Polish Legion in France. Rifleman, 1919.
438. Czechoslovakia: The Czech Legion in Russia. Cavalry corporal, 1919.
439. The Soviet Union: Red Army. Artillery man, 1919.
440. The Soviet Union: Red Army. Infantry man, 1919.

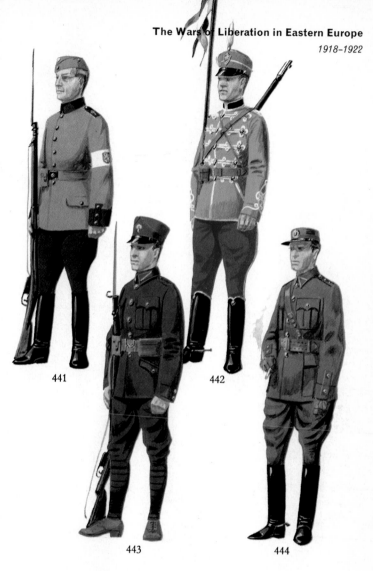

441. Finland: White Guard. Private, 1922.
442. Esthonia: Cavalry man, 1922.
443. Latvia: Infantry man, 1923.
444. Lithuania: Engineer Troops. 1st Lieutenant, 1926.

445. Germany: Air Force. Lieutenant (Flying Branch), 1939.
446. Germany: Infantry man, 1940.
447. Germany: The Navy. Commander, 1939.
448. Germany: Air Force. Parachute N.C.O., 1940.

449
450
451
452

449. Poland: Infantry. Captain, 1939.
450. Denmark: Infantry man, 1940.
451. Netherlands: Infantry man, 1940.
452. Belgium: Infantry. Colonel, 1940.

453. Norway: Infantry. Private, 1940.
454. France: 37th Fortress Regiment. Corporal, 1940.
455. France: Army of the Air. Captain, 1940.
456. France: 24th Regiment of the Line. Infantry man, 1940.

457. Germany: 4th Armoured Regiment. N.C.O., 1940.
458. Germany: Field-Marshal, 1940.
459. Italy: Calabria Infantry Brigade. Corporal, 1940.
460. Italy: Air Force. Captain, 1940.

461
462
463
464

461. Great Britain: Royal Air Force. Sergeant, 1942.
462. Great Britain: Infantry, 1st Corps. Private, 1942.
463. France: The Foreign Legion. Corporal, 1942.
464. Great Britain: Infantry, 8th Army. Private, 1943.

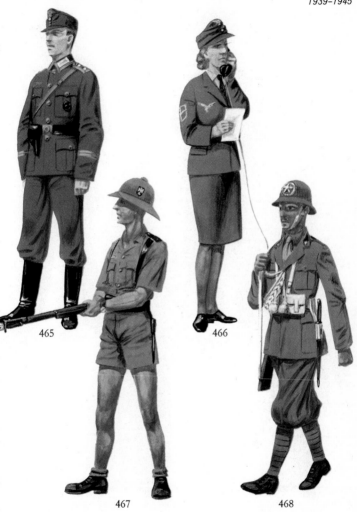

465. Germany: Naval Artillery. Senior N.C.O., 1943.
466. Germany: Air Reporting Service. Auxiliary, 1944.
467. Germany: Afrika Korps. Infantry man, 1943.
468. Italy: African Rifles (Cacciatori d'Africa). Private, 1939.

469

470

471

472

469. The Soviet Union: Field Artillery. 1st Lieutenant, 1940.
470. The Soviet Union: Infantry man, 1943.
471. The Soviet Union: Administrative Service. Sergeant, 1943.
472. The Soviet Union: Air Marshal, 1943.

473

474

475

476

473. Germany: Waffen SS. Lieutenant, 1943.
474. Hungary: Hussar Regiment. Hussar, 1940.
475. Rumania: Infantry man, 1940.
476. Finland: Infantry man, 1940.

477. Croatia: Bosnian Infantry. Corporal, 1943.
478. Slovakia: Infantry man, 1942.
479. Italian Social Republic: Parachute Section. Private, 1944.
480. Germany: Don Cossack Division. N.C.O., 1944.

481

482

483

484

481. Jugoslavia: Captain on General Staff, 1941.
482. Greece: Infantry. Lance-corporal, 1940.
483. Great Britain: Field-Marshal, 1944.
484. Great Britain: The Parachute Regiment. Parachutist, 1944.

485
486
487
488

485. U.S.A.: Parachute Infantry. Parachutist, 1944.
486. U.S.A.: Infantry. Enlisted man, 1944.
487. Great Britain: Infantry man in Jungle dress, 1945.
488. Japan: Major of Cavalry and Infantry man, 1943.

489
490
491
492

489. U.S.A.: Naval Aviation. Lieutenant, 1944.
490. Great Britain: Queen Alexandra's Imperial Military Nursing Service,
Lieutenant, 1945.
491. U.S.A.: Infantry man in jungle uniform, 1944.
492. U.S.A.: U.S.M.C. Women Marines. Top sergeant, 1944.

The United Nations Troops

since 1950

493. Great Britain: The Argyll and Sutherland Highlanders. Officer of the Korea Force, 1950.
494. U.S.A.: Light Artillery. Officer of Korea Force, 1950.
495. India: Military Police. Lance-corporal of Gaza Force, 1958.
496. Ireland: Infantry. Sergeant bagpiper of Cyprus Force, 1963.

497. Norway: Infantry man of Gaza Force, 1961.
498. Denmark: Infantry man of Gaza Force, 1958.
499. Sweden: Infantry man of Gaza Force, 1961.
500. Nigeria: Infantry. Sergeant of Congo Force, 1963.

501

502

503

504

501. Finland: The Cadet School. Army Cadet, 1965.
502. Norway: His Majesty's Royal Guard. Guardsman, 1958.
503. Denmark: Royal Life Guard. Guardsman, 1965.
504. Sweden: Royal Life Guards Squadron. Captain, 1954.

Contemporary
Guard Units, etc.

505

506

507

508

505. France: Republican Guard (Cavalry Section). Corporal, 1966.
506. Italy: The Carabinieri. Man, 1961.
507. West Germany: Artillery lieutenant, 1966.
508. Netherlands: Guard Fusilier Regiment 'Prinses Irene'. Officer, 1966.

509

510

511

512

509. Great Britain: Gordon Highlanders. Drum-major, 1958.
510. U.S.A.: Military Academy, West Point. Cadet, 1965.
511. Congo-Brazzaville: Republican Guard. Corporal, 1963.
512. Thailand: Royal Palace Guard. Captain, 1965.

HOUSEHOLD GUARDS BEFORE 1670

Uniforms in the true sense were first worn by the corps of guards established by rulers for their personal protection and prestige during the sixteenth and seventeenth centuries. Such troops might be recruited from the nobility or be mercenaries from abroad, or be supplemented by meritorious N.C.O.s. Guard corps have always been splendidly uniformed and equipped with the finest weapons, a tradition that, of course, still survives, except, of course, in the case of modern ceremonial guards like the Yeomen of the Guard, who wear carbine belts but have not carried actual carbines for centuries.

1. The Vatican (The Papal States). The Swiss Guard. Guardsman, 1506

The Swiss Guard was formed in 1506, and is the oldest active military unit extant. Besides its ceremonial function it provides the Papal residence with permanent military protection and is thus now equipped with modern small arms. Formerly there were Swiss guards and Swiss regiments in many countries (see 149, 174 and 319) but since 1859 the Swiss have been forbidden to enter foreign military service. Service on behalf of the Pope is an exception, and this Papal guard is always recruited from the Catholic cantons of Switzerland. Tradition has it that Raphael (or Michelangelo) designed the original uniforms, but there is no evidence for this, although the basis of the present uniform can be traced back to about the middle of the sixteenth century.

2. England: The Yeomen of the Guard. Yeoman, 1520

Today, *The Queen's Bodyguard of the Yeomen of the Guard*, nicknamed 'The Beefeaters'. This Bodyguard was formed in 1485 so it is older than the Swiss Guard (1). Nowadays its function is only ceremonial, its ranks being filled by seasoned army N.C.O.s, who consider it an honour to be selected. Just how the peculiar nickname originated is

not clear: the most probable origin lies in the fact that the guard wore the same dress as the server who was given the task of attendance at the 'buffet' at royal banquets. The guard certainly had its uniform well before 1520 by the time of a meeting at the Field of the Cloth of Gold between Henry VIII and Francis I, of France, when the two powerful monarchs tried to outdo each other in pomp. Apart from minor details, the same uniform is worn today. The 'Beefeaters' should not be confused with the Yeomen Warders of the Tower, who have a similar uniform, but without the carbine belt.

3. Spain: The Noble Guard. Guardsman, 1646

The King's Guard of Noblemen was established in 1646 and was recruited from the nobility serving in line regiments. To put noblemen into uniform at that time was unthinkable, so the armorial coat or 'surcoat'—a development of the surcoat formerly worn over the armour—was used to distinguish members of the guard. The surcoat, worn on active service only, gave its wearer a certain distinction, showing that he was in the King's service without in any way demeaning him. On the chest and back it was adorned with the Spanish royal arms, while the sleeves carried the cross of Burgundy, a Habsburg emblem.

4. France: Musketeers of the King. Musketeer, 1665

The best known of the aristocratic corps of guards is certainly the French king's musketeers, celebrated by Alexandre Dumas in his novels. On the *casaque*, as the surcoat is called in France, the musketeers wore a cross decorated with the lilies and tongues of flame comprising one of the emblems of the king of France. Red heels were reserved for the nobility in France, but the privilege spread to other countries where it proved less popular; they appear to be tolerated in England but Danish officers were forbidden to wear them. The first company of musketeers was founded in 1622, and when a further company was formed in 1661, the first retained the red flames on their crosses, the second being granted yellow ones. Cardinal Richelieu dressed his musketeers like those of the King, but in red surcoats and without lilies or flames on the crosses.

THE DUTCH WARS 1652–1678

The Franco–Dutch war was fought between France, England and Sweden on one side, and the Netherlands (Holland), Austria and Spain on the other. Various German states also took part on both sides. The main cause of the conflict was Louis XIV's wish to subjugate the Netherlands for interfering with his plans on various occasions. In the battles at Seneffe and Colmar the French defeated the Dutch and Austrians. The most notable battle was at Fehrbellin, in 1675, in which the Swedes were defeated by the Brandenburgers, thus losing the reputation for invincibility they had maintained since the Thirty Years War. In 1674 England, which had participated only half-heartedly, withdrew from the conflict. Neither side appreciably benefited when peace was concluded in 1678.

5. France: The 'Carignan-Sallières' Regiment. Ensign, 1665

The French officers enjoyed considerable freedom in choice of uniform, which, however, was often of the same colour as the cuffs of the other ranks. Current fashion had a considerable influence. By this way originated the very short coatsleeves, revealing the lavish shirtsleeves, the lace-trimmed cravat, and flowing ribbons. But the ribbon on the right shoulder had the practical function of retaining the sword-bandolier in position. Note that the colours of the ribbon are the same colours as in the standard. Ensign was the lowest commissioned rank, and the ensigns undertook the duty of carrying the colours. The 'Carignan-Sallières' Regiment played an especially notable part in the French colonisation of Canada.

6. France: Amiral de France Regiment Officer, 1670

Grey woollen uniforms were introduced for the French infantry in 1670, and attempts were made to equip the officer with uniforms matching the men's in principal features. The latter nevertheless retained the choice of cut and details. The then fashionable braiding also influenced uniforms, usually with variations according to rank. In general officers' uniforms in an individual regiment were trimmed in a similar manner. The real distinction for an officer was the gorget, originally part of the armour of a knight and the last piece to be worn.

7. France: The Dauphin's Regiment of Dragoons. Officer, 1675

At this period the French dragoons were still mounted infantry, so in dress they followed the custom for this branch of the service. However, their uniforms were generally red. The royal regiments or units with a member of the royal family at the head, were an exception they wore blue uniforms to mark their status. Their relation to the infantry was manifested by wearing a variety of leggings with spurs, instead of boots. The cord loops at the shoulders which originally retained the bandolier continued to be a distinguishing feature of the dragoons in many armies when the bandolier became obsolete. The peculiar cap was characteristic of French dragoons up to 1763 (68). At this period they were armed with muskets carried on their backs by means of the musket sling. The broad-brimmed hat got in the way when the musket had to be taken off or slung in a hurry, hence the choice of the cap. The regiment shown was formed in 1673.

8. France: Swiss Regiment 'Greder'. Musketeer, 1673

Although they wore grey uniforms after 1670, the French infantry regiments were distinguishable by the contrasting colours of their cuffs and stockings. In addition it was also possible to alternate between brass or tin buttons, group the buttons singly, in pairs (as in 6), or in threes (as in 7) while the pocket flaps could be vertical (6) or horizontal (5), so it is not surprising that there was a different uniform for each infantry regiment which numbered one hundred in the French army before the Revolution. At first the Swiss regiments in French service wore grey uniforms, but later red, with contrasting cuffs. The regiment shown was formed in 1673.

9. England: Foot Guards. Musketeer, 1660

Today, the *Grenadier Guards*. These Foot Guards were formed in 1656 by the prince who later became Charles II of England, during his exile in the Netherlands. They were recruited from among Royalist émigrés. The guards wore the uniform illustrated when they paraded before the King when he left the Netherlands in 1660. It has a number of old-fashioned features: the leather jerkin (or buff coat) and the bandoliers date back to the style of the Civil War. Since they all wore red lower garments it was, in effect, a kind of uniform. The Guards officers were clad in more up-to-date fashion (see 5) consisting of a blue jacket with red cuffs, and well adorned with gold braid. The trousers and hose were red, and the hat had red and white plumes.

10. England: King's Troop of Horse Guards. Officer, 1670

Today, *The Life Guards*. Originally an aristocratic guard, they were formed by Charles II during his exile in the Netherlands. Over the jerkin or buff coat the officers wore a great coat in the characteristic colours of the English 'royal' regiments, red and dark blue. The fashionable short sleeves did not reveal, like some others, the lavish shirtsleeves of the period, but the gold-braided sleeves of the buff coat.

11. England: Coldstream Guards. Tangier, 1669

The uniform illustrated is one of the earliest examples of adaptation of military dress to climatic conditions. Both officers and other ranks in the Tangier garrison wore uniforms of red material signifying the 'King's Coat'. While the men had to make do with these, the officers and sergeants also had a form of tropical dress, grey throughout and evidently in lighter weight material. Thus they were not notably different in appearance from civilians. The coloured hat band and ribbon provided a form of regimental identification. The hat with the shallow crown was the ultimate in fashion at the time; in this instance it may have been a form of 'boater'.

12. England: Dragoon, 1672

The headgear of the English dragoons was fur trimmed, as giving a more dashing appearance. Their boots were a lighter and more flexible pattern than those of the troopers, which, from the earlier soft top boots (3, 4) had evolved into rather stiff footgear with leg-pieces of stiff jacked leather (15). This was certainly with the object of protecting the legs of the wearer while riding in close formation. However, when the large tops were done away with, there was a tendency for the boots to fill with water in wet weather, and they were provided with a small hole in the heel, to act as a 'scupper'. The New Model Army, formed under Cromwell, was dressed entirely in red. The royal troops wore variously coloured uniforms, but red finally predominated, to last until 1914, as the full dress of infantry and dragoons.

13. Netherlands: Artillery Officer, 1668

A dark uniform was chosen for the artillery in most armies from the outset. In the days of black powder and muzzle-loaders the artilleryman's was not a particularly clean craft. Originally the artillery was indeed a craft, for which a man had to serve an apprenticeship and take a trade-test. Fully trained gunners were an elite, who closely guarded the secrets of their profession. During the period when the Netherlands had no head of state, the officers' sash was crimson. When a prince of Orange was again called to head the nation in 1672, the orange sash of the House of Orange was restored, and is still worn.

14. Hesse: The Landgraf's Leibwache. Musketeer, 1660

In 1914, *Fusilier Regiment von Gersdorff* (*Kurhessisches*) nr. 80. Being a type of guards unit, the Landgraf's Leibwache had a uniform from early days. This was in the colours of the Hesse arms; silver, blue and red. Since the Thirty Years War, the musketeers carried their side-arms in a bandolier over the right shoulder, while from the left shoulder hung a number of small, leather-covered, flask-shaped containers called powder-chargers (8–9 and 20). Each container carried a measure of powder for one shot, to facilitate reloading the muzzle-loading musket in battle. Lead shot was carried in the pouch attached to the bandolier. The powder horn, slung with the pouch, was for the fine priming powder, to be poured onto the priming pan. At one time the Life Guards were formed from the remainder of the Hesse regiments which had taken part in the Thirty Years War. In 1821 they were included in the Electoral Hesse Life Guards Regiment, which itself became part of the Prussian forces in 1866.

15. Saxony: Graf von Promnitz Cuirassiers. Trooper, 1660

At this time cavalry, in the strict sense, consisted of regiments of troopers or cuirassiers, descendants of the original heavily armoured knights. Armour diminished to a cuirass or breastplate, or, in certain cases, simply a helmet. The cavalry shown here are wearing well polished cuirasses and helmets, but on active service these were often painted black. From earliest times the cavalry wore a jerkin or leather coat of black wash-leather. It was originally sleeveless, showing the sleeves of the garment beneath, but later it had sleeves of thinner leather. A special feature of the leather coat was that it was not buttoned, but fastened with hooks or loops, as otherwise the cuirass would press on the

buttons and cause discomfort to the wearer. Apart from the cavalry sword, units of this type carried two pistols in special saddle-holsters.

16. Bavaria. Steinau Infantry Officer, 1670

The Bavarian infantry were first put into uniform in 1670. Originally each regiment had its own uniform colour, but the special 'Savoy' blue later became the commonest and in 1684 was used for all the infantry. Light blue remained characteristic of the Bavarian infantry up to 1914. The regiments were recognizable by cuffs of a contrasting colour, while the colours of the Bavarian house and arms—blue and silver—appeared in the crest, scarf and sword bandolier. At this time infantry officers in all armies were equipped with a shafted weapon, either a half pike or a partisan. In the British Army they were replaced in 1710 by the espontoon as it was called. Before the end of the eighteenth century these weapons for officers had disappeared in all armies.

17. Austria: Saxe-Coburg Regiment. Musketeer, 1690

In Austria, until 1780, the regimental commander had the task of deciding on the appearance of the uniforms. However, uniforms of grey woollen cloth were cheapest and hence commonest and it was natural to choose pale grey as the basic colour when a standard uniform was wanted for the infantry. When the choice was made by the regimental commander it might well occur that several regiments had the same colour. There were, however, variations through the wearing in some regiments of breeches and hose in the regimental colour. In others these items were grey. As regards the leather equipment, a new system was becoming general: the side-arms, as in the cavalry, were worn from a waist belt.

18. Austria: Artillery. Gunner, 1671

Although the Austrian infantry uniform was made of light woollen material, for practical reasons the darkest possible

148

wool was chosen for the artillery. The darker natural wools were often brownish, so while the infantry uniforms tended to become whiter, the artillery uniform became really brown (345). As shown here, the gunner carried a priming powder on a red sling carried over his shoulders. The piece of equipment with the long shaft is a linstock. There were good practical reasons for its length: first, the burning slow-match was kept away from the open powder-barrels, and second, the cannon could be fired from a safe distance, to avoid the holder being struck when the recoil caused the cannon to run backwards. The white shirtsleeves can have been worn only on parades and similar occasions. On active service the gunner certainly wore a long-sleeved grey vest under the jacket.

19. Brandenburg (Prussia): The Electress Dorothea of Brandenburg's Regiment. Musketeer, 1681

As early as the year 1632 the Elector Georg Wilhelm of Brandenburg was at the head of Life Guards dressed in dark blue, but there were no regulations in existence for general uniforms for the infantry until 1685. Dark blue was prevalent, and this colour characterized the Prussian infantry until 1914. When the regiment illustrated here was formed in 1676, however, they wore red uniforms. Thus it seems to have been the custom for regiments connected with the spouse of the sovereign to wear red, as manifested by Denmark (21), England and France. It is also noteworthy that in Brandenburg, Denmark and England these regiments wore green cuffs. They were introduced in Brandenburg in 1686. The regimental lieutenants wore crimson uniforms and the captains violet. The musketeers carried a cartridge pouch with a fabric-covered top, adorned with the eagle of Brandenburg and embroidered with the Electress' initials. Cartridge pouches were worn at this time instead of the small, flask-shaped wooden containers that had been suspended from the bandolier. Evidently the reason for the change was that a new method of

loading the musket had become general. Instead of the earlier, separate powder and shot, the troops now had a measure of powder packed together with the shot in a small paper container henceforth to be called the 'cartridge'. Such cartridges were best carried in a pouch where cleaning equipment for the musket could also be kept.

20. Savoy: Regiment 'Guardie'. Musketeer, 1664

At this period the Duke of Savoy maintained an army uniformed on the model of the French, but with the difference that the guards regiment wore greatcoats with two rows of buttons. In hot weather and on parade the greatcoat could be buttoned back, so that the appearance of the lining and waistcoat, or 'camisole' as it was called, became of greater importance than formerly. When the regimental characteristics of the uniforms were established, the colours of these details became important.

THE SCANIAN WAR 1675–1679

The Scanian War was fought between Denmark and Sweden. Danish war aims were to recover the former Danish provinces east of Øresund. The war commenced with the Danish conquest of Wismar in the Swedish settlements in North Germany. After a fortunate start in the main seat of the war, in Scania, Denmark won a great victory at Lund, in 1676. But despite further Danish good fortune on the Norwegian frontier and at sea, it ended inconclusively. Sweden's ally, France, declared war on Denmark and invaded, and Sweden emerged without loss of territory.

21. Denmark: Queen's Life Regiment. Pikeman, 1675

King Christian IV had attempted to introduce uniforms for his national regiments before his entry into the Thirty Years War, but it was not until the time of the Scanian war that they were worn to any significant extent. The regiment illustrated, like its counterparts in other countries (19) was clad in red and green. In 1677 the cuffs and stockings were blue and in 1679, yellow. Subsequently, red and yellow became the regimental colours until 1785. A certain proportion of an infantry regiment at this time was equipped with pikes. Formerly the principal infantry weapon, these remained the best defence against cavalry, as well as being a useful defensive weapon when attacking fixed positions. This regiment was equipped as a dragoon unit in 1657. For notable bravery during the siege of Copenhagen (1658–1659) it was promoted to the status of Queen's Regiment, which it still enjoys.

22. Denmark: Prince George's Regiment. Staff officer, 1675

At one time, Christian IV led his guards regiment dressed in blue with white trimming, and later it became traditional for Danish guards or royal regiments to wear blue. During the Scanian War, the King's and Queen's regiments were, however, dressed in red while regiments led by a prince were in blue with contrasting cuffs, varying in colour according to the regiment. In Denmark it was the custom for the officers to wear uniforms in which the principal colour was that of the men. Contrasting ostrich feathers in the hat were a privilege reserved for senior officers. The gilded gorget was general among infantry officers. White silk scarves, trimmed with gold, were worn only by officers of guards regiments. The high boots indicate that the officer is a member of the staff. All infantry officers, even the regimental commanding officer, paraded on foot, but on active service the staff were generally mounted. But they dismounted to attack, and led the assault on the enemy position on foot, with 'partisan' in hand. Prince George (Jørgen), the commanding officer of the regiment illustrated, married Princess, later Queen Anne of England, in 1683.

23. Denmark: Life Regiment of Cavalry. Trooper, 1675

During the Scanian War the Danish cavalry generally wore leather buff coats, but light grey, often almost white coats were also worn. Like the infantry, the dragoons apparently wore red, blue, green or grey uniforms. The grey hat, as shown, is of an earlier pattern, in use since the Thirty Years War, and at this time evidently being supplanted by a smaller and stiffer type in black felt (21 and 24). The coming of the paper cartridge made it possible to arm the cavalry with a form of musket, the carbine. When the soldier was mounted, the lattern was worn in the carbine hook of the wide bandolier. The small bandolier supported the cartridge-bag.

24. Denmark: 1st Fyn National Regiment. Musketeer, 1676

Today, *Fyenske Livregiment*. Green uniforms or distinguishing marks were characteristic of the Fyn regiments for many years. Especially popular were the green jackets with yellow cuffs originally worn by the 2nd Fyn Regiment, while the 1st wore grey coats with green cuffs. When the two regiments were combined in 1676, the new unit took over the uniform of the 2nd Fyn. The royal monogram and crown on the hat were characteristic of Danish infantry at this time. The weapons of the Danish army during the Scanian War were very up-to-date. The matchlock muskets were replaced by the flintlock, and the earlier bandolier with the wooden powder containers disappeared.

25. Sweden: East Gotland Regiment. Musketeer, 1675

Today., *K. Livgrenadjärregementet*. As early as 1575, the Swedes had regulations for the uniforms of the national regiments. Later an attempt was made to make uniforms correspond in colour to the flag and arms of the district from which the regiment was recruited. French influence played a large part in the early Swedish uniforms, particularly in the form of vertical pocket-flaps on the coat. Especially characteristic of Swedish uniforms at this period was the cap prescribed instead of the hat. As shown, the cap could be trimmed with fur or similar material, or it could also resemble the cloth cap with the loose bag of the French dragoons (27).

26. Sweden: Skaraborg Infantry Regiment. Ensign, 1675

Today, *Skaraborg Armoured Regiment.* The Swedish officers, too, had considerable liberty in choosing the details of their uniforms. Nevertheless the gorget was generally worn as a mark of rank. It appears from a regulation dating from 1688 that the captain's gorget was gilt with the king's monogram under a crown in blue enamel, while lieutenants and ensigns wore silver-plated gorgets with the initials in gold. A characteristic feature of the uniforms of Swedish officers at this time was the belt with sword-slings often covered with gold or silver braid. The sash was not worn at this time, but it reappeared later (146).

27. Sweden: Hälsinge Infantry Regiment. Musketeer, 1675

Today, *Hälsinge Regiment.* The regional coats-of-arms, after all, gave insufficient possibilities for colour variation, so that other, non-heraldic, colours such as brown or green were brought into the uniforms. Instead of more or less conspicuous shirt-sleeves below the cuffs, the Swedish rankers' uniforms, for everyday use at any rate, revealed the long narrow sleeves of the waistcoat.

28. Sweden: National Cavalry. Trooper, 1676

In the Swedish cavalry only the breastplate from the earlier armour was retained, but, in compensation, this plate was made bullet-proof and held in position by cross-straps at the back. For the sake of convenience it became the custom to hook the skirt corners of the buff coat together when mounted. This led to the use of more decorative, fabric trimming for the reinforcement of the coat-skirts, in the regimental colours, and on this basis developed the first distinctive regimental features in cavalry uniform. (87 and 114.) During the

Scanian War, when many Danish and Swedish regiments wore virtually the same uniform, both sides had to put on some conspicuous sign of their identity before a battle. At Lund in 1676, for instance, the Danish regiments wore a white armband, and the Swedes a wisp of straw. Hence the origin of the tradition that the straw cockade worn today by certain Swedish regiments is a mark of bravery awarded for their conduct at Lund.

THE WAR OF THE PALATINATE 1688–1697

Under pressure of Louis XIV's threat to occupy the Palatinate, as security for his sister-in-law's inheritance, a number of German states, in conjunction with Austria, Spain and Sweden, pledged themselves to uphold the unity of Germany. When war broke out, they were joined by England, the Netherlands, and Savoy. The French fought with distinction on all the battlefields, the most celebrated of which were Steenkerke and Neerwinden, in 1692 and 1693 respectively. The Palatinate was entirely laid waste by the French. William III, however, captured Namur in 1695. When France wished to free her hands for the coming problem of the Spanish succession, Louis XIV contented himself with an allowance for his sister-in-law.

29. Spain: Dragoon, 1690

Conceivably because of the influence of the earlier cavalry coats made of leather, a yellow uniform was introduced for this branch in Spain. It is of interest that all the Spanish cavalry and dragoon regiments at this time wore red cuffs. The cavalry still wore their helmets and cuirasses. Among the equipment one notes, especially, the bayonet carried on the right side. This was the plug bayonet which could be fitted to the muzzle of the firearm. But this was inconvenient, in that it was impossible to fire the weapon with the bayonet fixed. Before the end of the seventeenth century, contrasting cuffs (51) were introduced regiment by regiment in the Spanish cavalry.

30. Austria: Infantry Regiment 'Deutsch-meister'. Fifer, 1700

In 1914, *'Hoch-und-Deutschmeister'* Infantry Regiment no. 4. From an early period, each company had at least one 'tambour' or drummer whose function was to transmit the commander's orders to the company by prearranged beats and rolls on the drum. On the march he provided—as he still does—the marching rhythm. There were also fifers or flute-players to play marches or popular tunes to march rhythms. When the regiment was fully assembled, the drummers and fifers formed a single body under the drum-major (170). Special attention was paid to the uniforms of fifers in all armies. Later, when uniforms were strictly enforced, theirs was the last to come within the regulations. The regiment shown here wore grey uniform with pale blue cuffs, and these facings appear in the uniforms of the drummers and fifers. Characteristic of the uniforms of the 'music' was also the rich braiding. The brass container on the cloth-covered bandolier was for carrying the fifes, of which each player had several. The name of this regiment originated in the fact that, when formed in 1695, its first head, the Palatinate Duke Franz Ludwig, was also head of the Teutonic Order of Knighthood. Hence his title *'Hoch-und-Deutschmeister'*.

31. Hanover: Infantry Regiment 'von Podewils'. N.C.O., 1687

This regiment, formed in 1631, was among the oldest in the Hanoverian army. The uniform consisted of both old and more recent features. The wearing of the coat open, showing the waistcoat, seems quite modern, while the leather trousers for the infantry, and the neutral colour of the stockings look rather old-fashioned. The plain shoes were usually laced, although by this period it was becoming the custom to wear buckles and to colour them black. Both officers and N.C.O.s in many armies from the earliest

times carried a shafted weapon, the halberd. This was considerably shorter than the pike, and so called a 'pole-arm'—the word 'arm' not being applied exclusively to firearms at this time. The white hat feather and the red neckerchief with gold fringe is an early instance of the later more general use of distinguishing features for the unit. The regiment was awarded these for good conduct during an inspection at the Lido in 1685. It was in the service of the Venetian Republic during the war against the Turks in 1685–1688.

32. Bavaria: Puech Infantry Regiment. Musketeer, 1682

Here the leather equipment is a mixture of old and new: the old bandolier for the side-arm (21) is worn with the modern cartridge pouch. The white neckerchief, worn at the time by both civil and military was tied, as shown, with a contrasting ribbon. In many armies a red ribbon, or 'necktie' as it was called, was popular. The most usual, but also the hardest to keep clean, was a white ribbon but black, and less frequently other colours were worn. When the neckerchief went out, the cravat was tied round the neck outside the shirt-collar, but the traditional colours were retained, as they were when the cravat at the neck lost its character of a fastening, and was sewn in position. Later, black neckcloths became general, although in certain armies up to a later date red indicated regiments with an ancient tradition.

33. Savoy: Artillery. Gunner, 1698

Until the middle of the eighteenth century the Sardinian (Savoy) artillery wore dark blue. At this period the sword was being replaced by the heavy backsword cutlass, as a side-arm for gunners. The cutlass originated as a short weapon used in the chase, and its scabbard provided extra space for other knives. This was useful for the artillery, since the reamers and bit used by the gunners could thus be carried so as to be readily accessible at all times.

34. Netherlands: Life Guards of Foot. Musketeer, 1691

The Life Guard of Foot accompanied William of Orange to England in 1689 when he became king, but they remained a Netherlands regiment. Before his death in 1702 they returned to their homeland. Their colours, blue and orange, the livery colours of the House of Orange at the time, were reserved for the Netherlands guards regiment (80).

35. France: Gardes françaises Regiment. Grenadier, 1697

This regiment, founded in 1563, was a field unit. In peacetime it shared guard duties at the royal residence with the Swiss Guard (149). Like other French guards regiments it was put into uniform at an early period, its regimental colours being those of the livery of the Royal house; blue, white and red, a combination reserved before the Revolution for the guards and other privileged units. The shoulder knots were also very ornamental at this time, and restricted to specially distinguished units. In peacetime this regiment carried red cartridge pouches, with yellow edges and the French arms embroidered in gilt. The grenadiers were specially picked infantry trained in the use of hand grenades as well as in the usual weapons. At this time the grenade was an alarmingly primitive weapon, dangerous to its user. It consisted of a hollow, iron sphere, filled with powder and fitted with a fuse. The grenadier carried a slow match to ignite it. His duty was to proceed at the head of the column of assault to clear the way, and hold the enemy down with his grenades. Curiously enough, the grenadier cap (36) had not yet been adopted by this regiment.

36. England: Queen's Troop of Horse Grenadiers. Grenadier, 1688

In 1678, all squadrons of the Horse Guards were reinforced with mounted grenadier units. These units did not consist of the nobility but were recruited on a general basis. The grenadiers were actually dragoons, and equipped as such.

Because the grenades occupied the wallet carried on the bandolier, the cartridges for the musket were kept in a small pouch on the belt. The grenadier section was uniformed in a manner different from that of the ordinary squadrons. Their coats were à la polaque and their cuffs blue, while their rich braiding was in the squadron colours: blue for the 1st, green for the 2nd, and yellow for the 3rd.

THE GREAT NORTHERN WAR 1700–1721

In the Great Northern War, Sweden stood alone against Denmark, Norway, Poland–Saxony, Prussia and Russia. The conflict began with the Swedish *blitzkrieg* against Denmark in 1700, which resulted in Denmark hastily suing for peace. She entered the war again in 1709. The most celebrated battles of the war were at Narva, in 1700, Klissow, 1702, and Poltava in 1709. Denmark fought bravely but unsuccessfully at Halsingborg in 1710 and Gadesbusch in 1712. In 1718, Charles XII was killed before the fortress of Fredriksten in Norway, and the following year Sweden made peace. The result of the war was the breaking of the Swedish dominance in the Baltic, and a more important role for Russia in European affairs. Denmark's attempt to reoccupy her former provinces east of Øresund was a failure.

37. Denmark: Grenadier Corps. Grenadier, 1709

The Corps of Grenadiers was formed in 1701 of grenadiers from the enlisted regiments. Of guards status, they wore especially elegant uniforms. Coats were à la polaque, richly braided in front and with pointed (Polish style) cuffs. The pouch, which served both for grenades and for cartridges, bore the embroidered royal monogram under a crown. The headgear was an early form of grenadier cap. The special duties of the grenadiers (see 35) meant that the usual wide-brimmed felt hat was impractical so, like the dragoons, they were equipped with the tall cap. The idea that the felt hat got in the way during the process of throwing the grenade is mistaken: the grenadiers threw underarm. It was the slinging of the rifle, as with the dragoons, that required the special headgear. To give the grenadiers a more impressive appearance in keeping with the élite troops they were, a pointed peak was added. Originally, as shown here, it was fabric covered and richly embroidered. The Grenadier Corps, with the Foot Guards, won undying glory at Halsingborg in 1710, when they held out to the last man although the remainder of the Danish force took part in a retreat that was more like a rout.

38. Sweden: The Drabant Corps. Drabant, 1700

The Drabant Corps was formed at Humlebaek on Zealand during the short campaign against Denmark in 1700. The unit consisted exclusively of officers. (A drabant was the equivalent in rank of a captain of horse in the other regiments.) The Corps wore quite lavish uniforms. The widely accepted belief concerning the simplicity of Caroline uniforms is a myth that must have originated in the king's own simplicity in dress.

39. Russia: The 'Nichegorodski' Infantry Regiment. Musketeer, 1711

Peter the Great's plans to make Russia a great European power included the creation of an army on Western lines. From this time, then, the Russian uniforms were designed according to Western European models, and apart from certain exceptions it was only at the end of the nineteenth century that a Russo–Slavonic cut returned to favour. The colours of the first uniforms were chosen by the head of the regiment, but Peter the Great, influenced by the armies adopting a single uniform among his opponents and allies, introduced a dark green standard uniform in 1720. This colour remained characteristic of the Russian infantry until 1914. The shape of the headgear, as shown, was characteristically Russian. It was also practical for use in the north, because the coloured

capband could be pulled down round the neck.

40. Russia: Dragoons Officer, 1701

From the start, the Russian dragoon regiments preferred pale grey or white uniforms. A soft hat seems to have been worn rather than the cap. The brim, formerly left to choice, and usually turned up at one side only, was by now strictly according to fashion with the brim secured on three sides. This was the origin of the tricorne. Originally this assumed the plan form of an equilateral triangle as shown, but later the front corner was secured at the top, giving a more bicorne appearance.

41. Sweden: Life Guards. Musketeer, 1709

Today, *Royal Swedish Life Guards*. Charles XII equipped his guards with new and splendid uniforms in 1699. The officers gleamed with gold braid and the N.C.O.s with silver braid on coats and hats. The corporals and privates had yellow cuffs, and the officers and N.C.O.s dark blue uniforms throughout. Several illustrations of the Life Guards at the time show a yellow trimming on the breast of the jacket resembling a lapel, but this was not the practice in Charles' time. The variegated uniforms of the Swedish infantry (25–27) were replaced in 1687 by a dark blue, standard uniform with yellow cuffs and waistcoat for preference. The cavalry continued to wear the buff coat, but a cloth coat in dark blue throughout was gaining acceptance. Officers and N.C.O.s of the line regiments were required to wear rich trimmings of gold and silver braid. Later, as the war continued, raw materials for uniforms were in short supply and many of the units formed in the last year of the conflict were clad in plain grey.

42. Saxony: Life Guard of Horse. Officer, 1700

From 1695 the Saxon infantry and cavalry wore red uniforms. The Life Guard of Horse was equipped like the grenadiers. The grenadier cap shown here is a further development of the earlier form (37). The tapering crown now joins the topmost point of the peak, with the tassel projecting above it. The ornamentation on the cap could be made of metal, but embroidery was still commonest at this time. The officer's neckerchief was not in the Saxon, but in the Polish colours, red and silver. This resulted from the fact that in 1697 the Elector Augustus I, of Saxony, became king of Poland also, hence the Polish royal colours were added to the Saxon.

43. Poland: Light Horse. Trooper, 1702

At this period, the Polish army was being modelled on Saxon lines and was uniformed accordingly. The greatest progress was manifested in the infantry, but the cavalry, still essentially aristocratic, was influenced by the traditions of medieval chivalry. The exclusively aristocratic regiments were heavily armoured and richly clad. The lighter cavalry with the task of 'mopping up' were more modestly clad in national Polish costume. An attempt was made in certain regiments to give this a certain uniformity by the use of a single colour. But true uniform was as yet unheard of.

44. Brandenburg (Prussia). Infantry Regiment 'von Schlabrendorff'. Musketeer, 1700

In 1691 all the Brandenburg infantry were ordered to wear dark blue uniform coats; the guards units with white cuffs and the others with red. By judicious management of the possible alternative colours for under garments and braiding, each regiment was successfully provided with its own uniform. The fabric-covered cartridge pouch cover became obsolete, and more utilitarian black (but well polished) pouches came in. In some countries decoration continued in the form of metal ornamentation, of which the regiment illustrated provides an example. The pouch carried a crowned *cartouche*, with the electoral monogram in hammered brass, on the flap, which was itself bordered in red.

THE WAR OF THE SPANISH SUCCESSION 1702-1714

The War of the Spanish Succession involved Austria, England and the Netherlands on one side, and France, Spain, Bavaria, Portugal and Savoy on the other. During the war the latter two changed sides and joined France's enemies. The cause of the war was the ascent of a French prince, Philip of Anjou, to the Spanish throne, which the Hapsburg's considered they were themselves entitled to. The most important battles were at Hochstadt, in 1704, Ramillies, 1706, and Malplaquet in 1709. The outcome was Philip's retention of the throne of Spain, while the enemies of France were placated with French and Spanish cessions of territory mainly in the Netherlands and Canada.

45. Austria: 'Bayreuth' Dragoons. Grenadier officer, 1713

Although the Austrian infantry and cuirassiers were all dressed in grey, the dragoons were allocated blue, red and green uniforms (89). In 1711, grenadier companies were formed in the Austrian dragoon regiments. The officers in these companies, as was the rule in the infantry, were armed with fusils to show that the grenadiers were picked troops. These dragoons were often given rich clothing: the grenadier cap decorated with fur (bearskin) was a forerunner of the later bearskin cap. It is worth noting that the officer here is wearing a waistcoat instead of a shirt, with sleeves and cuffs, the latter being worn outside the cuffs of the coat and fastened by small straps attached to the cuff buttons.

46. Austria: 'Hasslingen' Infantry Regiment. Musketeer, 1713

Although it was decided in 1708 that all the Austrian infantry were to wear grey, it was some time before the change was effected. Thus in 1713 certain regiments were still wearing the old variegated uniforms. Other regiments, again, had white uniform coats. An unusual feature was the fabric-covered buttons worn by many regiments. Leather trousers were for winter use, and the normal trousers were made of linen. The N.C.O.s in several regiments wore coats of the same colour as the men's cuffs, a feature that was going out, nevertheless. The green sprig in the hat was the Austrian (Imperial) field badge, always worn on campaign.

47. Netherlands: 'Van Friesheim' Infantry Regiment. Grenadier, 1701

Uniforms began to be worn more generally in the Netherlands around 1680. Up to 1730, both infantry and cavalry were dressed in grey with contrasting cuffs varied according to the regiment. Originally blue was reserved for guards regiments, but after 1730, blue coats came in for the infantry also. The grenadier cap shown here has a peculiar shape, but its origin was identical with that of the tall pattern. The crown is not so lofty, but the top tassel shows that it stems from the cap. The pouch in the bandolier was used for the hand grenades, so the cartridges for the musket were carried in a small pouch at the belt. The brass container on the bandolier, the 'match-holder' (*lunteberger*), was for the slow-matches for igniting the grenades. The container was perforated, so that the burning match could be carried in it without being estinguished. Note that the green sprig in the hat was also worn by Austria's allies.

48. Great Britain: The Princess of Wales's Own Regiment of Foot (later the Queen's). Grenadier, 1715

Today, 1st Bn, The Queen's Regiment (*Queen's Surreys*). Kirk's Regiment of Foot, formed in Tangier in 1661, was the oldest line regiment but one in the British Army. In 1678, British infantry regiments were reinforced by the addition of a grenadier company. Early grenadier caps seem to have been round and trimmed with fur (12) but this type was soon displaced by fabric caps with embroidered fronts, which were to become more popular in England. The trimming of lacing on the coat seems, to

begin with, to have been confined to the grenadiers. Lapels on the front are notable: originating when the double-breasted coat was buttoned back. These lapels became in time the most popular decorative feature on uniforms in almost all armies.

49. France: 'De Bourbon' Regiment. Drummer, 1713

Until 1767 it was the custom in the French Army for the drummers in infantry regiments to wear the livery of the regimental commander. Regiments with the king as head dressed their drummers in the Royal blue livery. In 1767 this was adopted by all the French regiments except those with the queen or a prince of the blood as head. Until the Revolution these latter retained the livery colours of the regimental head for the drummers. The regiment shown here, led at this time by the duke of Bourbon, had drummers dressed in the duke's livery colours, with silver braid on the sleeves as a further distinctive mark. The drums were made of wood, painted in the livery colours, and adorned with the arms of the regimental head. The method of carrying the drum is unusual.

50. France: 'Royal Cravattes' Cavalry Regiment. Trooper, 1701

Like the infantry, the French cavalry generally wore grey from the beginning, but certain regiments wore red, and the Royal regiments were in blue with red cuffs. The principal regimental markings were contrasting patterned lacing on the saddle-cloth and holster-caps. Under the cloth coat the trooper wore a leather waistcoat with sleeves. To save wear, the cloth coat was packed and carried on the saddle during exercises and marches, and the trooper wore the waistcoat in lieu of the leather coat or jerkin. The cloth coat was worn in battle, on parade, guard duties and other special occasions. Note that the French cavalry, at quite an early period, wore black polished spurs. This regiment entered French service in 1667.

51. Spain: Numancia Dragoon Regiment. Private, 1707

Around 1700, the yellow uniform coat of the Spanish dragoons was replaced by a green one with contrasting cuffs according to the regiment, but the shoulder-knots were always yellow. At the same time, a special type of headgear came in —a development of the stocking cap, as was also the grenadier cap. The crown was contrasting, but its ancestry is revealed by the pompon on top (47). The crown was green, but the front piece, with a curved (not pointed) top, was cloth-covered in the regimental colours and plain except for a gold-braided edge. In 1719, the yellow coats came in again and the cap was replaced with a soft hat, later again replaced by a fur-edged cap.

52. Bavaria: Leib Regiment. Musketeer, 1701

In 1914, the *Bavarian 10th Infantry Regiment, 'König'* (69). Blue and white, the colours of the Bavarian arms, are again found in the uniform of this distinguished regiment. All the Bavarian infantry wore pale blue coats at this time, but white cuffs and rich braiding were reserved for the guards. To spare the knitted stockings and protect the legs when the going was rough, a form of gaiter or legging was coming in, made of grey or plain material, in winter usually wool or homespun, in summer of linen. Very early this was fitted with a strap under the instep, but at first it was not buttoned up the side, as later. It was loose enough to be pulled on, and was supported by a garter at the knee.

53. Savoy: Marine Regiment. Musketeer with Colonel's Colour, 1701

Guards regiments and artillery in Savoy were dressed in blue (20 and 33) from the commencement. But infantry of the line were dressed in pale grey until the middle of the eighteenth century. An exception was the Naval Regiment, which was dressed in red with green cuffs and under garments. When the blue uniform came in for infantry of the line, the Naval regiment wore it also. Though it had been the custom for the men to wear their long hair loose, corresponding to the full-bottomed wigs of the officers, at this period they were commencing to enclose it at the nape with a ribbon or hair-bag. Later the hair was gathered at the nape and was plaited into a pigtail; the sideboards were curled also. The military pigtail was always tied with a black ribbon.

54. Denmark: Prince Carl's Regiment. Musketeer, 1701

Today, *'Prinsens Livregiment'*. In Denmark a standard uniform was introduced in 1691, when the entire army was ordered to wear light grey coats with contrasting cuffs in regimental colours. Exceptions were the guards regiments and The Queen's Regiment (21). Breeches and stockings had to match the cuffs, and the rosette in the tricorne was usually the same colour. In 1711 red uniforms were introduced generally, but the re-uniforming took a relatively long time, and was not complete until 1720. The red uniform was of similar cut to the grey, but the change of colour involved a change of regimental colour also. This regiment, founded in 1657, was loaned to England and the Netherlands in 1700, and won considerable renown in their service during the War of the Spanish Succession.

55. Hanover: Von Bülow's Dragoons. Officer, 1706

Although the Hanoverian infantry were dressed in red uniforms quite early, the cavalry throughout wore white with contrasting cuffs according to the regiment. Waistcoats and breeches were leather and the former was curved at the bottom and trimmed in the regimental colour like the old buff coat. The men wore coats without braiding and carried a cartridge pouch in a bandolier over the left shoulder. When the Silesian and Hanoverian forces were combined in 1705, the Hanoverian officer's yellow sash was introduced. This regiment, founded in 1688, distinguished itself in the War of the Succession several times while fighting on horseback, although the Hanoverian dragoons were still considered at this time as mounted infantry.

56. German Empire: Salzburg Regiment. Musketeer, 1705

As a prince in the direct line of succession, the Prince-Bishop of Salzburg was pledged to supply a regiment to the national army. This regiment was recruited in the Prince-Bishop's district. It was dressed after the Austrian style (46) and wore gaiters or leggings. The wide belt was for the cartridge pouch, and the narrow one for the knapsack, the forerunner of the later pack. Officers and N.C.O.s in this regiment wore red coats with white cuffs.

THE WAR OF THE POLISH SUCCESSION 1733–1735

The War of the Polish Succession broke out at the death of Frederick Augustus I of Saxony in 1733, because both his sons, Augustus II and Stanislaus Lesczynski, laid claim to the throne of Poland. Augustus was supported by Russia and Austria, while France, Sardinia and Spain sided with Stanislaus. When peace was concluded in 1738, Frederick Augustus was recognized as king, while Stanislaus, as compensation, received Lorraine.

57. Poland–Saxony: The Guard Cuirassiers. Officer, 1734

While the union between Poland and Saxony lasted there was considerable mutual influence in military dress. So sometimes it is not easy to distinguish whether a particular unit is Polish or Saxon. The unit in question is an example: in some respects it is Polish, in others Saxon, but the general tendency is very Polish. The considerable amount of armour is suggestive of the Polish knights, and the winged helmet is notably Polish also. The sash is worn in Polish style, with the tassels on the right side. On the breastplate are the arms of Poland–Saxony within a crowned *cartouche*. The men's buff coats were unlined and trimmed with white cord with

two red stripes. Their coats carried no braid, their armour no coat of arms or gold edging, and the helmets no crest.

58. Poland–Saxony: Foot Guards. Bagpiper, 1732

The Polish guards are one of the few military units on the European mainland to have been equipped with bagpipes as a standard issue. At this time, their uniform was red with pale blue cuffs and under-garments, but to emphasize the status of the unit, the bagpipers were dressed in a form of national costume with the livery colours of the house of Wettin. The ram's head bagpipes are of a type still found in Eastern Europe. In the illustration they have an inflation tube, as distinct from other Polish bagpipes known as 'elbow-pipes', which are inflated by means of bellows carried under the arm.

59. Poland–Saxony: Guard Musketeer. Officer, 1735

This guards corps was not a field unit, but had the exclusive task of protecting the king and the royal residence. The officers wore elegant uniforms with silver trimming according to rank, and shoulder bands on both shoulders. The officer shown is on the staff. A striking detail is the sword bandolier which certainly still serves its original purpose but has become mainly non-functional in shape.

60. Russia: Infantry of the Line. Grenadier, 1740

When the green, standard uniform was instituted in 1720, the entire Russian infantry had red cuffs and lower garments, which certainly did not conform to the general principle at the time that the uniform should indicate the regiment. The only means available in Russia at this time of distinguishing the individual unit through the uniform was to include the arms of the town after which it was named on the metal mounts of the pouch and on the plate of the grenadier cap. In Russia the grenadier cap developed on somewhat different lines than in the

West, in that the crown has risen above the front plate.

THE WAR OF THE AUSTRIAN SUCCESSION 1740–1748

The War of the Austrian Succession, including the First and Second Silesian Wars, was fought between Austria, Great Britain, the Netherlands and Russia on one side and Prussia, Bavaria, France, Spain and Sweden on the other. Later, several German and Italian states also took part on both sides. The principal cause of the war was Karl Albrecht of Bavaria's claim to the Habsburg possessions on the extinction of the male line at the death of Charles VI in 1740, although Maria Theresa had long been recognized as heir to the throne. The most important battles were at Mollwitz in 1741, Dettingen in 1743 and Hohenfriedburg in 1745. The war commenced with Frederick the Great of Prussia's invasion of Silesia in 1740. In 1742, Prussia and Austria made peace, on condition that Austria ceded Silesia, but in 1744, Prussia re-entered the war for a short period. When peace was concluded in 1748, Maria Theresa's right to the throne was recognized by all the warring powers, but Prussia retained Silesia.

61. Austria: Emmanuel of Portugal Cuirassiers. Captain, 1740

In 1740, despite attempts to do so, it had proved impossible to impose a common uniform on the Austrian army. The regimental commanders still had considerable influence on the appearance of uniforms; often it was their personal arms that shone on the saddle-cloths and holster caps instead of the imperial eagle. The cuirassiers originally wore buff leather coats, but these were soon replaced by white cloth coats. Cuffs and under-garments had been red, blue or green, but red now became general. Since, however, waistcoat and breeches could be red or—like the buttons, white or yellow—it was possible to provide each cuirassier regiment with its own uniform. The cuirass consisted at this time simply of a breast-plate. For the men the straps and lining were made of wash leather. The Austrian, or more precisely the Imperial, sash was in the colours of the Imperial arms—gold and black. When the Elector Karl Albrecht of Bavaria became Emperor of Germany in 1742, the former Imperial Army became the Royal Bohemian-Hungarian Army or, as it was generally called, the Austrian Army. It was then decided that the sash should in future be natural green with gold or silver. When the Imperial dignity was again enjoyed by the Habsburgs in 1745, the black and gold sash was restored.

62. Austria: Nádasdy Hussars. Man, 1743

Since, in 1526, the Hungarian crown had passed to the Habsburgs, the Hungarian soldiers served in the Imperial army. The best known of them were the Hungarian cavalry, or hussars. The regiment shown here, founded in 1688, was the oldest regular hussar regiment in the Austrian army. From the first the hussars wore uniforms in the Hungarian national style. Specially characteristic were the cord froggings on the jacket, which owe their presence simply to the fact that the now conventional buttonhole sewn in the fabric had not yet reached Hungary where the national dress originated. Instead jackets and coats were fastened with the aid of loops and cylindrical buttons, known as olivets. The tight trousers, short boots and fur-lined jacket carried over the shoulder likewise originated in the national dress. It must be emphasized that this furred jacket, over the shoulder, is called a pelisse, while the jacket proper worn by the hussars is called a 'dolman'. Until 1757, the head of the regiment could decide the colour of the uniform of the hussars. The excellent horsemanship of the hussars, and the terror they inspired in battle, induced other armies to establish hussar units, at first composed of recruits from Hungary, and later of native troops.

63. Austria: Kökényesdi Hungarian Infantry Regiment. Private, 1742

Like the hussars, the Hungarian infantry were uniformed in national Hungarian style. An order of 1733 specifies a blue 'attila' (jacket), bright red trousers, and a cap of black felt, but the heads of the regiments altered the uniform as they thought fit. Both the Hungarian hussars and infantry had a special hair-style, consisting of a plait at the nape, and one over each temple. The long moustaches were worn either with the points turned down or boldly upwards (19–92). This regiment was formed in 1734.

64. Austria: Vasquez de Binas Italian Infantry Regiment. Grenadier drummer, 1740

The basic colour for the Austrian infantry uniform officially remained light grey, but in practice white cloth was used at this time. The coat had lapels and cuffs in the regimental colour. The waistcoat had either one or—as shown here—two rows of buttons, depending on the regiment. The grenadier cap was taking on the form that later would develop into the bearskin cap, but its ancestry in the stocking cap still showed in the braid-trimmed crown which was in the regimental colours. The outer or protective stockings had become thoroughgoing gaiters, or more precisely, spatterdashes, with buttons on the outside. They were usually black, but in hot weather, during peacetime or on parade, white were worn. In many regiments the drummers wore coats of the same colour as the regimental cuffs, or with richer braid trimming. But economy was often enjoined in this detail, and in 1755, it was prescribed that the drummers were to be distinguished only by the 'swallows' nests' or wings on the shoulders. The regiment shown, which was formed in 1721, was recruited in Lombardy.

65. Prussia: Fürst Moritz Infantry Regiment. Grenadier, 1741

Under Frederick William I, the soldier-king, the Prussian army was greatly expanded. With regard to uniforms, as a result of scrupulous economy, coat became both tighter and shorter, in order to save cloth. Lapels were beginning to be adopted, but by no means all regiments wore them. The under-garments were white, pale yellow or, as shown here, straw-coloured. Field equipment included a knapsack of coarse leather and a water-bottle. The decoration on the plate of the grenadier cap was no longer embroidered, but pressed in sheet brass and of open pattern so that the lining beneath was visible. The cap was thus more durable and the brass ornamentation could be kept as bright as the buttons on the uniform. Prussian grenadier officers did not wear the grenadier cap, or carry a musket, as in most other countries, but the tricorne and *espontoon*. The regiment shown, which was formed in 1713, was led by Prince Moritz of Anhalt-Dessau.

66. Prussia: The Artillery. Bombardier 1740

In 1914, *Prince Augustus of Prussia's Field Artillery Regiment* (*1st Lithuanian nr. 1*. The uniform of the Prussian artillery was essentially the same as that of the infantry. The coat was dark blue throughout except for the lining. Black collars and cuffs first came in in 1798. The special bombardier's cap, of black oilcloth with brass ornamentation was introduced in 1731. Some of the reamers formerly carried in the cutlass scabbard were now kept in the powder-flask belt. The bombardier's rank was indicated by gold lace on the cuffs. When the side boards were curled, it became the custom to powder the hair as in civilian life, but this did not apply generally among the men under campaign conditions, but only on parade and during guard duty in peacetime. But the officers always had to have powdered hair or to wear white perukes.

67. France: Royal-Comtois Infantry Regiment. Musketeer, 1740

This unit, founded in 1674, being a royal regiment, wore blue cuffs. The uniform of the French infantry was standardized

n 1736. Coat and waistcoat have, in this
nstance, remained wider and longer
han in Prussia. Generally speaking,
French uniforms at this time were not
so tight as the Prussian. About 1740,
uniforms began to be fitted with collars
n the regimental colours. The number
of buttons on the cuffs and pocket flaps
and the number and shape of the latter
were also distinctions carefully maintained, since the traditions thus represented dated back to the initiation of
uniform. On campaign the infantry were
kitted with knapsacks or a pack carried
on the back, but in this field also there
seems to have been greater liberty than
n Prussia.

68. France: De Beauffremont Dragoons. Man, 1740

This regiment, founded in the Franche
Comté, in 1673, like other French
dragoon regiments not led by princes of
the blood, was dressed in red. The
colours of the cap and tunic, among
other details, indicated the regiment.
Shoulder cords were discontinued and
instead a fringed epaulette was introduced for securing the belt of the cartridge pouch. Dragoons nearly always
wore the coat skirt corners hooked
together, a custom that was also coming
n for the infantry. In 1750 a tricorne
hat was prescribed for dragoons, after
which the cap was worn only in barracks.

69. Bavaria: Leib Regiment. Grenadier, 1740

n 1914, the *Bavarian 10th Infantry
Regiment, 'König' (52)*. With the introduction of lapels the Leib Regiment
was allotted black as a regimental colour,
while the lace trimming was reduced.
The pale blue trousers gave way in 1748
to white. The grenadier cap, which had
generally been worn without decoration,
was fitted with a metal plate around
1740, with ornamentation in relief. In
most armies, grenadiers were privileged
to grow moustaches, while other branches
were clean-shaven according to current
fashion. In several armies, the privilege
became a duty, and grenadiers not

suitably endowed by nature had, on
service, to wear false or painted-on
moustaches. Grenadiers with blonde
moustaches had to blacken them for
parade; moreover, the moustache had
to be constantly waxed so that the points
pointed boldly upwards.

70. Palatinate: Graf von Hatzfeld Carabiniers. Officer, 1748

In 1914, the *Bavarian 5th Chevaulegers-
Regiment, 'Archduke Frederick of Austria'*. The Palatinate Electorate, of which
the army was combined with the Bavarian
in 1777, maintained at this time an army
uniformed in general after the Bavarian
pattern. In both, the cavalry regiments
were clad in white coats with contrasting
cuffs according to the regiment. The
blue and white hat-bow or cockade is
noteworthy. In many armies it was
black, but it could also, as here, be in
the colours of the royal house (33, 50,
52 and 74-75).

71. Saxony: Queen's Regiment. Drummer, 1745

The red uniforms of the infantry of
Saxony were replaced in 1734 by white.
In 1742, the lapels were discontinued
and regiments could be identified only
by the colours of their cuffs and under-
garments. The button arrangement is
apparently of Polish origin, and seems
only to have been adopted by the Foot
Guards and the Queen's Regiment. The
other infantry regiments had equally
spaced buttons. The distinguishing mark
of the drummer is the yellow lace and
the decorations on the shoulders. These
'swallows' nests' could, as shown, be in
the regimental colours, but they could
also be in the basic colour of the jacket,
and contrasting only in the lace (64).
The chevron-shaped trimming on the
sleeves was very popular, and was used
in many countries over a long period.

72. Saxony: Artillery. Gunner, 1740

In 1914, the *Royal Saxon 1st Field
Artillery Regiment no. 12*. In 1917, green
coats with red cuffs and collars and brass
buttons were introduced throughout the

Saxon artillery, a colour combination that lasted until 1914. The gunners could button over the lapels in cold or rough weather, so that they showed only at the top, and under these circumstances the belt and side-arms were worn outside the coat. At this time, the artillery was generally losing its character of a craft-guild, but this branch still required basic training. Besides handling his guns a well-trained artilleryman had also to be a pyrotechnist, both when dealing with signal rockets for military purposes, and for firework displays. The senior artillery N.C.O.s had thus been called 'pyro-technists' or 'fireworkers' for some time while their younger comrades had the more military title of bombardier.

73. Russia: Preobraschenski Guards. Grenadier officer, 1740

This regiment, formed in 1683 and raised to the status of a guards regiment by Peter the Great in 1700, was the most noted infantry regiment in the Russian army (399). The uniform illustrated was adopted in 1732. The headgear was a grenadier cap of peculiarly Russian type (97) and adorned with a large plume of feathers. The distinguishing mark of the regiment was the red collar; the 2nd Russian guards regiment, the Semenov-ski, had pale blue collars. The officers in the regiment's musketeer companies wore tricorne hats with gold braiding and were armed with espontoons. For this reason they did not wear the red bando-lier with the cartridge pouch over the left shoulder. The men's uniform was like the officers', but without gold trim-ming and with the leather equipment light brown and without braiding (97).

74. Spain: 'Soboya' Infantry Regiment. Ensign, 1748

After 1710, the Spanish infantry wore pale grey and later, white coats, with contrasting cuffs and tunics according to the regiment. Breeches were generally white, and stockings red. In 1730, white linen spats were introduced. From the outset, coats were worn open while the coat skirts of the other ranks were

hooked together. Lapels were first intro-duced in 1767.

75. Sardinia: 'Sardinia' Regiment. Musketeer, 1744

While the Guards regiment and the artillery wore blue uniforms (20 and 33) the Sardinian infantry, from the outset, wore pale grey (white) uniforms. The naval regiment (53) was an exception to this. The regiments differed from each other in the colours of their cuffs and collars. The under-garments were either the same colour as the cuffs or pale yellow. The grenadiers wore fur caps and carried sabres. All regiments carried cartridge pouches with red edges. In the 1750's, the entire infantry were given dark blue jackets.

76. Naples: General, 1740

At this period, the kingdom of Naples maintained an army that was uniformed predominantly according to the French pattern. Special uniforms for generals were first adopted in many armies about the middle of the eighteenth century. Before that time, generals usually dressed as they pleased, or wore the uniform of one of the regiments they commanded, often with the addition of certain dis-tinguishing features. A well-known sign of the general was the 'plumage', a trimming of ostrich feathers round the edge of the hat brim. It is still worn by generals in many armies on ceremonial occasions. Hitherto, princes had worn uniform as rarely as possible, for in-stance in wartime or during inspections. Exceptions were Charles XII of Sweden, and Frederick Wilhelm of Prussia, who both normally wore uniform. The general here is decorated with the Order of Constantine.

77. Hanover: Horse Grenadiers. Trooper, 1742

The Grenadier Squadron, founded in 1742, together with the *Garde du Corps* Regiment, comprised the Hanoverian mounted guard. Both units were dressed in red. Notice the regimental colour of the trimming on the waist coat. Like the dragoons, the grenadiers were recognizable by the shoulder-cords worn on the right side. The front of the grenadier cap carries the British arms in embroidery above, indicating that after 1714 the Electors of Hanover were also kings of Great Britain. Below is the Lower Saxony crest, the running White Horse. On the cover of the cartridge box, cut in brass and resting on a backing of red fabric is the electoral and royal monogram, surrounded by the insignia of the Garter.

78. Great Britain: Major-General Howard's Regiment of Foot (The Buffs). Private, 1742

In 1914, the *East Kent Regiment—The Buffs* (401). The regiment shown, which can trace its origins back to 1572, became part of the English army in 1665. The regiment's nickname, later to become official, comes from the buff-coloured facings on the red coats adopted on the latter occasion. In the 1740's British uniforms were becoming regularized. The patterned lacing was no longer reserved for grenadiers, but had become a regimental feature. Most British regiments wore red waistcoats although they could be of the facing colour. The bulky leather equipment was characteristic of the British army at this time. The picker and brush for cleaning the touch-hole of the musket were carried on two thongs in which the end of the pouchbelt terminated.

79. Schwarzburg: Infantry Regiment 'von Diepenbroik'. Officer, 1740

As a prince in the direct line of the succession, the prince of Schwarzburg had a duty to supply contingents to the national army, as it was called. In the War of the Spanish Succession these contingents wore white uniforms with red cuffs. In 1734, the distinctive colour was changed to pale blue, which included the waistcoat. At the end of the eighteenth century the Schwarzburg infantry were given dark blue uniforms (219).

80. Netherlands: Foot Guards. Pioneer, 1750

The orange cuffs and under-garments earlier worn by the Foot Guards (34) were replaced at an early period by red, and again around 1750, as regards the breeches and stockings, once again by white. At this time there were sappers or pioneers in nearly all regiments of most armies. Like the grenadiers, the pioneers were a form of shock troops, with the task, among other duties, of removing palisades and other defences. They also constructed them, and were thus equipped with an axe and often also with a sabre with saw-toothed edge. They also wore leather aprons and gauntlets. The sappers, who were chosen from among the tallest and strongest troops, were uniformed somewhat similar to the grenadiers.

THE STUART RISING IN SCOTLAND 1745–1746

The discontent of the Highlanders resulting from union with England grew until in 1745 they invited the Stuart Pretender, Prince Charles Edward, to lead them in the cause of independence from England and to regain the throne for the Stuarts. The Prince was received with enthusiasm, but after fighting a series of brave battles, the rebel army suffered a fatal reverse at Culloden in 1746, after which the rebellion was put down by the English troops.

81. Great Britain: The King's Own Regiment of Foot (later 4th Foot). Officer, 1743

Today, *The King's Own Royal Border Regiment*. At this time the British Officers could still indulge their choice with regard to the braid trimming on their uniforms. The only restriction was that the choice of gold or silver depended on whether their men had brass or pewter buttons. Likewise the gorget was silver or gilt according to the buttons. The royal regiments wore dark blue cuffs and lapels, with dark blue breeches for parades. On the march, the troops wore gaiters made of brown cloth or linen, while the officers wore boots.

82. Hesse-Kassel: Prince Maximilian's Regiment. Grenadier, 1750

In 1914, *'Kurhessisches Infanterie' Regiment nr. 82.* The Stuart rising was put down by the English, partly with the help of troops hired in Hesse. At the time the uniform of the Hesse army was largely on the Prussian model. All infantry regiments wore cuffs and lapels of the regimental colour, while the lining, visible when the coat skirts were hooked together, was generally red. Lace trimming was worn only by regiments led by royalty. Around 1750, breeches of the same colour as the waistcoat were adopted. As regards the grenadier cap, at this time fronts entirely of metal were being adopted. The grenadier is holding a cap worn by a contemporary English regiment, namely Viscount Harcourt's (Oxfordshire) Regiment.

83–84. Great Britain: The Black Watch (later 42nd Foot). Bagpiper and corporal, 1745

Today, the *Black Watch* (*Royal Highland Regiment*) (132). This regiment, which can trace its origin back to 1729 and is the oldest Highland regiment in the army, became part of the latter in 1740. Its uniform is an adaptation of the Highland dress. The red jacket with cuffs in the regimental colour (buff) indicated adherence to the British army. In 1742, the jacket was trimmed with white lace at the button holes, and the buttons were arranged in pairs. The mark of rank of the corporal is the shoulder knot on the right side. The kilt could be either a *feileadh beag* (philabeg), that is, a kilt as worn today (509) or a *breacan-an-feileadh* or 'belted plaid' as shown here. A green breacan or tartan of a particular pattern or 'sett' was used for both types, and was later called the 'Government' or 'Military' pattern (or sett). About 1745, a small red stripe was introduced into the sett of this tartan. For the piper's kilt a red tartan of a sett reminiscent of the later Royal Stuart

Tartan was used. The stockings were made from cloth of a pattern later called the 42nd or Old Pattern. On normal service heavy shoes were worn, with buckles, but for mountain operations *cuarons* or light shoes of thinner hide were used. The cap or 'Highland bonnet' (493) was sometimes made with a red rim with slits through which a white ribbon could be passed, so that the cap could be adjusted for size. Later this developed into the chequered rim of the Highlander's headgear (132, 253 and 509). The pouch or sporran was, of course, part of the Highland dress and supplemented the pockets. Musket and side-arm, in this instance the broad sword, were standard issue while the dagger or dirk, and pistols with iron or brass butts—also customarily carried by the Highlanders — were usually purchased by the individual, but sometimes by the unit. Besides the side-arm, the pipers could also carry dirks. Each company had one piper and one drummer. The earlier type of bagpipes, as shown, had only two 'drones' or bass pipes, but pipes with three drones were coming in. The piper's banner was paid for by the captain of the company and usually carried his crest, a custom still maintained in certain regiments. The regimental grenadiers seem to have worn caps of the conventional type for the period, but in 1747, they were allowed to wear fur caps.

THE SEVEN YEARS WAR 1756–1763

The cause of the Seven Years War was Frederick the Great's wish to secure his position in Silesia, and to counter the threat of an anti-Prussian coalition. His opponents were Austria and her allies France, Russia, Saxony and Sweden. A large part of the 'national army' was also at the disposal of Austria. Prussia was supported by Hanover and Great Britain. Her fortunes in the conflict varied. Frederick the Great was generally weaker numerically, but this was compensated for by his military genius and the qualities of the Prussian troops. The most significant battles were at Rossbach and Leuthen in 1757, Kunersdorff in 1759 and Torgau in 1760. In 1762 Russia and Sweden withdrew from the conflict, to be followed by France. When peace was concluded in 1763 the European balance of power remained unchanged, but Prussia was henceforth recognized as a great power.

85. Prussia: Von Ruesch Hussar Regiment. Hussar, 1757

In 1914, the 1st *Leib Hussars*. The first Prussian hussar regiment was formed in 1721, but at the commencement of Frederick the Great's reign this branch was enlarged to include ten regiments. One of the best known of them was certainly the 'Black' hussars shown here, formed in 1741 and whose special mark was the death's head and crossbones on the cap. This macabre emblem was often copied subsequently, especially by units wishing to advertise their reckless bravery (240, 258, 301 and 473). Instead of the fur cap, the 'death's head hussars', like the Austrian pandours (92), wore soft caps. The felt cap, also called the 'flügelmütze' or 'schackelhaube' had a loose flap normally wound round the cap but which could be worn hanging loose for parades and in battle. The style of the hussars uniform followed, or was similar to, the Hungarian. Nevertheless, in the Prussian and certain other armies the leg covering took on the form of the 'esquavar', a pair of close-fitting trouser legs made of fabric worn with a pair of leather breeches (107). The other Prussian hussar regiments wore green, red, blue and white uniforms.

86. Prussia: Margraf Friedrich von Bayreuth Dragoons. Officer, 1757

In 1914, the 2nd (*Pomeranian*) *Cuirassier Regiment, 'Königin'*. Originally in white uniforms, the Prussian dragoons were given pale blue coats after the War of the Austrian Succession. The lace trimming on the men's uniforms was matched by embroidered gold or silver loops in elegant rococo style. These, the most characteristic manifestation of the rococo influence on uniforms, were very popular in the Germanic countries. Each regiment has its own pattern. The loop often terminated in a small tassel. The sash, which remained in use until 1918, was in the armorial colours of the Hohenzollerns, which were also the Prussian regional colours. The officer is decorated with the Prussian order *Pour le Mérite*. The regiment shown was formed in 1717, and in 1731 the Margrave Frederick of Brandenburg-Bayreuth became its head. The regiment won such renown at the battle of Hohenfriedburg in 1745 that it was allowed its own special grenadier march on parade.

87. Prussia: Von Seydlitz Cuirassiers. Trooper, 1762

Around 1735, the original buff leather coats of the Prussian cavalry were replaced by garments of straw-coloured cloth or kersey. When soiled, they were treated with a kind of 'blanco'. When it proved difficult to obtain the correct colour, and the regiments began to present an inconsistent appearance, it was decided that white should be used instead. Around 1780 the cavalry coats began to be made from the outset from white material. Since 1735 the cuirassiers waistcoats had been called *chemisettes*. A *sabretache* as it was called was carried from the belt of the broadsword or *pallasch* to compensate for the uniform's lack of pockets. Irrespective of the regimental colour, all regiments had a red edging to the lining of the cuirass. In 1762, a white plume of feathers was introduced for the headgear of the entire Prussian cavalry. This regiment, founded in 1690, had in 1757, the famous cavalry leader, Frederick Wilhelm von Seydlitz as its commander.

88. Prussia: Erbprinz von Hessen-Kassel Fusilier Regiment no. 48. Drummer, 1759

The regiment shown was formed as a field-infantry or field-fusilier regiment in 1756. The distinguishing feature of its uniform was the wearing of the fusilier cap as it was called, instead of the tricorne. This resembled the grenadier cap, but had a lower front. The waterproof cloth crown, decorated with brass, terminated at the top in a moulded flaming grenade. Grenadiers in the Prussian fusilier regiments always wore the grenadier cap. The braid trimming on the drummer's uniform varied from regiment to regiment, but lavish braiding on the sleeves was popular. Notice the leather apron, to give protection against the rubbing of the drum.

89. Austria: Erzherzog Josef (Archduke Joseph) Dragoons. Man, 1763

A regulation dating from 1757, specifying dark blue for the Austrian dragoon regiments proved impossible to maintain, partly on account of the war conditions. Hence the regiments mainly wore green, red and blue uniforms, and one of them was dressed in white. When, later, the dragoons developed into medium-heavy cavalry, the light cavalry in most armies were supplemented by the formation of *chevauléger* regiments, or light cavalry regiments which were uniformed similarly to the dragoons.

90. Austria: Bethlen Hussars. Officer, 1760

In 1914, the 10*th Frederick William III of Prussia Hussar Regiment*. Dark blue was prescribed in 1757 for the hussars also, but this regulation, as in no. 89, was not observed. The hussar officers displayed considerable lavishness in the decoration of their uniforms. Cords and trimming were finer than the men's and of gold or silver. Valuable fur was used for cap and trimming, while the sabretache was usually a sumptuous piece of gold or silver embroidery work. The officers wore moustaches like the men, and hair styles were in the current fashion.

91. Austria: Graf Franz Gyulai Hungarian Infantry Regiment. Musketeer, 1759

This regiment, formed in 1702, was the oldest regular Hungarian infantry regiment in the Austrian army. In 1747, grenadier companies were formed in the

Hungarian infantry regiments, and in 1749 the dress of the latter regiments underwent a change which brought them more into uniformity with the Austrian infantry. The former frogged outer garment was replaced by a white *caputrock* (overcoat) and the fur or soft cap by a tricorne hat. The Hungarian aspect was retained in the braided *dolman* worn instead of the waistcoat, and in the tight trousers with low ankle-boots—which were, however, virtually 'shoes'. The latter two features were worn in the same manner until after the commencement of the First World War.

92. Austria: Gradisca Slavonian Frontier Regiment. Man, 1759

To defend his frontier possession against the Turkish power, the emperor maintained in them a number of frontier regiments, composed partly of Croatian and Serbian immigrants. Their uniforms, like those of the Hungarians, had marked national characteristics. The regiments could be distinguished by different uniform colours, but brown predominated and later became the general colour for all the frontier regiments. The footwear, the *opanker*, is noteworthy; it was the national footwear of the common people in many Eastern European countries until quite recently. As the frontier guards had to pay for their own outfit, protective leather patches made their appearance. The curious water bottle made of wood later became general throughout the Austrian army. All the frontier regiments carried a red cape on the back, together with a pack containing the soldier's essential possessions. In 1760, a white *caputrock* matching those of the Hungarian regiments was authorized as regulation, and the *opankers* were replaced by Hungarian boots. Eventually, the government took over the expense of the outfitting.

93. Saxony: Prince Xaver Infantry Regiment. Musketeer, 1756

No comprehensive changes in the uniform of the Saxon infantry had taken place since the War of the Austrian

Succession (71). After the surrender of the Saxony army at Pirna in 1756, the regiment shown was enrolled in the Prussian army as the Jung-Bevern Regiment.

94. Saxony: Brühl Dragoon Regiment. Dragoon, 1756

At this time the Saxon dragoons usually wore red coats and tricorne hats. The grey coats of this regiment are thus worthy of note. The shape of the cap is reminiscent of those of the Spanish dragoons (51).

95. Sweden: North Scania Cavalry Regiment. Trooper, 1757

There had been little change in the Swedish uniforms since the Great Northern War. There had been a certain simplification and a less buttoned-up style but overall the army had an old-fashioned appearance, when it took part in the Seven Years War. The leather coat which had gone out of use, on account of cost, during the Great Northern War, was reintroduced in 1727, but was not used again after 1735, and subsequently worn only on parade.

96. Sweden: Södermanland Infantry Regiment. Grenadier, 1757

Today, the *Royal Södermanland Armoured Regiment*. In 1756 there was a complete change in the Swedish infantry uniforms, when it was decided that, in future, all regiments should have yellow collars, cuffs and breeches with their dark blue coats. Only the cavalry retained the old regimental colours. The stockings that remained the prescribed wear seem rather old-fashioned. Leggings seem first to have been used during the Seven Years War.

97. Russia: Infantry of the Line. Grenadier, 1756

With the exception of a new shape for the grenadier cap, instituted in 1752, there had been little change in the uniform of the Russian infantry (60) since 1740. The regiments still carried the civic arms on the front of the grenadier

cap and on the cartridge pouch, now entirely covered with a brass plate. In 1763, coats with red lapels came in, and grenadier caps of the usual type with metal front plates. At the same time the regiments were permitted to wear a strap on the left shoulder, as a regimental mark. Since the designs of the shoulder straps were under regimental control, they varied considerably in shape and colour combination.

98. Russia: Artillery. Gunner, 1757

Since the time of Peter the Great, the Russian artillery had been in red, originally with dark blue and later with black cuffs. Since these artillerymen, as in many other armies at the time, were still equipped as infantry, they carried as well as the powder flask on a shoulder-belt, a cartridge pouch at the belt. In 1757, a brass top was introduced for this pouch, with the Czarina's crowned monogram.

99. Russia: Moldavian Hussars. Hussar, 1756

Five hussar regiments were formed in Russia around 1740. Three were allocated fur caps, the others *flügelmutze* like the Prussian hussars. The all-yellow cap shown here is most unusual. Later these regiments were given black pelisses with red loops, and black caps. The monogram on the sabretache is that of the Czarina Elizabeth Petrovna.

100. Russia: Pandour Regiment. Grenadier N.C.O., 1756

In 1752 four pandour and four hussar regiments were formed in Russia, from a group of Serbian colonists in Southern Russia, immigrants from the Austrian Turkish frontier possessions. The uniforms of the pandours resembled those of the Austrian frontier regiments. There were certain divergences, for instance the round cuffs on the *caftan*. The yellow boots were worn only on parade; for daily use black boots or *opankers* were worn. The grenadiers were distinguished by the grenadier cap plate on the soft hat. On the plate, as well as the crowned monogram of the Czarina, there was oddly enough a device from the region colonized by the Serbians. The ordinary pandours wore a smaller plate on their caps. The gold braiding on the cuffs was the mark of the N.C.O.

101. Hanover: Von Scheither Infantry Regiment. Grenadier, 1756

Besides wearing braided buttonholes, until 1756 the Hanoverian infantry also wore lapels, cuffs, cuff-flaps and coats trimmed with lace, like the British (104). In 1763 the coat lining and waistcoat colour was changed throughout to pale yellow or straw. The adornment of the grenadier caps should have been uniform throughout all regiments, but it varied considerably nevertheless. Most regiments, like the British, wore caps of the embroidered variety, but some had caps with metal ornamentation. Caps with fronts entirely of metal were not used by the Hanoverians.

102. Hanover: Von Müller Dragoons. Grenadier officer, 1761

The Hanoverian dragoons wore white coats until 1766, and then dark blue came in. The cavalry regiments also wore white coats without the lapels. The skirts of the waistcoat were edged with a border in the regimental colour on the inner side, but this was not visible until the skirts were hooked back under campaign conditions. The officers wore cartridge pouches on field service.

103. Great Britain: 11th Dragoons. Man of light squadron, 1757

To make up for the lack of light cavalry, light squadrons were formed in the British dragoons regiments in 1756. They wore the relevant regimental uniform, but with lighter equipment and individual caps. Perhaps the most fundamental difference was that the horses were markedly less heavy than usual. The boots were called 'jockey boots', and were lighter than normal cavalry boots, while the headgear was the jockey cap—in reality a form of helmet of stiff

jacked leather and with a brass comb. The leather equipment was narrower and lighter than that of the dragoons. As always in the British army, there were many variations on the theme. For instance, the tuft on the helmet of the regiment shown should have been half buff and half red, according to the regulations. The light cavalry were also called hussars.

104. Great Britain: 20th Regiment of Foot. Grenadier, 1759

Today, the *Lancashire Fusiliers*. The British Infantry uniforms were standardized in 1751. The style was generally the same as before, only a little more close-fitting in accordance with fashion (and as a result of economies). The leather equipment became somewhat narrower. The grenadier cap of the embroidered pattern was established. The grenadiers wore the hair with a plaited pigtail, which was tucked up under the cap. The regiment shown, formed in 1688, won great renown at Minden, in 1759, and was presented with a laurel wreath after the battle. In recent times, the colours have been adorned with a wreath on the annual parade to commemorate the battle. On the same occasion, the entire regiment put roses in their caps, to commemorate the fact that the officers and men wore roses as a field-emblem during the advance to Minden.

105. France: Royal Lorraine Infantry Regiment. Grenadier, 1756

This regiment was formed as the Lorraine militia in 1744, but was considered, nevertheless, as a regular regiment. Uniforms of the French infantry at the time were white throughout. The grenadiers, who earlier wore grenadier caps of British type, had, in many regiments, adopted the fur cap which, however, varied somewhat in style. The bearskin was first authorized in 1763. The red sword-knot and the red grenades on the buttoned-back flaps of the coat were peculiar to the grenadiers, and lasted until the introduction of the service jacket. It was becoming the custom to wear the waist belt, with the side-arm, over the shoulder, crossing over the cartridge pouch belt. The method was prescribed for infantry of the line in 1779.

106. France: Royal Regiment of Cavalry. Trumpeter, 1756

The blue, red and grey uniforms of the French cavalry included lapels in 1750. The principal distinction of the regiment was still the contrasting colour of the patterned lace on the saddle cloth and holster caps. The leather equipment was white in certain regiments, and in others still yellow. The royal livery, worn by trumpeters in the royal regiments, could be varied somewhat according to the arrangement of the lace. The banner on the trumpet, with the royal arms, was confined to these regiments.

107. France: Berchény Hussars. Hussar, 1756

The 59th cavalry regiment, founded in 1720, was the oldest hussar regiment but one in the French army. All the four French hussar regiments were composed of foreigners, generally Hungarians or Germans. They all wore practically identical uniforms. The principal regimental distinction was the colour of cuffs, collar and cap. The latter in France was called the *mirliton*. Up to 1751, the French hussars wore fur caps. After the Seven Years War, they were dressed in green with red trousers, but the regimental features were virtually unchanged.

108. France: Maison du Roi Chevau-légers. Trooper, 1760

This guards squadron, which stemmed from the army of Navarre, was included in the French guards in 1589 when Henry of Navarre became king of France. Like other French guards units, it won various privileges in the course of time, partly in the form of rank. The squadron ranked immediately before the musketeer corps (4) and this status was expressed in the uniform. Gold and silver was the special royal braiding and could only be worn by permission.

Private troopers ranked with lieutenants. When the French kings accompanied the army to war, they wore the uniform of this squadron.

109. Bavaria: Electoral Guards. Guardsman, 1760

In 1914, the *Hartschier Life Guards*. This guards unit could trace its origins back as far as the middle ages. At the time of the Thirty Years War, the unit was mounted; later it became a dismounted palace guard, but retained boots and spurs for certain dress. The uniform illustrated remained unchanged apart from the influence of the mode, until 1858. The coat with the black velvet lapels is almost hidden by the sleeveless *casaque*, which was worn only on special guard duty, and which had the same origin as the *casaques* of the French musketeers (3 and 4). The peculiar weapon, the *couse* (or *glaive*) as it was called, remained in use for household duties as long as the regiment survived. Guard service was a reward for long-service officers.

110. Württemberg: Infantry Regiment 'von Roeder'. Grenadier, 1757

The Württemberg infantry were dressed in white until 1745. In that year yellow coats and red waistcoats were introduced, but in 1752 the former was replaced by dark blue in Prussian style. Grenadiers and musketeers in all regiments wore shoulder-knots. During the Seven Years War, the Württemberg grenadiers had to wear white linen covers to their caps, to distinguish them from the Prussians.

111. Brunswick-Wolfenbüttel: Leib Regiment. Drummer, 1760

At this time, the Brunswick army was uniformed entirely according to the Prussian pattern. The yellow coat worn by all the drummers was characteristic. It was of very similar cut to that of the ranker of the same regiment, and sometimes had lapels, cuffs and collar in the regimental colour, with 'swallows nest' wings and sleeve trimming.

112. Baden: District Regiment Baden-Baden. Grenadier, 1760

In 1914, the *1st Baden Leib Grenadier Regiment no. 109*. The Margraves of Baden-Baden and Baden-Durlach each undertook to supply one infantry and one dragoon regiment to the national army, as it was called. The uniform was very reminiscent of the Prussian, but the bearskin grenadier cap indicates the influence of nearby France. The Baden-Durlach district regiment had red lapels and cuffs, and a grenadier cap with a plate.

113. German Empire: Frankish District. Ferentheil Infantry. Grenadier, 1760

The infantry in the national army at this time was uniformed either in white, after the Austrian example, or in dark blue. Grenadier caps with peaks, and fur caps were both worn. Most grenadier caps had plates of metal throughout, but the earlier type with metal ornaments or open work on the plate were still used.

114. Saxe-Gotha: Garde du Corps. Trooper, 1760

This minute guards unit, with its 75 men, horseless despite their imposing cavalry attire, was typical of the German lilliput state at the period. Their sole duty was to parade in their decorative uniforms at the prince's residence. The model was evidently the uniform of the Prussian cuirassiers.

115. Schaumberg-Lippe: Carabinier Squadron. Trooper, 1756

The corps maintained by Graf Wilhelm of Schaumberg-Lippe-Brückenburg from 1753 was in direct contrast to the foregoing. Though it likewise totalled 75 men, they were mounted and on black Spanish stallions, and all were trained and daring riders. The uniforms seem anachronistic. Under the black armour was worn a long coat of black leather, with a bearskin band on the helmet. The leather pieces on the sleeves proved themselves impractical in the long run and were discontinued in 1759. The officers wore a coat with a plain red lining, and polished armour with gilded edges. Despite its armour, the corps was a light cavalry unit.

116. German Empire, Upper Rhine District: Artillery Fireworker, 1760

In peacetime, the district artillery was normally allocated to the national fortresses, which were maintained by the artillery branch. At this time the uniforms were dark blue throughout, with red or black. The dark green uniform worn by the Upper Rhine District artillery was something of a curiosity.

THE FRANCO-BRITISH COLONIAL WARS 1756-1763

France suffered as a result of her participation in the Seven Years War, because Great Britain took the opportunity of waging war against her not only in Europe but in the colonies, and with such success that France lost much territory in India and North America.

117. Great Britain: Royal Navy. Commander, 1756

Uniforms were adopted for naval use at a very late stage. The officers were the first to wear them. Uniforms for the seamen date from a relatively recent period. British naval officers first wore prescribed uniforms in 1748. They were blue and white throughout, a colour combination that persists in the 'number ones' or ceremonial uniform of British naval officers. Gold lace varied according to rank, and was especially lavish on ceremonial dress. The uniform shown was for daily use.

118. Great Britain: Light Infantry in North America. Man, 1758

Various items of the infantry man's normal equipment were made lighter as a result of the campaign in the forests of North America. This applies especially to the equipment of the light companies of specially picked men from the regiments, who were trained to move and fight in the forests. The uniforms were stripped of all lace. The sleeves of the coat were attached instead to the jacket, which became the principal garment, and the now sleeveless coat was used as an outer garment. As shown here, the coat is rolled up with the pack which, for the first time, is carried high on the back by means of two straps. The water-bottle was carried below the pack, and a powder horn under the right arm. A tomahawk was also carried below the cartridge pouch, which was carried on a narrow strap. Two pockets made of leather or rawhide were sewn to the breast of the jacket, for carrying shot and flints. Trouser-leggings were worn instead of knee-breeches and boots. The hat that had been cut down to a cap, which had black flaps over neck and ears. The troops were allowed to be unshaven on active service, which frequently resulted in some picturesque growths of hair and beard.

119. France: 'Volontaire de Bussy' in India. Grenadier, 1756

Military power in the North American colonies usually consisted of forces from the regular armies of the various countries concerned. In India, on the other hand, this task was performed with the aid of troops maintained by the trading companies. Generally consisting of native personnel, these troops were, for the most part, uniformed like the troops of the mother country, but with distinctive details added. This French trading company regiment was dressed in pale blue and red, and therefore very similar to the royal colours. The hair style and the bearskin must have been torture to wear under the Indian sun. See also the colonial troops under 365–80.

120. France: Royal Navy. Commander, 1763

As early as 1728, officers in the French galley fleet wore red, whereas the officers of the sailing fleet had adopted the royal colours, blue and red, a combination that persisted for a long period. Each squadron of the French fleet at this time had its own distinguishing colour. About

the year 1765, the collars on naval officers' uniforms were made in the colours of their respective squadrons. In the 1780's, the officers were granted permission to wear white waistcoats without lace for normal duty.

THE POLISH STRUGGLE FOR NATIONAL INDEPENDENCE 1768–1772

On the death of Augustus III of Poland in 1763, Russia enforced her choice for the succession, Stanislas Augustus, by sending troops into Poland. So the new king of Poland was simply a puppet of Russia. To stem the encroachment of Russia, a number of Polish nobles formed the Confederation of Bar in 1768. They demanded, among other things, greater protection from the Catholics, and tried to enforce their demands by sending an army against Warsaw. But the latter was destroyed by the superior Russian forces. In 1769 Prussia and Austria joined the conflict to prevent Poland from falling entirely into Russian hands. The result, however, was the combination of the three powers in 1772 in the first partition of Poland, in order to avoid war.

121. Poland: Royal Hussars. Captain, 1770

This corps performed guard and escort duty, and its uniform combined remnants of the Saxon influence with the national Polish tradition. It was in the national style but the colour, inherited from Saxony, was red. The cap, called the *konfederatka*, was the national Polish headgear (280 and 437), later replaced by the uhlan headdress (164 and 196). This type of baton was a development of the medieval battle-mace or club used to smash the armour of one's opponent and which, in Poland, became the mark of the specially distinguished officer.

122. Poland: Confederation Cavalry. Man, 1769

The majority of the confederation army had no uniform, but because the men

171

wore folk dress, the result was a certain uniformity of dress. However, certain cavalry units, as in previous periods, attempted a form of uniform.

123. Russia: Chevalier Guard. Man, 1772

The Chevalier Guard, established by Peter the Great in 1724, was the most distinguished unit in the Russian army. The type of light armour forming part of the uniform was peculiar to the guard at this time. The headgear consisted of a helmet with neckpiece. At the front the headdress was adorned with the Russian spread-eagle in open metal relief, above the protruding peak. The helmet was topped with a large plume of feathers that hung below the shoulders. The curiously shaped additions to sleeves, breeches and boots were a form of armour-protection, of metal plates joined by chains. The shoulder belt, too, was a form of armour, consisting of metal links on a pale blue underlay. The pale blue supervest worn over the tunic was almost hidden by the bandoliers. The supervest was a further development of the surcoat and the casaque (3–4 and 109) which, in its ultimate stage, was virtually a cloth cuirass. On the breast and back the supervest was decorated with the stars of the Order of St Andrew (208 and 250).

124. Russia: General Field-Marshal, 1768

In 1764, a standard uniform was prescribed for Russian generals, with a number of rows of gold embroidery, according to rank, along the edges of the coat and waistcoat and on the cuffs. Only generals wore gold embroidery along the seams of sleeves, shoulders and back. As a special distinction they also carried a marshal's baton, a development of the baton of authority (121). The field-marshal in the illustration has been decorated with the Order of St Andrew, with brilliants, and with the Grand Cross of the Order of St George. The latter was a military order which could be awarded

for individual bravery or for distinguished leadership.

THE AMERICAN WAR OF INDEPENDENCE 1776–1783

Discontent with the treatment of the British settlements in North America by the British government caused thirteen of the colonies to declare themselves independent in 1776. The conflict between the British troops on the spot and the Americans, which had been in progress since 1775, now attained the dimensions of a war. The Americans possessed only militias of very mixed quality, while the British army consisted of seasoned troops, including various regiments hired in Germany. Nevertheless, the Americans managed to defeat the British at Trenton, in 1776, and Princeton in 1777. The capitulation of a British army at Saratoga the same year encouraged France to enter the war in 1780, when the situation was critical for the Americans. She despatched a reinforcing army to America, and in 1781 a combined Franco-American force once more brought about the surrender of a British force at Yorktown. When peace was concluded in 1783, the independence of the former colonies, as the United States of America, was recognized.

125. U.S.A.: Washington's Guard. Man, 1776

There were militia units in the British North American colonies from the commencement. Many of them were uniformed, but as each company could choose the uniform it preferred, there was little uniformity when larger forces were assembled. Various militia units and the 'minute men' as they were called formed up in the clothes they were wearing at the time. Thus it was a motley army over which Washington assumed command in 1775. He himself wore a dark blue jacket with buff coloured cuffs, lapels and breeches. His guards were responsible for headquarters security and were composed of picked men dressed similarly to himself. The problem of commanding such a variously clad army as the Americans resulted in Washington's early initiation of marks of rank for the officers. They took the form of hat cockades. Field officers wore a red or pink cockade, captains yellow or buff, and lieutenants green. Generals and staff officers could be recognized by coloured bands worn across the chest between coat and tunic in the same manner as the grand cross ribbons.

126. U.S.A.: 1st Georgia Regiment. Private, 1777

Up to 1778 the shortage of clothing in the American army was of almost catastrophic proportions and any idea of uniformity had to be abandoned. In 1776 the problem of providing some form of uniform caused Washington to advise the states to equip their troops with 'hunting shirts', which originated in the type of body garment common in the frontier areas, where they were worn by trappers. His argument was that, besides being cheap and practical, they led the enemy to believe that he was merely up against irregular troops. The regiment shown seems to have had no uniform except this 'hunting shirt' which was worn by the officers also. In 1778 it adopted wool or linen leggings (140) instead of leather knee-breeches.

127. U.S.A.: 3rd Continental Artillery. Officer, 1776

This regiment was established as the Massachusetts Artillery Regiment in 1775. At first the ranks were not uniformed, but the officers wore the uniform as illustrated. By 1778, however, this was one of the best-dressed units in the American army. The other ranks wore white cross-belts, red plumes in their hats, and white spatterdashes. In 1779 the uniform of this regiment was adopted for the American artillery branch throughout, the only change being the adoption of the red lining of the coat, with yellow lace trimming for the men. Curiously enough the red British sash was retained in the American army right up to modern times.

128. U.S.A.: 2nd Canadian Regiment. Corporal of light company, 1778

This regiment was formed in 1776 as a result of recruiting in various American states, but the majority of the troops were Canadians. In 1775, Congress decided that the American army was to wear brown uniforms, because brown seems to have been the only colour of material locally available everywhere. All shades of brown thus dominated the appearance of the American army during the war in North America. In 1779 the regiment adopted red collars, lapels, cuffs and linings, but the under garments remained white. When cockades were introduced as a mark of rank for officers in 1775, a shoulder strap or epaulette was adopted for N.C.O.s, red for the sergeants and green for corporals. The jacked leather headdress shown—peculiar to light companies—consisted of a round crown and plate. The remainder of the regiment wore the tricorne hat. Various American regiments used British leather equipment taken as booty. The picker and brush for cleaning the priming-hole were carried on chains from the pouch belt.

129. Great Britain: 37th Regiment of Foot. Grenadier officer, 1776

Today, the *Royal Hampshire Regiment*. In 1768 the British infantry were issued with a new standard uniform which was generally used during the war in North America. Bearskin was now used for the grenadier caps of several regiments, with a black metal plate and white metal ornamentation. Loops and tassels were not official, but were nevertheless worn in many regiments. The grenadier officers wore epaulettes on both shoulders, and the other officers a single epaulette on the right-hand side. Normally the officers wore braiding of gold or silver round the buttonholes of the coat, but this practice was abandoned during the war in North America. The boots and the water-bottle were also wartime equipment. Normally the officers carried their cartridge pouches on a white belt.

The American War of Independence 1776–1783

130. Great Britain: 64th Regiment of Foot. Private, 1777

Today, *The Staffordshire Regiment* (*The Prince of Wales's*). By now the uniform prescribed for the British infantry in 1768 had lost much of its braiding, but frequently the buttonholes of the coat were still surrounded by patterned braid. The under-garments and the lining of the coat were now always either white or buff. Leggings were worn on campaign instead of half-length gaiters. The knapsack was replaced by a rectangular pack usually made of white goatskin. The sabre was no longer worn by musketeers, leaving only the bayonet on the waist belt. On active service the latter was often worn over the shoulder, crossed with the cartridge-pouch belt.

131. Great Britain. 5th Regiment of Foot. Man of light company, 1778

Today, *The Royal Northumberland Fusiliers*. When the light companies of the British infantry regiments were established during wartime, the regulations prescribed the composition of their equipment. Coats, for instance, were to be reduced to jackets, the hats replaced by caps, and the cartridge pouch carried on a belt. The red waistcoat was a special mark of the soldiers in light companies. Sometime after the commencement of the war in North America, the uniforms were stripped of lace trimming. Several regiments were permitted to wear special headgear instead of caps: as a consequence helmets reminiscent of those of the light dragoons were very popular. The officers of the light companies who, as grenadier officers, were armed with muskets, wore similar uniforms to those of the men, but without lace and with epaulettes on both shoulders. When a pack was worn, often an axe was attached to it. Otherwise it was worn beside the bayonet.

132. Great Britain: 42nd Royal Highland Regiment of Foot. Private, 1783

Today, the *Black Watch* or *Royal Highland Regiment* (83–84). Pomp and splendour had for the most part vanished

from British uniforms by the end of the war in North America, at any rate when their wearers were on active service. The change was felt most severely among the Highland regiments. They had been compelled to hand in their broadswords and pistols as early as 1776. In 1778, kilt and sporran were also abandoned, and the regiment illustrated was given the same type of leg-wear as the other British infantry regiments. Legging-trousers were much worn in the last period of the war. The Highlander's cap was the only mark of the regiment. The feather in it was the first sign of what became a full-scale feather-bonnet (383 and 493).

133. Hessen-Hanau: Erbprinz Regiment. Grenadier, 1776

In 1914, *Fusilier Regiment 'Von Gersdorff'* (*Kurhessisches*) *nr.* 80 (14). The spread of the conflict in North America made it apparent that the British army was in no position to field enough troops to put down the American rising on its own. Consequently the British government once more (82) had recourse to the hire of German auxiliary troops. A total of 40,000 men went to North America from the following German states: Anhalt-Zerbst, Ansbach-Bayreuth, Brunswick, Hesse-Hanau, Hesse-Kassel and Waldeck. Because most of them were from the states comprising Hesse, the German troops readily became known as the 'Hessians'. At this period the Hesse uniform resembled that of Prussia, diverging only in minor details and, of course, in the initials and arms of the badges. The regiment shown was specially distinguished by cords on the shoulders. Mascots were also characteristic of the German regiments in North America.

134. Brunswick: Prinz Ludwig Dragoons. Dragoon, 1777

This was the only German cavalry regiment to serve in North America, but because it proceeded there without horses, and because they proved unobtainable on the spot, it was forced to

174

rve on foot. Black boots were generally
orn. It proved impossible to part the
ragoons from their long broadswords.

35. Brunswick: Regiment 'von Riedesel'. Man of light company, 1776

s in the British infantry, some of the
ierman regiments that went to North
America .had light companies distin-
uished by different headgear. In this
istance, the cap is adorned with the
orse of Lower Saxony and a feather in
ie Brunswick colours. The leggings of
nen were summer wear only. They
iight be white or grey, but red, blue, or
rown stripes were also popular, and
ere worn by all the German units in
forth America. But the Brunswick
rummers and fifers still wore the yellow
niforms dating from the period of the
even Years War (111). Although this
giment had yellow lapels and cuffs,
iese distinctions were pale blue on the
rummer's uniform.

36. Hessen-Kassel: Rifle Corps. Rifleman, 1780

1 1914, *Kurhessisches-Jäger-Bataillon*
r. 11 (156). This jäger or rifle corps,
hich could claim to be the German
nit that gained most renown during the
ar in North America, was founded in
758 and composed of hunters and
»resters. The corps soon acquired the
ghting techniques of the Americans and
idians, and the well-trained hunters
nd woodsmen were more than equal to
ie American 'riflemen' as crack-shots.
ed by commanders who knew how to
ike full advantage of these qualities,
iey were consequently dreaded by their
nemies. From the outset the uniform
/orn by members of the corps was
iitable for jäger duties. In America the
lack half-boots worn at home were re-
laced by brown leather leggings. On
arade the riflemen wore green feathers
ver the green cockades (bows) in their
 its.

37. U.S.A.: New Jersey Infantry. Private, 1780

1 1779, when the supply problem ap-

peared to have been solved, Washington,
with the assent of Congress, established
a basis for the future uniforming of the
American army. The principal colour
was to be dark blue. The coats of the
infantry were to have white buttons and
white linings. Collars, lapels and cuffs
would be white for regiments from New
Hampshire, Massachusetts, Rhode Island
and Connecticut; buff for regiments
from New York and New Jersey; red for
those from Pennsylvania, Delaware,
Maryland and Virginia; and dark blue
with white lace on the button holes for
North and South Carolina, and Georgia.
It was simultaneously decided that knee
breeches were to be replaced gradually
by gaiter trousers or overalls. In 1782 it
was decided that the whole of the infantry
were to have blue coats with red lapels
and cuffs. In 1780, as a mark of respect
to the French troops on their side, a
white cloth centre was ordered to be
worn on the black cockade of the
American troops (142).

138. U.S.A.: 2nd Continental Light Dragoons. Drummer, 1780

In 1780 parts of this regiment were
detached for light infantry service for
which they wore shoes and overalls. The
trumpeter had to act as drummer instead.
As usual, when dragoons carried out
infantry duties it proved impossible to
separate the men from their long broadswords. Although the regulations of 1779
concerning the American army uniforms
specified white collars, lapels and cuffs
for dragoons, in this instance these
details were buff-coloured. The chevron
loops on the sleeves do not indicate rank,
or the fact that the wearer is a musician,
but were worn throughout the regiment.
As a form of 'standard' the drum carries
the badge of the regiment.

139. U.S.A.: Marine Corps. Marine, 1780

Since 1776 the predecessors of the
'leathernecks' of today officially wore
green jackets, first with white and, after
1779, with red collars, lapels, cuffs and
linings. The basic colour of the uniform

was changed to dark blue in 1797. In 1780, epaulettes were ordered for officers in the American army. Field officers wore them on both shoulders, captains wore a single epaulette on the right side, and lieutenants one on the left.

140. U.S.A.: 4th Massachusetta Regiment. Man of light company, 1781

This regiment wore blue and white, in accordance with the 1779 regulations for American army uniforms. Like the British light companies, these units in the U.S. army wore shorter coats, or jackets, and a special form of cap. The trimming at the shoulders, the so-called 'wings' made of material of the same colour as the lapel, was attached to the jacket. The dark blue oilcloth pack, and the blue water-bottle carry the regimental insignia in white. The regimental drummers wore white uniforms with dark blue facings.

141. France: 'Touraine' Infantry Regiment. Officer, 1780

In 1763, uniforms of the Prussian style, as they were called, were prescribed for the French infantry. In France, however, the Prussian spareness of style became more elegant. In 1776 the distinctive colours of the regiments were grouped. Each group covered six regiments, which wore the colours either on both cuffs and lapels, or on cuffs or lapels alone, with yellow or white buttons providing an additional distinctive feature. This regiment had pink, the Royal Regiments blue, and the Princes' Regiments red as identification colours. Other special colours were sky-blue, black, violet, iron-grey, chrome-yellow, crimson, silver-grey, orange and dark green. On active service captains and lieutenants, like the men, carried muskets and leather equipment.

142. France: 'Gâtineau' Infantry Regiment. Grenadier, 1780

At this period the French grenadiers did not wear fur caps, but instead were distinguishable by red pompons, red epaulettes, and a flaming grenade in the regimental colour. as ornament on the coat-flaps. The light infantry or *chasseurs* wore a green pompon, green shoulder straps and a hunting horn on the coat flaps; fusiliers (musketeers) a pompon in the company colour, white epaulettes edged in colour and heraldic lilies on the coat flaps. In several regiments the grenadiers and light infantry also wore epaulettes in the appropriate colours, a detail which was first prescribed in 1788. One of the first orders to be issued by the commander of the French auxiliaries when they arrived in America was that they should wear a black American rosette (137) on their white cockades, in response to the similar gesture accorded them by the Americans.

143. Great Britain: Queen's Rangers. Hussar, 1781

Although many of the American colonists joined the struggle for liberation, a certain number, nevertheless, remained loyal to the British crown. Some volunteered for service with the British forces, and several corps of loyalists, or 'provincials' were formed from them. One of the most renowned was The Queen's Rangers, which was formed in 1776, and which at that time consisted of eleven infantry companies, comprising one grenadier, eight battalion, one light and one Highland company (the latter wearing the kilt and carrying the bagpipes). The corps also included one squadron of hussars, three squadrons of light dragoons, and one light cannon. Like other 'provincials', this corps always wore green, unlike the loyalist units, which after 1778 changed to red coats. The reason for this was that green uniforms were not conspicuous and were thus very suitable for light troops. The tall headdress was adopted to avoid confusion with the American forces. It is not surprising that the uniforms of the hussar squadrons were not more in the hussar style, because even the British light cavalry were earlier called 'hussars' (103). It was to be some years before complete hussar uniforms won their way into the British army (254 and 256).

144. France: Lauzun's Legion. Hussar officer, 1780

Lauzun's Legion was formed in 1780 for service in the colonies, and consisted of foreigners recruited for service with France. Part of the Legion, including among others 300 hussars, was included in the French expeditionary force that went to North America. The Legion's hussar officers were uniformed in a somewhat different style from their men. These latter wore black *mirlitons* with yellow lace, pale blue pelisses with black fur trimming, yellow trousers and white cord and braiding. The style of the infantry uniform in the Legion was the same as that of the infantry of the line. The coat was pale blue, with white lining, yellow edging, cuffs and brass buttons, the waistcoat pale blue and the trousers red.

RUSSO-SWEDISH WAR 1788–1790

The war was begun by Gustavus III in 1788, mainly to alleviate the domestic political situation by attempting to draw the attention of his people to the pressure being exerted by Russia. But the laurels he hoped to win remained unplucked, and little use was made of the victories won by the Swedish home fleet at Hogland and Svensksund. Owing to the already complicated European balance of power, Sweden avoided any cession of her territories at the conclusion of the war.

145. Russia: Life Cuirassier Regiment. Cuirassier, 1788

Experimentation in the sphere of uniforms marked the period between the Seven Years War and the Revolutionary Wars. In 1786 a reform of the dress of the Russian army was commenced in a manner that, at the time, must itself have seemed very revolutionary. The whole army was now to wear uniforms of similar style and the different branches were to be distinguishable only by the colours and equipment. Nevertheless, the cuirassier regiments were given regimental marks on their yellow coats, in

the form of, respectively, black, pale blue and dark blue collars, lapels and cuffs. The carabineers and light cavalry (the *chevaulegers*) were uniformed in dark blue and red, the former with yellow and the latter with white buttons.

146. Sweden: East Gotland Cavalry Regiment. Officer, 1788

Today, the *Life Grenadier Regiment*. 1779 also saw the commencement of revolutionary reforms in uniforms in Sweden, but on very different principles from those that prevailed in Russia, in that here a uniform in the 'national' style introduced by Gustavus III was chosen. The previous colours were largely retained but were now distributed on the many borders of the tunic, as well as on the collar and cuffs. The officers' trimming at the shoulders had transverse bands or extensions. The tricorne hat was replaced by what was called a 'round' hat, of which the counterpart in civilian life was the ancestor of the top hat of our own period. The white armband was to commemorate the *coup d'état* in 1772, by which Gustavus III gained absolute power, and during which the officers who collaborated with him had worn similar bands. The officer shown has been awarded the Order of the Sword.

147. Russia: Line Infantry. Musketeer, 1788

The Russian uniform of 1786 was designed to provide the soldiers with a more practical form of dress than hitherto. The jacket could be moulded closely to the figure, the lapels buttoned over, and the turned-up coat tails fastened down in bad weather. The long trousers with leather trimming were more convenient than knee-breeches and boots. The peak on the cap provided protection from glare and the transverse crest was introduced to protect the head from sabre cuts. The two strips hanging down at the neck could be tied round the chin in cold weather—a combined neckerchief and ear protector. The traditional colours of the uniforms were retained.

Infantry regiments were distinguishable by the epaulette on the left shoulder. The dragoons wore the same uniforms as the infantry, but with yellow loops on the right shoulder. The disappearance of the pigtail, side-rolls and powdering of the hair is especially noteworthy. This was justified by the need to avoid time-consuming hairdressing. In 1796 the Russian uniform once more returned to pre-1786 styles, and the bicorne, pigtail and powder regained their place in the army.

148. Sweden: Kronobergs Regiment. Musketeer, 1788

Today, *The Royal Kronobergs Regiment*. Attempts had been made in the Swedish infantry to modify the garb of the lower limbs in the 'national style' uniform. Instead of short boots, thigh-length stockings were introduced, reminiscent of the *esquavars* of the hussars (85 and 107). Laced boots very like the Hungarian pattern (91) replaced the shoes and buckles. The infantry hat was formed from the old tricorne hat. Feathers in various colours were arranged across the crown of the hat to indicate the unit, in addition to the vertical feather, which was always yellow. In Sweden, unlike the situation in Russia, progress had not resulted in the elimination of pigtail and powder. In 1792 a further change in the Swedish uniform commenced. Knee breeches and gaiters were introduced once more, and the short coat took on a more sober appearance, but the round hat was retained. So Swedish uniforms reverted only in part to the pre-1779 period. A certain amount had been learnt from the experimentation.

FRENCH REVOLUTION 1792–1804

In the Wars of the Revolution, France, at least to begin with, stood alone against the rest of Europe. Prussia and Austria which declared war at the same time as France in 1792 were defeated the same year at Valmy and Jemappes. In 1793 the first coalition against France was formed. It consisted of Great Britain,

Austria, Prussia, The Netherlands Spain, Portugal and various German and Italian states. In 1794 the French defeated the Austrians again at Fleurus and the following winter conquered The Netherlands. The French fought brilliantly on other fronts, and in 1795, first the Prussians and later The Netherlands and Spain sued for peace. In 1796 the French army in Germany was driven back over the Rhine, but the pay-off came in Italy, where Bonaparte won his superb victories over the Austrians, at Lodi and Arcola in 1796, and at Rivoli in 1797. The whole of northern Italy came under French control and in 1797 Austria and Portugal concluded peace with France. To strike at the last opponent, Great Britain, Bonaparte occupied Egypt, from which he returned to take the field against the coalition of 1799, consisting of Great Britain, Russia Austria, Portugal, Turkey and various German and Italian states. In 1800 Bonaparte crossed the Alps and won another brilliant victory over the Austrians at Marengo. A further Austrian defeat at Hohenlinden the same year led Austria and Portugal to conclude peace in 1801. Great Britain sent an army to Egypt in 1800 and drove the French out in the following year. Russia had already retired from the war in 1799, and in 1802 Great Britain and Turkey made peace with France.

149. France: Swiss Guards. Grenadier 1792

The Swiss Guard was the oldest and most renowned Swiss regiment in the French army, and it fought bravely in all France's wars from 1562 onwards It was bound to the king by an oath of loyalty and proved it during an heroic defence of the Tuileries, when the palace was stormed by the Parisians on the 10th August, 1792. Of the nine hundred Swiss guards on duty that day, six hundred fell at their posts, and another two hundred died of wounds in prison. The Guard formed a brigade with the Garde Françaises Regiment and originally wore the same uniform as the latter, but with reversed colours. Hence their coats were red and blue and their stockings blue (35). In 1763 uniform 'à la prussienne' was introduced and remained thus until 1792. The uniform of the officers was decorated with silver braid, and the plates of their grenadier caps were silver plated. The musketeers wore the bicorne hat, with scalloped white lace round the edge.

150. France: National Guard. Grenadier, 1792

The National Guard, which was formed as a militia in 1789 under Lafayette, had grown to an army of 100,000 men in 1791. Its uniform was in the new French national colours, red, white and blue, which appeared also in the cockades. White knee-breeches and black half-boots should rightly have been worn, but shortage of cloth and convenience dictated the wearing of long linen trousers by most of the guard. Striped trousers, especially in the national colours, were much worn. Originally the grenadiers were to have worn bearskins, but for economy's sake they were replaced by bicorne hats, with a red pompon made of horsehair (151). The lack of supplies and equipment, combined with the reluctance of the revolutionary volunteers to conform to the regulations, tended very frequently to cause the National Guard to present a' somewhat motley appearance.

151. France: Artillery. Gunner, 1792

After 1670 the French artillery were organized as infantry, so their uniforms tended to be in accord, with the exception of the uniform colours, which were always dark blue and red. The gunners were also armed like the infantry. The red distinction worn in the hat was adopted during the revolution.

152. France: 39th Infantry Regiment. Fusilier, 1792

The trial of more practical uniforms than hitherto held in France after the Seven Years War, did not result as in Sweden and Russia in any thoroughgoing reform.

The long coat was retained. In 1791, however, cuffs which turned up were introduced on it but this was hardly a change of military significance. At the same time a helmet was introduced for the infantry, and this was certainly a result of the experience gained in the attempt. However, the uncertain conditions prevailing in the revolutionary period dictated that only a portion of the infantry were issued with it, while the remainder continued to use the old tricorne hat. In 1790 the national cockade was introduced throughout the army (150). It was worn on the left-hand side of the headdress. At first the colour sequence varied, but later it became fixed in the order—from the outside—of white, red and blue. In 1791 it was decided that the regiments should have numbers, not names. In 1793, dark blue coats were introduced for the entire infantry, like those of the National Guard (150), and the regiment could be identified only by the numbers on their buttons. Nevertheless, it was some time before the white uniform disappeared from the ranks of the army.

153. Austria: Infantry Regiment nr. 42. Fusilier, 1792

In Austria, too, there was an attempt to evolve uniforms more suitable for active service, in the period after the Seven Years War. The white basic colour was threatened, but trials of a grey uniform held in 1775 were not satisfactory. The style, however, was changed. Lapels disappeared, and the coat was made fuller, but in such a way that it could be buttoned to the figure. In 1770 the *casquet*, as it was called, was introduced. The plate at the front was made of leather, and the crown of felt. Lace edging was abandoned in 1780, and the brass plate, earlier adorned with the imperial monogram, bore after 1790 the Austrian double-eagle emblem. The cockade was in the imperial colours. The officers retained the tricorne hat, but after 1789 officers working with the other ranks had to wear the same headgear as their men, so as not to present a target for enemy marksmen. The pack was still the knapsack, worn over the right shoulder.

154. Prussia: Infantry Regiment 'Teufel von Birkensee'. Sharpshooter, 1792

While Frederick the Great was alive the uniforms of the Prussian army remained virtually unchanged. Certain changes took place after 1786; the contemporary tendency towards more practical uniforms for active service being felt also in Prussia. The lapels which, in the final year of Frederick's life, were sewn firmly to the coat, were once more made to button over, with the consequence that the coat had to be made fuller. The bicorne hat was replaced by the 'casquet' which, in this instance, was quite unlike the type worn in Austria for example. Here it was a wide-brimmed felt hat turned up at front and back. The flaps were retained by straps buttoned to the crown, the idea being to make it possible to drop them to provide protection from sun and rain (162). The front flap bore the royal monogram in pressed metal. Grenadiers, on the other hand, wore a flaming grenade and a white plume instead of the pompon. After 1787 each company contained ten sharpshooters. They were used for dispersed engagements. They were picked men, armed with rifled firearms, and were distinguished by similar types of pompon or sabre-tassels as were worn by the N.C.O.s.

155. Hessen-Darmstadt: Chevauléger Regiment. Officer, 1798

In 1914, *Garde-Dragoner-Regiment* (1 *Grossherzogl. Hess.*) *nr.* 23. This regiment was formed in 1790. The uniform illustrated was worn by the officers for normal duty. The ceremonial dress had black lapels and silver lacing. The casque or helmet is of a type used especially by light troops (135).

156. Hessen-Kassel: Light Infantry Battalion. Man, 1793

In 1914, *Kurhessisches-Jäger-Bataillon nr.* 11. Formed in 1793, this battalion was incorporated into the Jäger Corps (136) in 1795. While the latter had retained the uniform which they had worn with distinction in the American War of Independence, the newly-formed battalion was provided with a uniform based on the uniform seen in America. The braid trimming and the short leggings are noteworthy in this connection. Curiously enough, it is evident that the free-flowing hairplume on the headdress was not popular, and its wearer has carefully rolled it up in corkscrew curls. The basic colour of the uniform was paler in shade than that of the Jägers.

157. France: General, 1797

A special uniform for generals was introduced in France in 1724. It was dark blue with gold embroidery in an oak-leaf pattern and was worn with a red waistcoat. In 1770 epaulettes were introduced, and in 1791 the red waistcoat was replaced by a white one. During the revolution the epaulettes were dispensed with, as incompatible with the new principles of equality—and with the title 'Citizens General'. Meanwhile, the new national colours had made way, not only in the cockade, but also in the hat plume and sash. In 1803 epaulettes according to rank were once more introduced.

158. France: Hussards de la Liberté. Hussar, 1793

In addition to the National Guard (150) a number of free corps were formed in France during the revolutionary period. They had resounding names and a variety of uniforms. The hussar corps were especially popular, probably because of their colourful uniforms. Besides this unit, there were, for instance, the Hussars of Death, the Hussars of Equality and the Hussars of the Mountain. Their uniforms were as fanciful as their names. Thus the Hussars of Paris wore yellow uniforms, which was the origin of their nickname of the 'canary birds'. Some of the volunteer hussar corps later became line hussar regiments.

159. France: 5th Chasseurs-à-cheval Regiment. Trumpeter, 1797

In 1779, the first six permanent *chasseur-à-cheval* regiments were formed in France. From the beginning their uniforms were green. During the revolutionary period the style became more like that of the hussars: a green dolman, with white lacing and a *mirliton* as headgear. Usually the trumpeters' uniforms were in the regimental colour. This regiment had preserved the tradition, from the time of the monarchy, of permitting the trumpeters to wear a blue coat with white lace, patterned with red. Trousers and headgear were like those of the men, but the tricolour feather was the mark of staff personnel (193).

160. France: Light Infantry. Officer, 1793

Apart from the name and the uniform, the French light infantry regiments at this period were no different from the regular infantry. The uniform shown was prescribed in 1793, but there was considerable freedom with respect to detail. Each regiment seems to have had its own small and well-preserved deviation from the norm. For instance, waistcoats with one or two rows of buttons, in white or dark blue, and with or without borders, were in use among the various regiments. The carabinier and voltigeur companies of the light regiments corresponded to the grenadier and light companies respectively of the regulars. The troops of the ordinary companies in the light regiments were called chasseurs. Carabiniers and chasseurs wore red collars and red or green plumes respectively; the voltigeurs, yellow collars and green plumes with a yellow top (198).

161. Prussia: Hussar Regiment nr. 11. Officer, 1792

A change took place in the dress of the Prussian hussars in 1796 in that all regiments formerly wearing fur hats were now to wear the *schackel* cap. The *squavar* also went out of use, and leather breeches reached down to the ankles. To protect the costly leather trousers most regiments wore long overalls with buttons down the side (185); some overalls were grey, blue, or of the same colour as the leather breeches. Individual regiments, however, wore tighter fitting Hungarian trousers made of cloth, trimmed in hussar style. This regiment, the former Margrave of Ansbach-Bayreuth's Corps of Hussars, which entered the service of Prussia in 1792, wore pale blue Hungarian trousers. However, the officers of this regiment also wore trousers of 'Pompadour red' (like the pouch-belt shown). In 1803 the regimental uniform was changed.

162. Prussia: Fusilier Battalion 'Stuttenheim'. Fusilier, 1798

Although earlier the appellation 'fusilier' in the Prussian army simply meant that the soldier wore a special form of hat, it now came to indicate a specially picked soldier, trained in combat in open order, and hence a type of light infantry man. From the outset the uniform of the fusiliers had been chosen with this function in view. Consequently the basic colour was always green, and the regimental colour inconspicuous. The original white leather was darkened as a result of the experience gained, and the white inner garment changed to green. The fusiliers wore casques with metal ornamentation, until the shako was introduced in 1806.

163. Austria: Lower Austrian State Corps. Private, 1797

During the conflict with revolutionary France, Vienna supplied six volunteer corps, totalling 37,000 men in all, each of these units being recruited from the individual social groups. Consequently, the corps shown consisted exclusively of the nobility and state officials. Common to all the Vienna corps was the pike-grey colour of the jackets. The identification colour and the cut varied according to the individual corps. The cockade and the plume as shown here are in the Austrian regional colour. All members of the corps wore silver epaulettes.

164. Austria: 'Degelmann' Lancers. Man, 1796

The first Austrian lancer unit was formed in 1781, but it was not until the third partition of Poland in 1795, when a portion of the country was assigned to Austria, that the conception of more permanent Austrian lancer units on the Polish pattern took shape. In 1790 the green uniform later to be prescribed for all the Austrian lancer units was adopted by the Degelmann Lancers. The headgear was the Polish *konfederatka* later to be changed for the hat called the *chapka* (243).

165. Great Britain: Coldstream Guard. Man of light company, 1794

Today, the *Coldstream Guards*. The light companies in the British foot guards had their own special headdress. Broadly speaking, the evolution of their uniforms and equipment was as follows. The white legging-trousers of linen had already been introduced by the time of the American War of Independence. In 1782 leather equipment in the shape of the crossed shoulder belts were officially recognized, and the regiments began to adopt belt plates in brass, the officers' being silver plated or gilded to match the buttons, and with the number or device of the regiment. About 1785, in individual regiments, the more usual type of collar began to give way to a higher design, which became official in 1796.

166. Great Britain: 14th (Bedfordshire) Regiment of Foot. Private, 1794

Today, *The Prince of Wales's Own Regiment of Yorkshire*. Generally, the British regiments of the line followed the example of the guards with respect to uniform, apart from details peculiar to the latter. In 1784 they were recommended to wear black fabric leggings instead of the earlier linen pattern. After 1796 most regiments of the grenadier companies carried a white feather in their hats. The light companies' feathers were green, and the battalion companies which had either black or were featherless adopted white and red.

167. Netherlands: 12th National Regiment. Private, 1791

The Netherlands infantry at this period wore coats both with and without lapels. The waistcoats were either yellow or white. The grenadiers wore fur caps.

168. Portugal: Infantry Officer, 1798

Throughout this period, the Portuguese army followed the normal style of uniforming. In the middle of the eighteenth century the earlier red uniforms were replaced by dark blue, with coloured collars, lapels and cuffs. The cockade was in the colours of the Royal House.

169. Baden: Leib Regiment. Grenadier corporal, 1793

After the Seven Years War, the Baden uniforms became more and more like those of Prussia. At this time, the somewhat old-fashioned equipment was retained, but the cut, if only uncertainly, tended to follow prevailing fashion in uniforms. Although the grenadier cap with plate had become obsolete in Prussia, in Baden it was modernized by dispensing with the pompon. The plate carried the Margrave's monogram. Note the special shafted weapon carried by the N.C.O. which survived into the nineteenth century in most armies.

170. Bavaria: 2nd Fusilier Regiment. Drum-major, 1793

In Bavaria, too, the tendency of the period to make uniforms more convenient for active service had made itself felt. The tricorne hat had been replaced by a *casquet*, as it was called, intended to protect the head from sabre cuts. Coat and waistcoat were combined in a single garment, which certainly appeared to be a coat over a waistcoat, but was, in reality, a short coat. Coat tails were retained, but in a very abbreviated form. Trousers and leggings were combined in the form of a pair of trouser-leggings. To protect the shoulders from sabre strokes, epaulettes made of black leather with brass edgings were widely worn. The neckerchief had been replaced by a frilled white collar-strip, to protect the uniform collar from soiling, which was easy to change and launder. The uniform described was introduced throughout the army, and the various branches were distinguishable from each other only by the colours. In 1785 the infantry were given white coats (205). The belt and mace may be mentioned as the special features of the drum-major. Both as regards colour and pattern, the lace trimming was taken from the Bavarian arms, and the 'swallows' nests' were the common mark of the bandsmen.

171. Kur-Mainz: Hussar Corps. Hussar, 1790

In addition to a white-uniformed 'national army regiment', the Elector of Mainz also put his personal hussar corps in the field during the conflict against the armies of the French Revolution. The uniform was the normal style for the period. The *schackelhaube* or shako evidently has no flap. The monogram on the *sabretache* is that of the Electorate of Mainz.

172. German Empire, Swabian District: Württemberg Dragoons. Man, 1793

In 1914, *Lancer Regiment King Karl* (1st *Württemberg*) nr. 19. Although most of the regiments in the national army at this period wore uniforms almost unchanged since the Seven Years War, this unit in 1793 adopted the new uniform as shown. Formerly its uniform embodied black cuffs, collar and lapel. The brass shoulder straps and red border on the skirt turn-ups are noteworthy. .

173. Sardinia: Light Infantry. Officer, 1792

At this time the Sardinian army possessed a rifle (cacciatori) company in addition to light infantry. The former was equipped with plain, dark blue coats with white lining, and white waistcoat. The officers' sashes were blue and gold. Later the gold was discontinued, and in spite of the fact that Italy became a republic, the sash—still worn by Italian officers—became pale blue throughout.

174. Spain: Swiss Regiment 'Schwaller'. Private, 1795

After 1743, Swiss regiments were recruited for permanent service in the Spanish army, whereas formerly they had been engaged only in time of war. The Swiss regiments in France and Naples were dressed in red, but in Spain they wore blue with red collars, lapels and cuffs throughout. The Spanish infantry of the line wore white uniforms at this time (238).

175. Russia: 14th Rifle Battalion. Rifleman, 1797

At this time Russian infantry of the line and cavalry were still known by their special names, whereas the rifle battalions had numbers. In 1797 the Russian uniforms reverted to the pre-1786 style. Consequently coats, tricorne hats, and grenadier caps, as well as pigtails and powdering were reintroduced. For the riflemen, who had adopted plain dark green with a hat resembling that of the infantry of the line, in 1786, pale green coats and tunics were introduced in 1797. Each battalion had its colour. Among the more curious special colours may be mentioned apricot, raspberry, flame, coffee and fawn. The specially shaped cartridge pouch was worn on a waist belt.

176. Russia: Duke of Bourbon's Grenadier Regiment from Condé's Army. N.C.O., 1797

Originally formed of French emigrants in the service of Austria, the Condé's Army entered Russian service in 1797. The distinguishing colour was black, and the uniform to a great extent resembled that of the corresponding Russian units. Consequently the illustration shows to what extent the appearance of the grenadier N.C.O. of a Russian regular infantry unit followed the regulations of 1797, relating to army uniforms. However, only certain regular regiments wore the black-painted eagle on the plate of the grenadier cap; the majority had this emblem in relief. The mark of the N.C.O. was the gold braiding on collar and cuffs, the special pompon in the cap, and the cane.

CAMPAIGN IN EGYPT 1798–1801

177. France: 4th Light Demi-Brigade. Rifleman, 1799

The army that Napoleon sent to Egypt was uniformed in the normal French style, but service abroad under difficult climatic conditions resulted in various changes. By 1798 it was decided to replace the tricorne hat with a helmet, with a 'sausage' or *pouffe* on the crown, which was also to be in a particular colour or combination of colours for each half-brigade, and thus to serve as identification. The grenadiers were to carry a grenade emblem on their helmets, but were more frequently identifiable by a red *pouffe*. Insufficiency of suitable material resulted in the decision, in 1799, that dark blue cloth should be reserved for the artillery, green for cavalry, and red, black, grey, brown, etc., for the infantry. As shown in the illustration, the light troops were allocated pale green.

178. France: Dromedary Corps. Camel rider, 1799

For effective patrol service in the Egyptian desert the French army in Egypt found it necessary to form a dromedary corps. Armed with muskets fitted with bayonets, this unit was, in fact, a dromedary-borne infantry unit and thus fought on foot. Its uniform constantly varied, but had a generally hussar-like style. The headgear was, in quick succession, the turban, the bicorne hat and the shako of every conceivable pattern. The umbrella, which was carried also by other French units in Egypt, served, of course, as a sun-shade.

179. France: Coptic Legion. Man, 1799

The Coptic Legion was formed in 1798, and consisted of volunteers from the Christian population in Egypt, the Copts.

However, the Legion also later included Berbers, Arabs, Turks and Moors. The uniform was French in style. The grenadiers wore a red hairplume on their hats, as well as red epaulettes.

180. Great Britain: 50th (West Kent) Regiment of Foot. Officer, 1801

Today, *The Queen's Regiment*. In 1796 it was decided that the British uniform coat should be so designed that it could be fastened close to the figure, with lapels that could be buttoned up. The officers' coats were to have gold or silver lace on the coloured side of the lapels, at the buttonholes. Lace trimming on the red side also was non-regulation, but was, nevertheless, a common practice. For normal wear the British officers tended to wear their coats buttoned over, except for the upper buttons, so that the coloured side constituted a form of lapel. In Egypt, the bicorne hat was often replaced by a civilian hat, to give better protection from the sun. The latter assumed a military look with the aid of the feather adopted from the bicorne. The colours of the feathers were laid down as follows: white for grenadiers, green for light troops and red-and-white for musketeers (188).

FRENCH REVOLUTION 1792–1804

181. The Cisalpine Republic: Lombardy-Cisalpine Legion. Infantry officer, 1797

The Lombardy Cisalpine Legion, formed in 1796, consisted of Italian revolutionary volunteers, who fought for the French in Italy during 1796 and 1797. The infantry of the Legion wore uniforms in the new Italian national colours, red, white and green. The headdress was the 'Corsican' hat. The ranks wore white, crossed shoulder-belts (233).

182. France: Polish Danube Legion. Artillery man, 1799

The Polish Danube Legion, formed in 1796, consisted of emigrant Polish volunteers who fought for the French in Italy during 1798–1800. A mixture of French and Polish features were to be found in the uniform. The artillery uniform, in hussar style, resembled that worn by the French mounted artillery, but the head-dress, the *chapka* as it was called, was a further development of the Polish cap, which later became a stiff shako-type garment with peak, feather and cord.

183. The Batavian Republic: Light Infantry, Carabinier, 1801

When, in 1795, The Netherlands were proclaimed the Batavian Republic, the army was reorganized and uniformed on French lines. The regular infantry wore various combinations of white and red on their blue coats, so that the half-brigades were distinguishable one from the other. The light infantry half-brigades all wore the same uniform, which developed a resemblance to that of the French light infantry (160). The head-dress was a very early form of the shako, which was to be the fashionable military headdress for the next half-century. The shako seems to have been inspired by the headdress of the Austrian frontier regiments (92) but may also be a result of the experiments in uniform conducted in France after the Seven Years War. The basis of the popularity of the shako seems undoubtedly to have lain in the fact that it was the military counterpart of the civilian hat of the period, the top hat.

184. The Helvetic Republic: Light Cavalry. Trooper, 1800

When Switzerland proclaimed herself a republic in 1798, an army formed and uniformed on the French model was created, instead of the former cantonal militia. The cavalry was formed as light cavalry or *chevaulégers* and, like their French prototype, was uniformed in hussar-style, in the new national colours —red, gold and green. The infantry wore green uniforms with black collars, lapels and cuffs, and adopted the Corsican hat (181). The grenadiers had lemon-yellow epaulettes.

185. Russia: Pereaslavski Dragoons. N.C.O., 1803

The Russian army adopted a new style of uniform in 1802. The coat could now be buttoned to the figure, the lapels disappeared, and high, vertical collars and short coat tails were introduced. The principal colour for dragoons and light cavalry was pale green, the remainder of the army wearing dark green. For parade duty, the dragoons wore tight, white trousers and top boots, and for daily wear and active service, grey leggings. For the other ranks, these overalls were fitted with grey, fabric-covered buttons, and with buttons of metal for the officers. The helmet replaced the bicorne hat in 1803. The crest was plain black for privates, and white, with a black tip, for officers. In 1806, scabbards made entirely of iron were introduced, suspended from two slings. In 1807, the basic colour of the coat was changed to dark green, and it was provided with straps on both shoulders.

186. Prussia: Infantry Regiment 'Unruh'. Grenadier, 1801

The curious grenadier cap was ordered for the Prussian infantry of the line in 1799, but had already been introduced in the guards in 1798. A grenade badge, in brass, was placed above the Prussian eagle on its brass plate, both being mounted on the patent-leather front plate of the cap. Crown and peak were of felt, the latter bordered with white, the former covered with regimental-colour material. Drill or linen trousers, to protect the white cloth knee-breeches, came in 1794. Grey was their normal colour but frequent washing turned them white. Striped linen trousers, so popular elsewhere, were seldom to be seen on the Prussian infantry (245).

187. Austria: Light Infantry Battalion nr. 9. Officer, 1800

To make up the deficiency in light troops in the Austrian army, 15 light infantry battalions were formed in 1798 from a number of more or less free rifle corps, formed during the war against the armies of the Revolution. A light grey uniform was prescribed for them, and each battalion had its own colour, appearing on collar, cuffs and pipings. The head-dress was the helmet, introduced in 1798 throughout the army, with the exception of the hussars and certain other units. It replaced the former *casquet*.

188. Great Britain: 8th or King's Regiment of Foot. Grenadier, 1801

Today, *The King's Regiment*. Lapels on the uniform coats of infantry men were discontinued in 1797 and the coats of the other ranks were closed down the front by means of a single row of buttons. Buttonhole loops on either side were to be in lace, of the former regimental pattern. The buttons were arranged either singly or in pairs, and the lace trimming could be square-ended or pointed (131). Officers, however, retained the lapels on their coats, although a shorter style of garment, also with lapels, was prescribed for use in the field. The shoulder ornaments of the grenadiers (104) had developed with time into what were called 'wings', which were also worn by the light companies. The bicorne was replaced by a shako in 1799, officially called a cap, but popularly a 'stovepipe'. The original model was a heavy object made of patent leather, but this was soon replaced by a lighter version made of felt, with a patent leather peak. After this the grenadiers wore their bearskin caps on parade only, using the shako for all other duties. Officers, however, did not always wear the shako, but retained the bicorne hat (257).

THE NAPOLEONIC WARS 1804–1815

The Napoleonic Wars were a continuation of the Revolutionary Wars, and during them France, under Napoleon, especially towards the close, stood virtually alone against the remainder of Europe. In 1803 Great Britain again declared war against France, and in 1805 the Third Coalition against France was formed: it consisted of Britain, Russia,

Sweden, Austria and subsequently Prussia. In 1805 Napoleon defeated the Austrians at Austerlitz; in 1806 he defeated the Prussians, at Jena and Auerstadt, and in 1807 the Russians at Friedland. At the Peace of Tilsit, in 1807, Napoleon compelled the defeated powers to join the Continental System which had been proclaimed in 1806 and which was a blockade directed against the last opponent, Britain. To bring her to her knees, Denmark and Norway, Sweden and Portugal were forced to join the blockade. In 1807 Napoleon occupied Portugal and in 1808, Spain, which latter move turned out to be a blatant error because of the British successes in the Peninsular War. In 1812 Napoleon undertook his fatal campaign against Russia, which ended with the retreat of the Great Army and its piecemeal annihilation. The disaster resulted in a new coalition against France, consisting of Great Britain, Russia, Prussia, Sweden and Austria, which were later joined by several German and Italian states. After the defeat of Leipzig in 1813, Napoleon was compelled to retreat on all fronts, and after the fall of Paris in 1814, he had to abdicate and went to live in Elba. His desperate attempt to regain power ended with the defeat of Waterloo and his exile to St Helena in 1815.

189. France: Imperial Guard. Grenadiers-à-pied. Grenadier, 1804

The renowned Napoleonic Grenadiers could trace their origin back to the Consular Guard, formed in 1799. Their uniform was regularized in 1800. With their elevation to the status of Imperial Guard in 1804, only the buttons and the plate of the cap were changed, by the addition of the imperial eagle. In winter, and in the field, black leggings were worn. Up to 1810 the grenadiers wore plain, dark blue coats as a field uniform. In 1805 long, dark blue trousers were introduced for use on the march. There was a curious order, which lasted until 1807, that moustaches could be worn only from 1st March to 1st December, thus the grenadiers were clean shaven during the winter. But after this year, moustaches were made compulsory.

190. France: Imperial Guard. 2nd Conscrit-Chasseurs. Sapper, 1810

By now, the Imperial Guard consisted of infantry, cavalry and artillery. The guard grew steadily, and in 1814 it included no less than 112,500 men of all branches. Such an increase made it necessary to form new regiments consisting of levies. A distinction was thus made in the Imperial Guard, between the 'old' guard of veterans, and the 'young' guard of levies. This regiment was formed in 1809, and belonged to the young guard. The uniform was similar to that of the regular light regiments, but was distinguished by special epaulettes, and by the decoration on the shako (191). The sapper is equipped in the traditional manner, with the leather apron and gauntlets and, according to the custom in the French army, with the bearskin.

191. France: Imperial Guard. Pupilles or King of Rome's Guard. Boy, 1811

Napoleon's son, born in 1811, was given the title of king of Rome while still in his cradle. He had not long been born before his father formed a regiment in his name. Subsequently it was recruited from sons and nephews of fallen soldiers, of between ten and sixteen years old, who had to be able to read and write. The regiment was intended as an army cadet school or military academy, but it took the field with the other guard regiments. It was uniformed in the Napoleonic livery colours, green and gold, and wore the standard shako for 'young' guard regiments.

192. France: Imperial Guard. Corporal of Engineers, 1810

The engineer company in the Imperial Guard, formed in 1810 as part of the 'old' guard, acted as a fire guard, among other duties at the Imperial headquarters. The uniform was in the traditional artillery and engineer branch colours. To distinguish them from the foot artillery in the Guard, who wore a similar uniform, they were equipped with a helmet instead of a bearskin.

193. France: Imperial Guard. Chasseurs-à-cheval. Man, 1804

In 1800 a squadron of chasseurs-à-cheval was formed from Bonaparte's former staff guard during the Egyptian campaign, and in 1801 it was expanded to a regiment. It accompanied the Emperor on all his campaigns, and one of its squadrons was always on duty as escort and headquarters guard. In 1800 the uniform in the hussar style was introduced, to last with small changes until the fall of the Empire. The yellowish deerskin trousers were worn on escort duty and on parades. For normal service, green Hungarian trousers with hussar-style lace were worn and, in the field, dark green leggings with orange stripes, which were finally replaced by grey, with red stripes.

194. France: Imperial Guard. Dragoons. Trooper, 1809

Napoleon appointed the Empress Josephine patroness of the dragoon regiment of the Imperial Guard, formed in 1806. It was generally known as The Empress' Dragoon Regiment. The green uniform had been characteristic of the French dragoons since 1762. The brass helmet was introduced in the same year, but over a period it became more elegant in shape. The feather at the side was only worn on parade. The cuffs were like those of the foot grenadiers (189). Tighter-fitting grey trousers were worn instead of white (195) when in the field.

195. France: Imperial Guard. Horse Grenadiers. Corporal, 1815

The mounted grenadiers, whose uniform was very like that worn by the foot grenadiers (189), could, like the latter, trace their origin back to the Consular Guard, formed in 1799. For parade and ceremonial duty they wore white lapels, white waistcoats, tight, white trousers and long boots. They also flaunted a red feather over their cockades, but their epaulettes, frogging and leather equipment were as illustrated. The uniform shown was prescribed during the Hundred Days. The lace on the sleeves indicates rank. In 1804 it was laid down that only grenadiers and chasseurs (both mounted and dismounted), as well as the artillery, gendarmerie and service corps of the Imperial Guard were allowed to wear pigtails. The mounted and dismounted grenadiers wore a small silver flaming bomb emblem on the black ribbon with which the pigtail was bound. Gold earrings were so commonly worn by the old guard that they were virtually part of the uniform.

196. France: Imperial Guard. 1st Chevaulégers Lanciers. Lancer, 1810

Inspired by a mounted Polish guard of honour which had attended him during his entry into Warsaw in 1806, Napoleon decided to include a Polish cavalry regiment in the Imperial Guard. This regiment, recruited exclusively from among Poles, was formed in 1807. It was not issued with lances until 1809. The uniform remained unchanged throughout the existence of the regiment. As regards colour and style, it was treated as the Polish national uniform. The *chapka* was the national military headwear of the period (229–230). The French cockade worn with it carried a Maltese cross in silver—to show that the regiment was a national Polish unit in the service of France. On active service, the *chapka* was carried in a waterproof cover. For parades and ceremonial duty, the officers wore crimson trousers with silver braid.

197. France: 9th Line Infantry. Drum-major, 1809

The Napoleonic era must have been a real Eldorado for a uniform enthusiast. In addition to the variety of army uniforms, every branch of the services, indeed each regiment, very often had its special uniform. In addition, the individual commander of the regiment frequently attired his regimental drummers, musicians, sappers and others of *la tête de colonne* in the most lavish possible

manner. These people were the cuddly toys of the regiment, with uniforms not only adorned with braid, piping, tassels, epaulettes and plumes, but also in strongly contrasting colours. The old custom of dressing the drummers and musicians in the uniform colours reversed was retained, while the various regiments in their *tête de colonne* recalled the uniforms they had worn at an earlier period—in this instance the uniform used during the Egyptian expedition. According to the principle adopted before the Revolution, when the drummers and musicians wore the royal livery colours, it was decided in 1810 that in the future they were to wear green and gold, the Napoleonic livery colours.

198. France: 5th Light Infantry Cuirassiers. Sharpshooter, 1808

The shako adopted for the French Light Infantry in 1801 had the feather at the side. In 1806 the plume was placed at the front. Certain light regiments, however, adopted the 1806-type shako worn by the infantry of the line, with a V-shaped leather trimming on each side. Among the divergences from the standard may be mentioned the yellow flaps on the cuffs, and the yellow edging of the waistcoat (160). In 1812 a more modern style was adopted for the cutaway coat of both the light and line infantry. It was fastened to the figure at the front, with the bottoms horizontal, and the lapels vertical (191), while the colours remained unchanged. The shako lost its hanging cords but acquired—for the grenadiers and riflemen respectively—a V-shaped trimming of red or yellow lace at each side.

199. France: 9th Cuirassiers. Trooper, 1805

The French cuirassier branch was formed in 1803. Whereas the cuirass was 'government issue', the regiments themselves were responsible for providing the helmet, so that it was possible to vary it in detail, from unit to unit. In 1805 the cuirassiers were issued with red plumes and epaulettes, and flaming bomb emblems on the coat flaps—the sign of élite troops. The regiments could be distinguished from each other by the colours of their collars, edgings and linings, combined with the colours of their buttons. Tight grey trousers were worn for field service (195 and 354). From 1811, the cuirassiers were armed with carbines, so they wore carbine belts combined with cartridge pouch belts. In 1812 the grenade on the cartridge pouch was discontinued.

200. France: 3rd Hussars. Hussar, 1808

In 1786 uniforms varying in colour according to the regiment were adopted as regulation for the French hussar regiments. This regiment, at that time the Esterhazy Regiment, was allocated a plain grey uniform with red frogging, while other regiments wore pelisse and overalls of a colour contrasting with that of the dolman. In 1802, the *mirliton* was replaced by a shako, with decoration varying from regiment to regiment. In addition to the sabretache shown, the regiment carried a black wallet with the regimental number in white (possibly the embroidered wallet fitted with a protective waterproof cover). This regiment was the only French hussar regiment to use black leather equipment; that of the others was white. The uniforms of the officers had silver frogging and braiding, the pelisse trimmed with brown fur, and crimson boots. It was the custom in the French cavalry of the line—except for the cuirassiers—for the 1st company in the regiment to be the élite company, corresponding to the grenadiers among the infantry. The men of this company had fur caps similar to those of the mounted light troops of the Imperial Guard (193) with red plume and red epaulettes. (The latter, however, were not worn by hussars.)

201. France: Foreign Troops. Croatian Regiment. Infantry man, 1813

It has been a long-standing tradition in the French army to include regiments of foreign recruits. During the Revolutionary and Napoleonic periods, the total of foreign regiments was considerably increased, often including the representatives of political factions or national minorities (179 and 182–2). At first the foreign regiments were uniformed in a manner which brought national characteristics into prominence, but later they adopted the French style, with national features only in details. Green seems to have been the favoured colour for foreign regiments, being worn by Irish, Hanoverians, Prussian and Italian units. The Swiss wore red, the Portuguese brown, and the Spanish white.

202. France: Marshal Soult's Staff. Captain, 1808

For French generals after 1790, the choice of adjutants was restricted to the officers of regiments under their command. Adjutants were distinguished by brassards in contrasting colours. In 1803, a dark blue uniform with pale blue collar was prescribed for them. The marshals of France dressed their adjutants in special uniforms. A hussar style was favoured, and the one illustrated, as regards style, is evidently the uniform that could be adopted by hussar officers on staff duty. This captain has been awarded the *Légion d'honneur* instituted by Bonaparte in 1802.

203. France: 15th Light Infantry. Cantinière, 1809

When armies were levied, the number of wives permitted to accompany the regiment on active service was laid down in the regulations. In view of the primitive supply and medical organization of the period, these camp followers were evidently indispensable to troops who, without them, would have had to fend for themselves or be looked after by their comrades when wounded or sick. In the days of black powder, when smoke lay thick over the battlefield, it was a fortunate company that possessed a Mother Courage who would venture out between the fighting ranks to administer a gulp of brandy as mouthwash and stimulant combined. There was no standard uniform for the camp followers, but various regimental commanders took the trouble to give them *cantinière* status and to see that they wore a form of uniform that showed their membership of the regiment. Often, however, it consisted simply of an inscribed brass plate, but in the uniform-conscious French army, these gallant women generally wore a dress adapted from the regimental uniform. The red tunic worn by the *cantinière* illustrated probably indicates that the *tête de colonne* of the regiment also wore red. This was a period when it was customary for the *cantinières* in various regiments to accompany the men on parades (308).

204. France: Imperial Navy. Sailor, 1808

Although the French naval officers had worn uniform for some time, up to now the seamen merely had a uniform outfit for service on board. The men had to provide their own dress for service ashore. There was, however, already a feeling that crews should be more appropriately dressed. Garments and hat suitable for ceremonial occasions on board, and for shore-leave, consequently became more generally issued.

205. Bavaria: 9th Line Infantry, 'Ysenburg Büddingen'. Man, 1807

In 1914, *Bavarian 9th Infantry Regiment Wrede*. The principal colour of the Bavarian infantry of the line coatees was changed in 1799 from white (170) to the former pale blue, and there was a change of style resulting in a more close-fitting coat. Meanwhile the *casquet* was replaced by what was known as a *raupe* (crested) helmet which became typical of the Bavarian army until 1886 (352). In 1803, a red feather was adopted for the grenadiers, worn on the left side of the helmet. In 1804 the rifles began to wear a green feather likewise, while in 1806 a round white-blue-white cockade was introduced throughout the army. The band over the peak of the helmet carried the name of the regiment, and the oval scutcheon the royal monogram. In 1807 the pack which had, up to now, been worn over the right shoulder, was

replaced by a knapsack. In 1814 red collars, lapels and cuffs were introduced for all regiments, which thus became identifiable only by the numbers on their brass buttons.

206. Bavaria: King's Chevaulegers Regiment nr. 4. Officer, 1809

The Bavarian Chevaulegers regiments, formed in 1790, were originally dressed in pale green coatees and *casquets* with white bands. In 1800 the *casquet* was replaced by a crested helmet, with a bearskin crest (comb) for the officers, and a white feather on the left side for parade duty only. In 1809 the dark-green basic colour was introduced. The grey leggings had been worn since 1804. For parades, tight white trousers and hussar-style boots were worn. The epaulettes were common to both officers and men. The former, however, were distinguishable by their sashes and silver shoulder-belt. The lace on the collar is a sign of rank. The officer shown is a first lieutenant. (See also 286.)

207. Württemberg: Infantry Regiment 'Franquemont'. Musketeer, 1809

In 1914, the 8*th Württemberg Infantry Regiment nr. 126, The Archduke Frederick of Baden*. The army of Württemberg, reorganized in 1807, consisted at the time of the former ducal, electoral and 'national' regiments which had survived the wars of the revolution. This regiment, in fact, was formed first in 1716. The uniform possessed many peculiarities. In 1799 a *casquet* reminiscent of the Bavarian style was introduced, but in 1807 the woollen crest was replaced by a crest made of horsehair. The band over the peak carried the name of the regiment, and the scutcheon the arms of Württemberg. The white feather was tipped in the regimental colour. The grenadiers wore a peculiarly shaped *casquet*. In 1811, the lapels of all the Württemberg infantry regiments were made dark blue like the coatee, after which only the collar, shoulder straps, cuffs and pipings were in the regimental colour. Crossed belts were introduced at the same time. In

1813 the crested helmet was replaced by a shako without any feather.

208. Württemberg. Life Guard of Horse. Man of Leibjäger Squadron, 1810

Since 1770, the Württemberg Life Guard of Horse wore uniforms varying with the squadron. At this time they consisted of one *garde du corps* squadron in red, with cuirasses, two squadrons of mounted grenadiers in blue and yellow uniforms with bearskins, and one squadron of *leibjäger* troops in the uniform illustrated. When the guards rode out as a body, however, they were dressed alike in the uniform of mounted grenadiers, with the exception of the *leibjäger* squadron, which wore green jackets. Earlier, the head-gear had consisted of a crested helmet similar to that worn by the infantry. Both the *garde du corps* and *leibjäger* squadrons wore the semi-heraldic or 'gala' coat. This had now attained its final form, in style resembling a cuirass, and was adorned with braiding round the edges, carrying the star of the Military Service Order on the breast and back. (See 123.)

209. Berg: Infantry. Regimental Pioneer, 1812

The Grand Duchy of Berg, formed by Napoleon in 1806, maintained at this time a contingent of troops uniformed in a style closely modelled on the French. The infantry, however, wore white with pale blue lapels. The cavalry, constituted as lancers in 1810, were dressed in green.

210. Berg: Artillery. Gunner, 1810

The Berg artillery also were uniformed in French style, except that the cut was more modern. The *habit veste* as it was called, was first introduced into the French army in 1812.

211. Baden: Regiment 'Margraf Ludwig'. Musketeer, 1804

The general change in the style of uniform coatee penetrated even to the Grand Duchy of Baden by 1803. In 1809 lapels and regimental colours were done away with, and all regiments wore red collars

and cuffs, which scheme, however, was again changed in 1813 by the reintroduction of regimental colours. In 1806 a form of crested helmet on the Bavarian pattern was introduced. The helmet mounts were in the same colour as the uniform buttons, but in 1810 brass mounts were introduced for all regiments of the line. The crest itself was curiously shaped, resembling most closely the Austrian model (187), in that the black upper portion was edged in the Baden armorial colours. In 1813, the crested helmet was ousted by the shako.

212. Baden: Hussar Regiment. N.C.O., 1812

The regiment shown, formed at the end of the eighteenth century, wore during its life, green and red with yellow and gold frogging respectively. In 1806 the shako was prescribed by regulation and, in 1807, long green leggings with red stripes. Like most of the other contingents of the Confederation of the Rhine, the Baden troops adopted the French marks of rank. Likewise, the grenadiers and light troops (*voltigeurs*) wore red and green feathers respectively, and epaulettes.

213. Saxony: Leib-Kurassiers. Trooper, 1812

In 1914, *The Saxon Guard Cavalry Regiment* (the 1*st Heavy Regiment*). This regiment, promoted to guards status for its part in the Battle of Friedland in 1807, could trace its history back to the Graf von Promnitz Cuirassier Regiment (15). At this time the Saxon cuirassiers usually wore a blackened cuirass consisting of just a breastplate. The riding coat was a modernized version of the old buff coat. The helmet was introduced in 1810, to replace a tricorne hat. A white feather was worn on the left side of the helmet on parade, with close-fitting white trousers. The regimental trumpeters wore red riding coats and red feathers with a crest on the helmet. They did not wear cuirasses. The officers had gold braid on their riding coats and gold-braid pouch-belts.

214. Saxony: Infantry Regiment 'Rechten'. Grenadier N.C.O., 1810

A new uniform style with shako was introduced for the Saxony infantry in 1810. Each brigade consisted of two regiments both with the same regimental colour, one having brass and the other tinplate buttons. Under field conditions the shako was worn in a waterproof cover, and the tight-fitting trousers were replaced by long linen or grey cloth trousers. Regimental marks and marks of rank were the same as in the French infantry, except for the fact that the grenadiers did not wear epaulettes. The musketeers had white tassels, and short white feathers tipped in the regimental colour in their shakos. N.C.O.s were recognizable by silver or gold braid on the upper portion of the shako and black-tipped feather, in addition to the stripes on the sleeve. In 1815 a green ring was introduced on the white cockade; lapels were discontinued and two rows of coat buttons became general. At the same time all regiments of the line adopted green collars and cuffs.

215. Hesse-Darmstadt: Guards Brigade. Musketeer, 1806

The parent unit of this guards brigade, formed in 1621, was later converted once more into a regiment. In 1914 the latter, as the Life Guard Infantry Regiment (1st Grand Ducal Hessian) nr. 115, was the oldest infantry regiment in the German army. After 1768, the uniform of the archduchy of Hesse-Darmstadt forces was virtually a copy of the Prussian uniform. In 1803 the infantry were formed into brigades and the uniform illustrated was prescribed by regulation for them. All brigades wore lace on their tunics, but collars, lapels, and cuffs were pale blue or yellow except for the brigade illustrated. In 1808 their swords were worn on shoulder-belts. The same year dark blue trousers with short, black leggings came in and, in 1809, the shako. It was simultaneously decided that in future lapels were to be buttoned over, except for parade duty.

216. Würzberg: Dragoon Regiment. Dragoon, 1807

Although the archduchy of Würzberg was not formed as such until 1805 Würzberg troops served in the so-called national army at an earlier period. Hence the uniforming was generally Austrian in style at that time. (For instance, the helmet was of Austrian pattern.) As in the Austrian army, the comb of the helmet bore a brush-like crest for parades. The Würzberg infantry wore white and red. In 1812 their uniforming became generally French in cut—though the colours were retained—and the helmet was replaced by a shako.

217. Westphalia: 4th Infantry Regiment Rifleman, 1808

King Jérôme of Westphalia had to hand over virtually the whole of his army to the control of his imperial brother, and the Westphalian troops fought bravely under Napoleon throughout Europe. The uniform of the Westphalian infantry of the line was very French in style at this time. The regiments, in pairs, wore dark blue, pale blue and yellow as distinguishing colours, on their white coatees. While one regiment of the pair had lapels in the distinguishing colour, the other wore them in white. In 1810, the uniforms were simplified and all regiments adopted dark blue trimming. The Westphalian grenadiers and jäger troops were identified like those of France. When the shako was worn in a cover, the feather was usually kept in a waterproof case also and attached to the sword. Tight white trousers were worn on parade duty.

218. Westphalia: Garde-Chevauleger. Trumpeter, 1808

Originally formed as a lancer regiment this unit should have worn helmets but at this time the lances had not been supplied, so they wore the shako. Both officers and men wore green coatees with red details. In the field, jackets without lace on the breast or shoulder bands were worn, and long grey overalls with red stripes.

219. Schwarzburg-Rudolstadt: Infantry. Officer, 1812

When the Confederation of the Rhine was formed in 1808, the states of Schwarzburg undertook to supply two infantry companies to the Prince's Battalion, as it was called. Consequently Schwarzburg-Sonderhausen supplied the 1st company and Schwarzburg-Rudolstadt the 2nd. Their uniforms were virtually identical. The men wore black leather equipment. During the war against revolutionary France, the Schwarzburg states for a time supplied a contingent uniformed in blue and red.

220. Schaumburg-Lippe: Infantry. Drummer, 1814

During the period of the Confederation of the Rhine the uniforms of the principalities of Schaumberg-Lippe and Lippe-Detmold were identical (222). But when Schaumburg-Lippe joined the enemies of Napoleon in 1813, with the other states of the Federation, its contingent of troops adopted a uniform of combined Prussian and Russian style.

221. Anhalt: Jäger-zu- Pferde (Light Cavalry). Trumpeter, 1813

At this time the states of Anhalt were pledged to supply to the Confederation, in addition to an infantry contingent (in green with pink collars and trimming), a light cavalry regiment. This unit also wore green jackets with pink and grey leggings and shakos. The yellow coatee with the pink regimental colour, and the somewhat old-fashioned bicorne hat worn by the trumpeter are exceptional.

222. Lippe-Detmold: Fusilier-Battalion 'Lippe'. N.C.O., 1807

Schaumberg-Lippe and Lippe-Detmold were together pledged to contribute a battalion of fusiliers and three companies to the Prince's Battalion, when the Confederation of the Rhine was formed in 1808. The uniform was French in style, although the headgear was reminiscent of the round hat introduced during the period of attempted reform of uniforms at the close of the eighteenth century

(146 and 148). With his knee-breeches, hose and buckled shoes the N.C.O. is clearly wearing off-duty dress, as it was retained in use well into the nineteenth century. Dress of this kind was worn by both infantry and cavalry. No self-respecting soldier, with the possible exception of a hussar, would be seen off duty in long or short boots. The jacket was altered to one that buttoned tightly to the figure, with vertical lapels, in 1812, but the colour remained unchanged. The shako was introduced at the same time.

223. Reuss: Infantry. Officer, 1812

The states of Reuss were pledged to furnish one infantry battalion to the Confederation of the Rhine at this time. In 1807 its uniform was established as a white tunic of Austrian style, with tight pale blue pantaloons, so that the battalion resembled the Hungarian infantry in Austrian service. This uniform remained virtually unchanged until 1822.

224. Waldeck: Infantry. Musketeer, 1812

The principality of Waldeck had to supply three infantry companies to the Confederation of the Rhine, of which one formed the 6th company of the Prince's Battalion. The uniform adopted was broadly that of the period. The black cockade was later replaced by a black–red and yellow national cockade. The brass plate on the shako carried the initials of the principality. As with several other small German states, the Waldeck troops adopted green uniforms after the Napoleonic wars.

225. Nassau: 2nd Infantry Regiment. Grenadier, 1810

This dark green colour for uniforms was introduced in the Duchy of Nassau in 1803. In 1808 black collars and cuffs, with orange lace, were introduced for the infantry, numbering two regiments. Lace of this kind was, however, dropped in 1809, and yellow edging was introduced instead. From 1808 the musketeers and riflemen wore the shako, while in 1810 the fur cap was introduced for the grenadiers. Caps of this pattern, normally for the élite companies in the French light cavalry, were worn also by light companies in individual French regiments of infantry. The latter probably provided the model for the headgear of the Nassau grenadiers. During the period of the Confederation of the Rhine, marks of rank and identification marks were the same as in the French army. The yellow leather equipment was typical of the Nassau uniforms up to 1866.

226. Saxe-Weimar: Light Infantry Battalion. Officer, 1812

After 1788 green and gold, the armorial colours of Saxony, were worn by the troops of Weimar. Up to 1812 the infantry uniforms were somewhat old-fashioned. The men wore the *casquet*, rather like the Prussian in style (154), and the officers the bicorne hat. When the uniforms were modernized in 1812 the shako was introduced, with the grand-ducal monogram at the front. The carabiniers (the élite troops) of this battalion wore orange feathers in their shakos. They also wore long grey trousers for normal daily duty.

227. Oldenburg: Infantry. Grenadier drummer, 1808

The principality of Oldenburg had to supply one battalion of infantry to the Confederation. The fusiliers and jäger companies wore hats rather like those of the Fusilier Battalion 'Lippe' (222). The grenadier company had an African drummer. This was a common custom in European armies after the middle of the eighteenth century, and indeed it lasted more or less until the First World War. Africans also played the percussion instruments in regimental bands, as well as the drums, and enjoyed wearing fanciful oriental-style uniforms.

228. Frankfurt: Infantry. Grenadier, 1806

The capital city of Frankfurt (*am Main*) was pledged to supply an infantry contingent—dressed in white and red—and a jäger unit, in green, to the Confederation. The white coatees of the infantry

had no lapels, and were fastened with a single row of buttons. The bearskin caps had white metal plates. The fusiliers wore the bicorne. In 1808, the infantry were ordered to wear a dark blue uniform and shakos on the French pattern. The pack was of the type commonest in the Napoleonic period.

229. Duchy of Warsaw: 1st Infantry Regiment. Sergeant-Major with regimental colour, 1810

After the duchy of Warsaw was formed, at the peace of Tilsit in 1807, an attempt was made to provide the newly formed army with a uniform of national Polish style. The infantry's first uniform had been in the national colours, crimson and dark blue (196) but later, contrasting collars and lapels were introduced. In 1810, however, a single uniform for all the infantry regiments was introduced, but because several regiments retained the identifying colours they had worn before, the common uniform was achieved only in part. The regiment illustrated, for instance, continued to wear its former uniform. The marks of rank were silver epaulettes and braided sleeves. Tight white trousers and short black boots were worn on parade. The grenadiers wore bearskin caps and red epaulettes. The white metal eagle worn on the *chapka* was to become the badge of the national army of Poland.

230. Duchy of Warsaw: 12th Lancers. Captain, 1812

At this period the Polish cavalry consisted of lancers, hussars and light cavalry (chasseurs-à-cheval) with a single regiment of cuirassiers. The lancer regiments, as might be expected in the Polish army, were in the majority. Their uniforms were very similar throughout. Individual regiments could be distinguished by the colours of collars, cuffs, trimming and trouser-stripes. Only certain regiments wore coloured lapels as regulation for daily duty, the majority apparently wearing lapels matching the collar only for parades and ceremonial duty. The style of attaching the retaining cord to the cap was peculiarly Polish (196).

231. Holland: Colonial Marines. Marine, 1806

Today, the *Marine Corps*. This colonial marine section, formed in 1801, was initially uniformed throughout like the army (183). But whereas the Netherlands marine regiments that were included in the army in 1795 wore yellow as a special identification colour, the corps of 1801 wore red. When the army was given a white uniform in 1806, the marine infantry retained dark blue and red, a combination of colours still worn by the marines of the Netherlands.

232. Holland: 7th Line Infantry Regiment. Drum-major, 1808

The Dutch uniforms were totally changed when Napoleon made the country a kingdom in 1806. The style was brought up to date, and white was adopted as the basic colour for the regular infantry. The regiments were distinguishable by the numbers worn on their shakos, and by the identification colours on their jackets. The regimental colours were pale blue, red, pink, dark green, pale green, yellow, violet and black. The grenadiers wore bearskin caps or shakos with red feathers and red epaulettes; the *voltigeurs* (light troops) shakos with green feathers and green epaulettes. The *tête de colonne* in all regiments wore very decorative uniforms. Long feathers seem to have been especially fashionable at the time in Holland. The band and sappers in this regiment wore yellow uniform jackets.

233. Italy: Infantry of the Line. Grenadier, 1805

The army of the Italian Republic was dressed in a style very similar to that of France, except that all details in blue in the French were green in the Italian army—in other words they wore the Italian national colour. Fusiliers wore the bicorne hat. However, when the country became a kingdom in 1805, the uniform was changed. The basic colour for the infantry became white, and the

regiments were distinguishable by various combinations of red, white and green, on collars, lapels and cuffs. In 1807 a French-pattern shako was introduced.

234. Sardinia: Infantry Regiment 'Savoyen'. Officer, 1814

The uniforms laid down in 1814 for the reorganized Sardinian army had, apart from the dark blue basic colour, an extremely Austrian style. Thus the helmet was undoubtedly on the model of the earlier Austrian helmet (187). Nevertheless, the officer's helmet shown here has an elegant and very Italian shape. The helmet worn by the ranks was of more modest dimensions. The comb carried a crest in blue, the colour of the royal house. French influence was revealed, however, in one detail—the epaulettes for the officers. In 1821 the shako was introduced.

235. Naples: The 7th Line Regiment 'Africa'. Grenadier captain, 1812

When Napoleon's brother-in-law, Marshal Joachim Murat, became king of Naples in the year 1808, so many regulations concerning the uniforming of the Neapolitan army were issued that only a proportion of them were ever put into effect. The uniforms of the regular infantry conformed most closely to the rules. Contrasting collars, cuffs and lapels on the white tunic distinguished the various regiments. The grenadiers wore the bearskin cap and the fusiliers the shako. This regiment, consisting entirely of Africans, wore white bearskin caps. The light infantry regiments wore dark blue uniforms, but were issued with pale blue ones in 1814.

236. Naples: 4th Light Cavalry Regiment. Trooper, 1815

The Neapolitan light regiments in the regular cavalry had earlier worn green uniforms, but in 1814 these were replaced by sky blue, with collars, lapels and cuffs in regimental colours. As in France, there were the élite companies in each regiment, with fur caps, in contrast to the shakos worn by the remainder of the regiment.

237. Spain: The Prince's Cavalry Regiment. Trooper, 1808

From the commencement of the eighteenth century the Spanish regular cavalry had worn white and the dragoons yellow since 1719. The dragoons retained their yellow uniform colour but the regular cavalry adopted dark blue coats, with contrasting collars, lapels and cuffs according to the regiment, in 1805. The ranks in the cavalry wore boot-shaped leggings. The emblems worn by certain Spanish units on their collars at this time were unique. They appear to have been a form of heraldic device. The cavalry wore a heraldic lion; the dragoon and light cavalry regiments a palm leaf with crossed sabre; the artillery a flaming bomb and the engineers a castle tower.

238. Spain: 'Princesa' Infantry Regiment. Grenadier, 1808

The white uniforms of the Spanish regular infantry had followed the general military fashion. In 1800 the coat, which had been cut away at an angle at the front, was modified to be buttoned to fit the figure and at the same time lapels were added, cut straight down (237). The regiments were distinguished by the colours of their collars, lapels and cuffs. Musketeers wore bicorne hats. The grenadiers' bearskins developed in a curious way in Spain: the fabric crown became so extended that it covered the whole of the back of the cap and even hung down the wearer's back. Normally the crown was of the same colour as the uniform collar and cuffs, and was adorned with the regimental arms in embroidery as well as a trimming of ribbon in a different pattern for each regiment. In 1812 the regular infantry were given dark blue uniforms.

239. Spain: Catalonian Light Regiment. Private, 1807

The uniform of the Spanish light infantry, in hussar style, was first introduced in 1802. The crested helmet was of

unusual shape, with a plate carrying the name of the regiment at the front. The leather equipment was of a kind previously characteristic of light dismounted troops, namely a cartridge-pouch normally worn at the waist (131, 136 and 175) but in this instance equipped with a strap for suspension from the shoulder. For footwear the Spanish national sandals were worn, undoubtedly to aid mobility. In 1806 it was decided that in future the light infantry were to wear dark blue tunics with contrasting collars, lapels and cuffs according to the regiment and, in addition, shakos with a feather on the left side. The oval plate from the crested helmet was also worn at the front of the shako as a form of decoration. The Prince's Cavalry Regiment (237), the 'Princesa' Infantry Regiment (238) and this regiment belonged to the Romana division which went to Denmark on the orders of Napoleon in 1808, where they attracted considerable attention because of their exotic appearance. Their 'paper cigars' (i.e. cigarettes) also made an impression; the Spaniards were the first to smoke them in Denmark. According to contemporary sources they all, from the youngest drummer-boys to the general, chain-smoked continually.

240. Spain: The 'Death' Regiment. Private, 1808

During the war against Napoleon, various units of the free-corps type were formed in Spain. They had fanciful uniforms as well as fanciful names. The uniforms for this regiment came from Great Britain. The red cockade and death's head on the shako were supplied locally, however.

241. Austria: Infantry Regiment 'Graf Erbach', nr. 42. Captain, 1811

Experience in the Austrian infantry with the helmet introduced in 1798, revealed that in the long run it was too expensive, so it was decided later, in 1806, to introduce the shako. The one illustrated was introduced in 1810. The braid ornamentation according to rank along the top edge of the shako became official for officers in 1811. The overcoat had already been mentioned in the Austrian regulations of 1798 concerning uniforms: and under subsequent rules it could be worn both on and off duty to protect the expensive white coat. It was fitted with collar, cuffs and buttons like those of the uniform coat. The waist-belt was prescribed in the same regulations: the plate was of polished steel, with the imperial eagle in gilded metal relief. For staff officers only, the belt was covered with gold braid with two black threads interwoven. It seems to have been the height of fashion in the Austrian infantry at this time to have the sling of such a length that the sabre or broadsword trailed along the ground. The idea was, perhaps, to imitate the cavalry, but the custom was entirely unofficial. A sash (61) was worn over the belt on duty, so that it was hidden (284).

242. Austria: Dragoon Regiment 'Baron Kneswick' nr. 3. Dragoon, 1815

In 1915, *The Kaiser's Dragoon Regiment, nr. 11.* The Austrian regulations of 1798 prescribed dark green coats for all dragoon regiments. In 1801 the colour was changed to white. To distinguish them from the cuirassiers who also wore white coats, the dragoons' collars were wholly in the regimental colour, in contradistinction to those of the cuirassiers, which had just a small rectangle on either side of the fastening. The helmet was very popular for dragoons and cuirassiers, and remained in use with them until after the commencement of the First World War. In 1836 the comb-crest (ridge) of the helmet worn by the ranks was changed to plain black. The dragoons wore long grey overalls with leather buttons on the outside, in addition to their white trousers. They were to be worn, stated the regulations, only when mounted and in cold weather.

243. Austria: 'Saxe-Coburg-Saalfeld' Lancers. Lancer, 1815

The four Austrian Lancer regiments were uniformed almost identically, and could be told apart only by the colour on the upper portion of the chapka, which was either yellow, black, red or white. Since these regiments were still considered as a variety of Polish unit, there was an attempt in the 1790's to bring their uniforms as far as possible into conformity with the national Polish style of uniform. Retaining cords with tassels were prescribed for the men in 1803, and in 1804 it was decided that there was to be only a single stripe on their trousers instead of the former two.

244. Austria: Regimental Surgeon, 1811

In addition to the actual fighting men armies have always included a certain number of specialists, with the task of procuring the supplies necessary to maintain fighting strength or with responsibility for the health of the troops. These 'non-combatants' have enjoyed various names and fluctuating status according to the period and the army concerned. Change, however, has generally been in the direction of greater recognition. The earliest to be recognized and given a uniform were the doctors, the barber-surgeons, as they were called, or field surgeons. As early as the middle of the eighteenth century doctors were to be found in uniform in most armies. Their importance in war, and consequently better standard of training, resulted in their uniforms coming more and more to resemble those of the officers. In the Austrian army the surgeons were in uniform by the end of the eighteenth century—a uniform very like the officers'—and in 1799 all qualified, that is, university-trained doctors were entitled to wear the token of commissioned rank, the ceremonial sword. The uniform shown was prescribed officially in 1811.

245. Prussia: 1st West Prussian Infantry Regiment nr. 6. Grenadier, 1810

In 1914, *The Graf Kleist von Nollendorf Grenadier Regiment (1st West Prussian) nr. 6.* The army formed by Prussia at this time was considerably smaller than the one put into the field in 1806. The uniform had been brought up to date, partly on the Russian model, and only certain details were reminiscent of the uniform of the earlier army. The basic colour of the tunic was now dark blue. Collar and cuffs indicated the province of origin of the regiment. For East Prussia the colour was brick-red, for West Prussia crimson, for Pomerania white, for Brandenburg bright red and for Silesia pink— later yellow. In 1817 all infantry regiments adopted bright red collars and cuffs. The white trousers were worn only in summer and on parade. For normal, daily duty, tight grey trousers (248) were worn, but were replaced in 1815 by long trousers with a red piping on the outer seam. The shako became official in 1807, but the grenadiers retained the old grenadier cap (186) until 1810, when it was replaced by a shako with a goats'-hair tuft. The musketeers' shakos were decorated at the front with the royal cypher; those of the fusiliers with a big cockade and clip as it was called (284). For normal duty the shako was worn in a black waterproof cover (247–248). In 1812, shakos on the French pattern with V-shaped leather trimming at the sides were introduced, and in 1813, shakos of Russian style. After 1810 the bayonet belt was worn over the shoulder, except on parade and, after 1812, over the shoulder only (283).

246. Prussia: 11th Reserve Regiment. Man, 1813

In 1914, *the Von Winterfeld Infantry Regiment (2nd Upper Silesian) nr. 23.* As a result of the financial state of the country, the regulations of 1812 affecting the Prussian reserves' uniforms were applied more widely. The colours of the regiment of origin were to be worn on jacket and cap. The illustration shows a reservist dressed according to the regulations except for the leather equipment, which should be black. During the armistice of 1813, a proportion of the reserve battalions were dressed in British uniforms of dark blue or green, and quite unlike the normal Prussian uniforms (240 and 254). The militia, which also took part in the campaign against Napoleon, wore dark blue jackets and *casquets* as standard.

247. Prussia: Neumark Dragoon Regiment, nr. 6. Captain, 1808

In 1914, *Grenadier Regiment zu Pferd Von Derfflinger (Neumark), nr.* 3. In 1808 the Prussian cavalry were divided into cuirassiers, dragoons, hussars and uhlans. Whilst the cuirassiers were uniformed very similarly to those of Russia (250) the dragoons officially wore jackets in the traditional pale blue colour, and with shakos resembling those of the infantry. The regiments differed from each other in their identification colours of crimson, bright red, black, pink, white or yellow. Their buttons were either of brass or white metal. Besides their normal uniform jacket, the dragoons also normally wore a *litewka* as it was called —a form of overcoat intended for winter wear but which was widely worn in the 1813–14 campaign. Its collars and shoulder straps were in the regimental colour. The officers wore marks of rank on their shoulder straps in the form of lace, always in silver, irrespective of the colour of the buttons. In 1813 epaulettes were introduced for the officers. The dragoons' sole form of leg-wear, the grey overalls, had side-buttons originally covered with grey material. In the regiments these were changed to plain metal ones which became official in 1812. In 1815 the buttons were done away with, and the trousers were fitted with a red stripe at the outer seam.

248. Prussia: 1st East Prussian Infantry Regiment, nr 1. Rifle Volunteer, 1814

In 1813, detachments of volunteer riflemen were formed in all the Prussian infantry regiments. They were to wear the same uniform as the relevant regiment, but the basic colour of the tunic was to be green. These men enjoyed certain privileges. For instance, all those with higher education were allowed to wear ceremonial swords, just as supernumeraries from the guards regiments were allowed to wear guards' lace on their collars. The white armband was the mark of the armies allied to Napoleon during the 1813–14 campaign.

249. Russia: Line Infantry. Musketeer, 1809

When the Russian army was given a new uniform in 1802 and the double-breasted coatee came in, it was decided that collars and cuffs were to have the same colour for all the line infantry regiments within the same inspection, and that the regiments were to be individually recognizable by the colours of their shoulder straps. In 1807 this arrangement was changed: collars and cuffs were to be red for the entire infantry of the line, but the regiments in the divisions as now formed were again to be identified by the colour of their shoulder straps. The colours were red, white, yellow, dark green (with a red edge), pale blue and pale yellow. During the introduction of the new uniforms in 1802, the grenadiers had retained their old type caps with brass plates and the grenadiers their bicorne hats. In 1805 shakos were introduced for the musketeers and likewise for the grenadiers in 1806. The shakos, which were provided with a V-shaped leather trim at the sides in 1807, were replaced in 1812 by a new type, with a concave crown (251). The original pompon decoration of the musketeers' shakos was discontinued in 1809, after which only cockades were worn. For the 1st battalion in a regiment, these were white, with a green edging; for the 2nd, green with white edging and yellow with red for the 3rd. The grenadiers had a black plume on their shakos, with a flaming bomb in brass. The guards infantry had a special decoration on their shakos, and wore yellow lace on collars and cuff flaps. (279.)

250. Russia: The Chevalier Guard. Captain, 1811

Since 1799, the Chevalier Guard belonged to the heavy guards cavalry, uniformed like the cuirassiers, with the addition of special guards distinctions. In 1802 the double-breasted jacket in the traditional white colour was introduced. White trousers and high boots were for parade duty only; for normal wear long grey overalls were adopted, like those of the dragoons (185). The woollen crest on the helmet introduced in 1803 was replaced in 1808 by a form of horsehair crest, and a chin-strap with 'scales'. But the officers retained the old type of helmet until 1811. Epaulettes were introduced in 1807. Again, in 1812, black cuirasses with red scalloping along the edges were added, the officers had gauntlets and it was ordered that the collar should in future be lower throughout the whole army, and fastened at the front. The special mark of the guards was the lacing on the collar and cuffs, and the star of the Order of St Andrew on the helmet.

251. Russia: 'Actirski' Hussar Regiment. Hussar, 1813

The Russian hussars' uniform remained unchanged when the new uniform was introduced in 1802. The *flügelmütze*, however, was replaced by a shako in 1803 and the edging of the sabretache, which was formerly curved, was straightened in 1809. In 1807, dark blue trousers came in to replace the former white ones, and in 1813 the shako as prescribed for the infantry in 1812. The cartridge pouch belt in Russian leather was later replaced by a similar one in black leather. The monogram on the sabretache is that of Czar Alexander I.

252. Russia: Ural Cossacks. Cossack, 1812

The uniform and arms carried by the cossacks at this time were, as might be expected, highly irregular. Baggy trousers and unofficial forage caps were the height of fashion. With the exception of the Bug regiment which wore green, all the regiments wore dark blue. The identification colour was pale blue for the Ataman regiments; for the other Don regiments red, for the Ural, Orenburg and Zhagare regiments carmine; for the Kalmuks yellow and for the Bug regiments white. The guard cossacks wore bright red jackets, dark blue trousers and fur caps with red crown.

253. Great Britain: 93rd Highlanders. Private, 1810

Today, *the Argyll and Sutherland Highlanders* (493). In addition to the 42nd Regiment (83, 84 and 132) there were four more Highland Regiments in the British army at this time. As regards uniform, they followed the example of the regular regiments in tunics and equipment. Kilt and stockings, however, followed the traditional pattern, and the headgear had begun to develop into the feather bonnet later to be worn by all the Highland regiments (509). On active service the cap was fitted with a black peak. The pouch or sporran was not often worn on active service.

254. Great Britain: 95th or Rifle Regiment. Rifleman, 1807

Today, the *3rd Greenjackets* (*The Rifle Brigade*). Experience in the American War of Independence resulted, in 1800, in the formation of an independent British rifle corps, which entered the line as the 95th Regiment. From the beginning they wore dark green uniforms with black leather equipment. The tight pantaloons were replaced during the campaigns in Spain and the Netherlands by dark green trousers, except for parade duty. The shako of the usual pattern was retained for all light troops when a new model was introduced in the British army in 1812. The sword was suitable for use as a bayonet. The officers' tunics were fitted with black frogging in hussar-style, and instead of gaiters they wore hussar boots with black tassels. The officer's crimson sash was like that of the hussar officers. Up to 1802, the officers wore a light dragoon helmet but it was then replaced by a shako, like that worn by the men. At the same time the officers adopted dark green pelisses with black trimming.

255. Great Britain: 3rd (or the King's Own) Regiment of Dragoons. Trooper, 1812

Today, the *Queen's Own Hussars*. The British Dragoon Regiments wore the bicorne hat and jacket with lacing at the

breast up to 1812, but this uniform was now modernized. An Austrian-style helmet became official, but was immediately changed, the woollen crest on the comb being replaced by a curved horsehair plume, giving the helmet a French look. The buttoned jacket was replaced by a closed coat which hooked together at the front. The cuirass, however, was not introduced. The white breeches worn earlier were replaced in 1811 by pantaloons made of plush. When these proved highly impractical, grey overalls with coloured stripes were adopted.

256. Great Britain: 15th Light Dragoons or King's Hussars. Offjcer, 1813

Today, the 15*th*/19*th*, *The King's Royal Hussars*. The late introduction of hussars in the British army was unusual. The light dragoon regiments in 1784 wore laced jackets, but they also wore helmets instead of hussar caps. Meanwhile progress continued; various light dragoon regiments had more or less officially adopted details, such as sabretaches and pelisses, that properly belonged to the hussar uniform. Finally, four light dragoon regiments in 1805 obtained permission to use the designation 'hussars' in parenthesis after the name of the regiment. This permission had scarcely been given before the regiments were fully equipped as hussars, and had adopted uniforms second to none for elegance—and expense. On active service, shakos and long white or blue overalls buttoned at the side, and with chains rather than straps under the instep, were adopted for convenience. This regiment also had red shakos for the officers, and black for the men.

257. Great Britain: The King's German Legion. Infantryman, 1812

This body, which included infantry, cavalry and artillery, consisted of officers, N.C.O.s and men sworn to service from the Hanoverian army disbanded by Napoleon in 1803 and who had come to Britain to join the colours. The uniform was as for the corresponding British units. The infantry of the line, of which all battalions wore the same uniform, wore the shako which was to be introduced in the regular British army in 1812. This, later known as the 'Waterloo shako' since it was worn at the battle in 1815, was made of felt and carried a decorated brass plate at the front. In the British army long trousers replaced the former tight white pantaloons and knee-length black boots worn by officers. During the Peninsular War the white overalls were nevertheless still the commonest, but in 1812 overalls of various shades of grey were dominant. So the illustration shows how a British regular infantryman as well as a member of the legion looked in 1812. The grenadiers wore 'wings' (188) like the light infantry, but the latter had a green feather and green cords on the shako in addition. The officers, who had worn the bicorne hat until 1812, adopted the same type of shako as the men in that year.

258. Great Britain: The Brunswick Black Corps. Infantryman, 1809

This corps, recruited in Bohemia in 1809, by Duke Frederick William of Brunswick-Oels, undertook British service during the Napoleonic Wars up to 1814. The uniform was very unusual, both as regards colour and style. Instead of the usual coat, the infantrymen of the corps wore what was known as a *polrock*, or Polish coat with black hussar braiding on the front. The skull and crossbones was worn by the whole corps, except for the sharpshooter company which had, in addition, a grey instead of a black uniform. There was also a squadron of lancers in the corps, who wore Austrian uniform (243).

259. Great Britain: Royal Navy. Able-seaman, H.M.S. *Tribune*, 1805

There was no official uniform for seamen in the British Navy at this period. They were, however, beginning to be kitted out from the store with a corresponding cut in pay. Various commanders, however, laid down a common form of dress for their crews, and this appears to have been the case with the *Tribune*. The name

of the ship on the hat band is noteworthy, since it is the identification mark of the ordinary seamen which was to become general. Where no dress was laid down for a ship's crew, it was by no means unusual for seamen—with their usual flair for neatness and seemliness—to fit out their blue jackets with anchor-buttons and white tape along all the hems and edges.

260. Great Britain: 2nd Greek Light Infantry. Private, 1813

During the war in the Mediterranean, two regiments of Greek light infantry were formed under British command, and on the British model. This regiment was formed in 1813. Both regiments were uniformed in a variation of the Greek national costume. The jacket, waistcoat and cap were in the traditional British uniform colour, red. The jacket, with its black cord embroidery had a somewhat East European appearance. The regimental colours were yellow and green. The *fustanella* (skirt), trousers and hose remained in Greek style. A similar uniform is worn today by the Greek king's Royal guard, the *evzones* as they are called (392).

261. Sweden: Kalmar Regiment. Private, 1814

For the Swedish infantry, whose uniforms partly returned in 1792 to the pre-1779 styles (148), jackets or coats with lapels which could be fastened close to the figure were made official in 1798. The round hat was made taller and fitted with a brass band which could carry either the royal monogram or the regimental emblem at the front. In 1806 the lapels were abolished, and the jacket was fastened by means of a single row of buttons. At the same time grey trousers were made official, and it was later decided that the whole uniform was to be in grey. The grey uniform never won favour, and already by 1809 it was decided to introduce blue jackets or coats. It was finally ordered in 1810 that the jacket or coat was to have two rows of buttons, a red collar, and red cuffs with blue flaps in all infantry regiments. It is understandable that these rapid changes in uniform caused much perplexity, particularly since the new uniforms were not to be used until the old ones were worn out. Various regiments did not carry out the regulations, but wore uniforms with collars and cuffs in the colours which had won favour among the various units. The brass band on the hat was technically done away with in 1810, but since it could not wear out, it was still worn by most regiments until the hats were abolished.

262. Sweden: Smålands Light Dragoons. Trooper, 1808

To judge from the steady stream of regulations concerning the uniforming of the Swedish cavalry at this period, it seems that a special uniform was laid down for each separate regiment. In 1799, the short jacket with the short, outlined lapels, was introduced. The knotted sash or hussar sash, as it was called, was already official for all dragoon regiments in 1795, and the same year it was decided that all the cavalry were to wear sabretaches. The hussar-style cap was introduced in 1801. For daily wear and in cold weather, dark blue riding breeches trimmed with leather and with 42 brass buttons had been in use since 1794. About 1810, the regiment, or a portion of it, appears to have adopted fur caps (218), fitted with peaks, yellow busby bags, and a white feather. In 1814 the regiment adopted shakos of Russian style.

263. Denmark–Norway: Norwegian Life Regiment. Grenadier lieutenant, 1807

Today, *The King's Regiment of Foot.* This regiment, formed in 1657, was named the Norwegian Life Regiment (*Norsk Livregiment*) in 1764. A Danish army order of 1785 prescribed the regimental colours for the infantry which, in the main, applied until 1842. The effort to make uniforms more practical took the form, in 1789, of the introduction of jackets of virtually Russian style

(147), and round hats. But the officers retained coats of the usual cut. The grenadiers adopted a form of head wear reminiscent of the Russian from 1786, but in 1803 this was replaced by a bearskin in virtually the Austrian style. For officers, the breeches and high boots were replaced by pantaloons and hussar boots in 1801. The same year, for the first time, marks of rank, in the form of epaulettes, were introduced for all officers. Since the ranks—which in 1803 adopted dark blue legging-trousers—wore white linen trousers for summer use, the officers adopted white or dark blue pantaloons to match. The poverty-stricken times that followed the loss of the fleet in 1807, meant that much of the expensive ornamentation on uniforms disappeared. In 1812 epaulettes and sashes, except for the field ranks, disappeared and in 1813 it was decided that henceforth grenadiers were to adopt the shako, already in use in 1801 for musketeers and light troops (297).

264. Denmark–Norway: Fyn Light Dragoons. Trooper, 1813

Today, *The Jutland Regiment.* The regiment shown, which was included in the Jutland Dragoons in 1932, was formed in 1670. The efforts to make the Danish cavalry more mobile resulted in the dragoon regiments being converted into what were called light dragoon regiments, with lighter mounts, hussar-type saddles and lighter arms. There were also some changes in the uniforms. This regiment adopted, from its formation in 1796, the casque (helmet) made official for light dragoons two years earlier. It had the name of the regiment embossed on the metal band over the peak. Instead of knee-breeches and high boots, the light dragoons were to wear pale yellow pantaloons and hussar boots. For daily wear and active service, the entire cavalry adopted dark blue overalls after 1797. After 1810, these were replaced by dark grey, since blue dyes were impossible to obtain because of the war. When epaulettes disappeared in 1812, marks of rank on the sleeves became usual for officers and N.C.O.s. Meanwhile cuff-flaps—to e pointed later—were also discontinued. he feather on the helmet was also bolished in 1813.

65. U.S.A.: New York Rifle Corps. Rifleman, 1812

he 'hunting shirts' (126) so popular uring the War of Independence, were lso prescribed for the American volun er corps, formed in the opening years f the nineteenth century. The prescribed olours were green and yellow, but the Maryland Rifle Corps adopted a red ringe.

66. U.S.A.: 16th Infantry Regiment. Enlisted man, 1812

oday, the *2nd Infantry Regiment*. Since he War of Independence, the American nfantry had worn dark blue coats with ed collars and cuffs. A regulation of 812 prescribed these colours, and a rimming of white lacing on the breast, ollar and cuffs. As a result of the army xpansion for the war against England, proved impossible to obtain sufficient lue material, so that a number of ackets were made in black, brown, reen and grey cloth. The gaiter-type rousers were in every conceivable shade f grey, brown and blue. In the summer, vhite linen uniforms were worn. In 1813 t was decided that the gaiter-trousers vere to be changed to trousers of normal ength. The same year all regiments dopted blue tunics; the uniforms were tandardized, while a new shako, similar o the British 1812 model, was intro luced.

67. Portugal: 1st Rifle Battalion (Caçadores). Rifleman, 1808

Vhen the Portuguese army was re ormed after the evacuation of the rench in 1808, the uniform adopted was f British style. The regular infantry, owever, were in dark blue, and the iflemen wore dark brown uniforms. The attalions could be distinguished by the olours on their collars and cuffs. The hako had a hunting horn with the attalion number on the metal strip over he peak, surmounted by an oval shield

with the Portuguese arms. The officers wore epaulettes and gold lacing at the breast and black hussar boots.

268. Netherlands: Belgian Militia. Infantry lieutenant, 1815

The Belgian regular regiments differed from the Dutch at this period in wearing shakos very like the British 1812 design. The Dutch regular regiments wore shakos with peaks front and back, with a large sunburst and the royal monogram over the front peak. The same shako was prescribed for the Belgian militia, but in 1815 it seems to have been worn only by officers. The regular regiments had white collars and cuffs.

LATIN AMERICAN WARS OF INDEPENDENCE 1807–1825

During the Napoleonic wars, Spain and Portugal underwent great disturbance, and as a result the long servitude of the Spanish and Portuguese possessions in Central and South America erupted in a series of conflicts which developed into lengthy wars of independence. The result was the liberation of a large part of these areas, and the formation of many in dependent states.

269. Argentine: 'Patricios' Regiment. Private, 1807

The colonial period saw the formation, beside the regular Spanish regiments, of military units manned from the local population in the Spanish possessions in America. This regiment was formed to resist the British invasion of the vice royalty of Buenos Aires in 1806. During the Argentinian War of Independence, from 1810–1816, the regiment joined the revolutionaries and later became the basis of the new national army. The uni forms were on European lines. The round hat was prescribed at the time for most of the Argentinian units in uniform.

270. Argentine: 'Infernales' Cavalry Regiment. Trooper, 1807

Like the foregoing unit, this regiment was formed to resist the British invasion of the viceroyalty of Buenos Aires in 1806 and later went over to the freedom fighters. The uniform was like that worn by the Argentinian dismounted riflemen. Other cavalry regiments wore blue with red collars and cuffs, red frogging at the breast, and red hussar lacing on the trousers. The majority of the Argentinian cavalry, however, were not uniformed, but wore the usual dress of the gauchos. The trooper is holding the Argentinian national cockade of 1812, which replaced the red Spanish cockade.

271. Brazil: Rio de Janeiro Militia. Infantry man, 1822

As in Portugal, the Brazilian uniforms were very British in style after 1808. The colours, green and yellow, which were to be the national colours of independent Brazil, were dominant in the uniforms of the national units. From 1822–1825, a green cockade over a yellow chevron was worn on the left arm, bearing the text 'Freedom or Death'.

272. Brazil: Diamantina Civic Guard. Private, 1824

Current uniform styles in Europe spread to South America, and were manifested in the use of shakos of post-Napoleonic type, among other details. White linen uniforms were common in summer. The Brazilian militia and civic forces were generally well and regularly uniformed at this time.

273. Mexico: Insurgent Army. Officer, 1814

It proved impossible to establish general uniforming in the insurgent army before 1820, during the Mexican War of Independence which lasted from 1810–1823. There were, however, certain attempts to do so. Indications of unit were often worn in the hat, drawn or painted on a piece of paper.

274. Mexico: General Iturbide's Independence Army. Light cavalry man, 1820

When General Iturbide, who had fought bravely against the Mexican insurgents

from the year 1810, went over to their side in 1820, the improved organization he was able to introduce was accompanied by improved uniforms. The infantry were mainly in blue, but red uniforms were also worn (291–2).

275. Venezuela: General Bolivar's Bodyguard. Man, 1820

This guards corps was formed as a personal bodyguard for General Bolivar one of the most renowned figures of the Latin-American struggle for freedom. I was thanks to his contribution that Venezuela and several other Central American states won their liberty. Their uniform was to some extent inspired by the Napoleonic mounted scouts. The colours, however, derived from the Venezuelan national colours, red, yellow and blue. The hussar braiding on the breast has a special shape in this instance. The remainder of the Venezuelan army wore pale blue.

276. Chile: Infantry of the Line. Private, 1820

During the Chilean struggle for freedom from 1810–1818, the national liberation army was uniformed only in part. There was no complete uniform until 1820. The shako carried the Chilean arms in front. The pompon was in the national colours: red, white and blue. The officer had silver pompons and the upper band on their shakos were in silver braid. They also wore silver epaulettes, pantaloons of the same colour as the coat, and black boots.

THE BELGIAN AND POLISH UPRISINGS 1830–1831

The 1830 July Revolution in France resulted in the long simmering resentment of the Catholic Belgian provinces against Dutch control breaking out in an armed rising. After four days of fighting, the Netherlands troops were compelled to evacuate Brussels, but Antwerp was bombarded in retaliation. With the intervention of the great powers in 1831, the war was brought to an end.

and Belgium was recognized as an independent kingdom.

277. Netherlands: Horse Artillery. Senior N.C.O., 1830

This artillery corps, formed in 1793, belonged, for the period of its existence to the élite troops of the army of the Netherlands. The corps wore a uniform generally like that worn at Waterloo in 1815. On active service the shako was worn in a form of waterproof cover. In 1841 a new uniform became official, entirely in the hussar style, with a dark blue dolman with yellow frogging, and a fur cap.

278. Belgium: Partisans of Capiaumont. Senior N.C.O., 1831

The Belgian struggle for independence resulted in the formation of various free corps, or civic corps. Their uniforms differed somewhat from those of the regulars. Although jackets were very popular in the free corps, many of their members liked to wear a form of smock or blouse, originating in the working dress of the period. The headgear was either a top hat or a cylindrical waterproof shako. The regulars wore French-style uniforms.

THE POLISH UPRISING 1830–1831

In the kingdom of Poland, too, which had been in personal union with Russia since 1815, the French July Revolution resulted in armed rising. At first the Russians had to vacate the country, but in 1831 the Polish national army suffered a decisive defeat at Ostrolenka from the returned Russian forces, which then besieged Warsaw. The rising was totally crushed, and Poland was placed under a Russian governor-general.

279. Russia: 12th Infantry Regiment 'Nishnij-Novgorod'. Private, 1830

The uniforms of the Russian army at this period were a development of those used during the Napoleonic wars. The 1828 model shako was certainly one of the tallest and narrowest of its kind in Europe. The regular regiments wore an eagle over a shield with the regimental number on their shakos, and those that had distinguished themselves in battle added a metal scroll with the (Russian) inscription 'For Distinguished Service'. On active service the shako was worn in a waterproof cover, with the designation of the regiment painted on it in yellow. The uniform coat had only one row of buttons after 1814, but red edging was added in compensation. The regiments carried their divisional numbers on their shoulder straps and the latter were red for the first regiment in the division and white for the second. In summer and for parades, white trousers were worn.

280. Poland: 10th Infantry Regiment. Captain, 1831

The Polish army, which remained independent of the Russian until 1830, had nevertheless a similar uniform. The basic colour for the infantry was dark blue, with yellow trimming. All the Polish regiments wore lapels, though they were confined to the guards in the Russian army. Buttons and mounts were made of white metal. The shako carried the Polish eagle. The regiments formed after the commencement of the rising generally wore dark blue jackets with collars and cuffs in the regimental colours, and blue or white trousers. Only two regiments wore the Polish cap or *konfoderatka*: the remainder wore casquets with Russian-style brims.

THE LONG PEACE OF THE 1830's

The 'eternal' peace proclaimed after the Napoleonic wars seemed very problematic. In Latin America there was fighting against the Spanish colonial dominance, and unrest also simmered in Europe but resulted in no actual conflict among the great powers. Army functions at this time were mainly of a police nature, which resulted in greater stress being laid on elegant parade uniforms than on practical dress for active service.

281. France: Infantry of the Line. Grenadier, 1833

With the restoration of the monarchy after the fall of Napoleon, white uniforms were introduced for the French infantry, but in 1820, dark blue tunics were once more adopted. In 1828 the identification colours of collars and cuffs were done away with, being replaced by red. In 1825 shakos became stiffer and more cylindrical, and their decoration up to the July revolution, the royal lily emblem, now became the gallic cock surrounded by a 'glory'. In 1835, a tapering shako was adopted. The most comprehensive change in uniforms was the adoption of red trousers in 1829. These were to become characteristic of the French army during the subsequent period.

282. Great Britain: 96th Regiment of Foot. Private, 1836

The most thoroughgoing change in the British infantry uniform after the Napoleonic wars was the introduction of a shako in the current continental style, to replace the 'Waterloo' shako. The first model, established in 1815, was replaced by a new type in 1828, with V-shaped leather trimming at the side. The battalion company feather, originally white and red, was replaced by a ball-tuft in 1835. The elegant star-shaped front plate was replaced for the ranks, by a simpler type in 1839. In the remainder of the outfit, the changes were not very radical. However, the contemporary tendency to fine down the uniform and provide a better fit had gained ground in Great Britain, to the extent that the soldier's uniform was relatively smart in appearance but far from convenient to wear on active service. The coat introduced in 1826 had a collar that closed under the chin, epaulettes, and—in 1829—flaps or slashes on the cuffs. Up to 1826 the officers wore lapels on their parade and ceremonial uniforms. In 1830 it was decided that, in future, gold should be restricted to the regulars, and that the militia were to wear silver. The other ranks retained lace in the regimental pattern until 1836, when it was replaced by white lace alone. Tight-fitting white breeches and white gaiters were in use for parades and ceremonial duties up to 1823, after which long white trousers were worn for special parades. The grey trousers were provided with a red stripe in 1833 (303).

283. Prussia: Guard Grenadier Regiment 'Kaiser Alexander'. Private, 1828

Since the end of the Napoleonic wars, the Prussian uniform conformed very closely to the Russian. Here, too, the general tendency towards closer fit and smarter appearance had gained ground. To improve the shape and fit of the coat and to emphasize the cut considerable padding at the chest was already the custom in most armies. The trousers were well braced up, and had straps under the instep so that they fitted with as few creases as possible. There was a tendency at this time, especially, to emphasize the uniform details which made the wearer look taller and slimmer, such as the shako, which was higher and narrower, and carried a long feather. As regards the leather equipment, the main problem was to make the pack sit securely on the back without the straps being too tight on the chest, a problem to which various solutions were sought (279 and 281–284). This regiment, together with the Kaiser Franz Guard Grenadier Regiment, was formed in 1814, and like the latter, obtained guards status in 1820. Both regiments carried the cypher of the Imperial honorary colonel on the shoulder flaps. Lace on the collar was first introduced in 1834. The Prussian infantry wore white legging-trousers at special parades until 1831, after which long white trousers were worn for such duties.

284. Austria: Infantry Regiment 'Graf Kinsky' nr. 47. Musketeer, 1837

The most noteworthy change in the uniforms of the Austrian infantry after the Napoleonic wars was the introduction of pale blue long trousers in 1836. The Hungarian infantry regiments had for ong worn pale blue tight trousers with hussar frogging in yellow and black cord. The shako was generally the same as had been introduced in 1807, but as it was tending to be used less and less on active service, it underwent various changes. The latest model, established in 1836, had peaks front and back, like the previous one. In 1840 a new model, without the rear peak, was introduced; it was also lower and parallel-sided. The grenadiers wore bearskin caps.

THE GREEK CIVIL WAR 1831–1832

The Greek struggle for freedom against the Turks in 1820 ended in 1829 when the great powers guaranteed Greek independence. A civil war between the political factions in Greece, which broke out in 1831, was brought to an end when in 1832 a national assembly chose Prince Otto of Bavaria to be king of Greece.

285. Greece: Infantry of the Line. Fusilier, 1832

During the struggle for liberty during 1821–1829, and the subsequent civil war, only in a few units was it attempted to establish a form of uniform. When Otto of Bavaria became king in 1832, the Greek army was uniformed with Bavarian assistance, and in Bavarian style. The grenadiers wore red shoulder adornments and red tassels on their shakos. These details were green for the rifles. In cut the artillery uniform was like that of the infantry, but in dark blue, with yellow buttons and crimson trimming. The cavalry were uniformed like lancers, in green and crimson. In 1851 a tapering shako made of leather was introduced, as was a service coat with a double row of buttons.

286. Bavaria: Chevaulegers-Regiment 'König'. Light cavalryman, 1833

To support King Otto, a Bavarian expeditionary force was sent to Greece in 1832, to remain until 1837. The Bavarian army uniforms had followed the general line of development. The long trousers of the cavalry were now the same colour

as the coat, and in 1826, regimental colours were once more introduced.

THE SPANISH CARLIST UPRISING 1834–1839

When Ferdinand VII bequeathed the throne, at his death in 1833, to his only daughter Isabella, his brother Don Carlos considered himself wrongly passed over. He had himself proclaimed king in the Basque provinces, provoking a prolonged civil war. With their outstanding leaders the Carlists were successful at the beginning, but after many desertions by his men in 1839 Don Carlos was compelled to abandon the struggle and seek refuge in France with his supporters.

287. Spain: Carlist Infantry. Private, 1835

The uniforms of the Carlists were scrappy in the extreme, generally consisting of items taken from the royalist troops. A common identification was the red Basque cap, worn by all the Carlist soldiers. The adoption of this cap was evidently a result of the early Carlist support in the Basque provinces.

288. Spain: Royal Guard Horse Artillery. Gunner, 1834

As with a number of other armies, the Spanish horse artillery were dressed in a hussar-style uniform. In the 1830's the Spanish cavalry adopted red trousers, and the mounted artillery which was considered as part of the cavalry, followed their example. The British influence on the Spanish uniforms after the Napoleonic period was, it seems, later followed by a preponderantly French influence.

THE MEXICAN WAR 1846–1848

When Texas became part of the United States in 1845, the Mexican protest resulted in 1846 in war with the former. An American army invaded Mexico, and in 1847 occupied the capital, Mexico City. When peace was concluded in 1848 Mexico relinquished all claim on Texas north of the Rio Grande del Norte, and also ceded New Mexico and New California to the United States.

289. U.S.A.: 1st Dragoons. Trooper, 1847

American uniforms had followed the general development. The dark blue coats, worn both on service and for parade duty, became close-fitting and narrow. In 1835 a tall cylindrical shako and pale blue trousers were introduced. During the war in Mexico the so-called 'undress'—a form of daily or working dress—was used for active service. The cavalry jacket had trimming on the curved back seam as well as on collar and edging. In 1835 a cap of the familiar pattern, but in black leather, was introduced. In 1841 caps of dark blue fabric were introduced. Yellow stripes on the trousers were official for corporals, sergeants and officers (326).

290. U.S.A.: Infantry of the Line. Enlisted man, 1847

The 'undress' for the regular American infantry consisted of a jacket of the same colour as the trousers, and dark blue cap for the entire army. In 1841 the single shoulder belt was abolished, and the bayonet was subsequently worn in a holder at the belt. The oval waist belt plate carried the initials of the Union, and the shoulder belt plate the American eagle (325).

291. Mexico: 1st Regular Infantry Regiment. Private, 1846

In the 1830's the Mexican infantry were dressed in dark blue, and in 1839 contrasting collars, lapels, cuffs and edging were introduced in regimental colours, so that each regiment was distinguishable by its own uniform. In 1840 it was decided that all infantry regiments were to have dark blue coatees without lapels, but with red collars and cuffs. In 1841, however, the 1839 uniform was once more introduced. The original shako, which had been of broad-top type, was replaced around 1840 by a shako of virtually cylindrical shape. There seems

to have been some latitude in the decoration of the shako. The ornamented plate with the Mexican eagle, and the regimental number is found in several variants.

292. Mexico: 7th Regular Cavalry Regiment. Senior sergeant, 1846

The Mexican cavalry came under the same regulations regarding uniform as the infantry. The 1840 uniform was pale blue, whereas the 1839 and 1841 styles were more variegated. This regiment originally wore white coats with pale blue facings, but in 1842 they adopted a uniform in the national colours throughout. Sergeants and senior sergeants wore silk epaulettes—green in the cavalry and red in the infantry. Sergeants wore epaulettes on the right shoulder only. Corporals wore a piece of lace obliquely over the cuff as a mark of rank. Whereas all metal items and ribbons are brass or yellow respectively in the infantry, in the cavalry they were white metal or white in colour. Unlike the Americans, who wore a form of battle dress during the Mexican campaign, the Mexicans, when they had uniforms on their backs, wore 'full dress' in the field.

EUROPEAN INSURRECTIONS 1847–1850

The decision of the Swiss Federal Assembly to use force against seven rebellious Catholic cantons in 1845 resulted two years later in the brief *Sonderbund* war. The result was that Switzerland remained undivided. The February Revolution in Paris in 1848 restored the republic in France, and also inspired unrest and revolt throughout almost the whole of Europe. In Germany the Prussian army was able to put down its revolution, whereas in Hungary and Schleswig-Holstein full-scale wars were developed against Austria and Denmark respectively.

293. Switzerland, Vaud Canton: Carabinier, 1847

After the Napoleonic wars the Swiss

uniforms were a cantonal responsibility. A uniform eliminating the cantonal characteristics was not introduced until 1852. Previously, nevertheless, the infantry had been dressed throughout in dark blue, and the light troops in green. As light troops, the carabiniers were armed with muzzle-loading rifles. To drive the bullet into position in the barrel a hammer was necessary, and this can be seen worn at the side of the cartridge pouch. As special equipment the carabiniers also carried a powder horn, suspended from a cord over the right shoulder. A special mark of the Swiss troops as a whole was the red brassard with the white Swiss cross, which remained in use until the First World War.

294. Prussia: 2nd Silesian Infantry Regiment, nr. 12. N.C.O., 1848

In 1914, the *Prince Karl of Prussia Grenadier Regiment* (*2nd Brandenburg nr. 12*). At the end of the 1830's there was some criticism of the current uniforms. It was said, and not without justification, that these were intended more to make the troops look colourful on parade than to provide them with protection and freedom of movement in the field. In Russia, which set the fashion in uniforms at this time, tunics and helmets were tried out, the latter based on cuirassier and dragoon helmets. Tunics had already been adopted to some extent at the end of the Napoleonic wars, in both the Prussian and the Russian armies, but were dispensed with. Whereas the experimental stage persisted in Russia, in Prussia the new ideas were seized on and adopted quite early. Long tunics and the spiked helmet were introduced in 1842. In 1847 new leather equipment was introduced, and the Prussian infantry assumed the appearance they were to retain in the main until the Second World War. The eagle adornment on the front of the helmet was variously designed for the guard and line units. The cockade was worn under the right-hand side chinscale fastener. In 1843 the horsehair plume on the helmet was introduced in the guards,

grenadiers, and certain regular regiments for festive occasions. The horsehair plume was generally white for the guards, black for the regulars and red for the bandsmen. The cartridge pouch was provided for at the belt, but until 1850 it was worn on the back. In this year the single pouch was replaced by two smaller ones, worn at the front, one at each side of the belt buckle. The buckle itself was adorned with a crown, and bore the inscription *Gott mit uns*. The spiked helmet and the tunic were introduced for the entire army, except for hussars and uhlans. The braiding on N.C.O.s' collars and cuffs had been worn unchanged since 1814 (341).

295. Hungary: Honvéd Infantry. N.C.O., 1848

The army put into the field by Hungary against Austria wore uniforms of definitely Hungarian style. The tunic with frogging was later to provide the model for hussar uniforms all over the world. The artillery wore the same uniform as the infantry, distinguished only by a white border and a white grenade on the collar. The mark of the N.C.O. was the red border to the collar and the braiding in national colours on the shako. The officers wore gold frogging and a red, white and green sash over the shoulder.

296. Schleswig-Holstein: Artillery. Train-constable, 1849

The army raised by the Schleswig-Holstein insurgents to fight Denmark was dressed in Danish uniforms at the beginning, which were soon changed for obvious reasons. By the end of 1848 a special Schleswig-Holstein uniform was beginning to be used in the army. This was quite modern, and closely resembled the Prussian uniform. The national eagle appeared on the spiked helmet and the national arms were worn on the breast. The artillery wore a ball as used in Prussia in 1844 on the helmet instead of the spike, which proved dangerous if worn during artillery duties. The infantry wore bright red braid, white shoulder straps, and white-metal buttons.

THE FIRST SCHLESWIG WAR 1848–1850

Unrest in Holstein during 1848 developed into a regular war against Denmark, because a Prussian army, at the request of the German Confederation came to the assistance of the insurgents. The conflict took place in Schleswig and Jutland, its principal events being the battles at Bov and Schleswig in 1848; the expedition from Fredericia in 1849 and the battle at Isted, in 1850. On Prussia's withdrawal from the war, the defeat of the Schleswig-Holstein insurgents at Isted compelled them to abandon the struggle. The outcome was that the duchies of Schleswig, Holstein and Lauenberg came under Danish rule.

297. Denmark: 1st Line Infantry Battalion. Private, 1848

Today, the *Danish Guards Regiment*. The Danish army was modernized as a result of the reorganization of 1842. Battalions replaced regiments and numbers replaced names. Uniforms were also standardized. The battalions were identified by the number on their shoulder straps and shakos in an otherwise identical uniform for all regular battalions. The coat was retained, though the tunic had been considered instead. Full leather equipment was worn on active service (299). White trousers and a white cord on the shako were worn for special parades. The dragoons wore the same uniform, but with pale yellow edging and helmets with brass mounts, while the artillery substituted dark blue for all pale blue and white details shown, and all their metal items were in brass.

298. Denmark: 2nd Rifle Corps. Bugler, 1848

Today, the *Jäger Corps*. Tunics were prescribed for the Danish rifles and engineer troops during the 1842 reorganization. The rifle troops retained the traditional colours, green and red, and the corps was identifiable by the number on shoulder straps and shako. The latter was like that worn by the

regular infantry, but had a green pompon. The shako was not specially popular, and this rifle unit was unlucky enough to 'mislay' its shakos during a voyage, so that it wore soft caps for the remainder of the campaign. The cap illustrated from 1842, was quickly replaced by the Hungarian style cap introduced in 1848. Musicians in other branches of the service wore the same kind of shoulder decoration as the rifles but invariably in the same colour as the uniform collar, and with lace of the same colour as the buttons. A certain number of line battalions were converted during the war to light battalions, and were given the same uniform as these rifles. In 1849 the rifle corps and light battalions were given dark grey trousers as a regulation issue. The engineers wore uniforms of dark blue throughout.

299. Denmark: 5th Line Infantry Battalion. Private, 1849

Today, the *Zealand Guards Regiment*. It was decided in 1848 that the red coat of the Danish army were henceforth to be replaced by dark blue service tunics. The latter were to embody bright red collar patches and edging for the infantry and crimson for the dragoons and artillery. The buttons were to be the same as were worn with the red tunics. Service tunics came in faster than was planned as a result of the war, and they were in use in all units by the end of the war. The shako was also dropped by the army in the field, and the old soft cap was quickly replaced by the 1848 model. An attempt to introduce the spiked helmet was abandoned because of the war. Throughout the conflict, the leather equipment was generally the old type with white bandoliers and covered knapsack strap. Black leather equipment was subsequently adopted, and a new arrangement, resembling the Prussian but black throughout, was to come into use in 1850 (339). During the war, marks of rank for the officers were practical and inconspicuous, but epaulettes and the sash introduced in 1842 were retained for parades and ceremonial occasions.

300. Sweden: West Gotland Infantry Regiment. Private, 1848

During the First Schleswig war, Sweden and Norway despatched a contingent of troops to Denmark, but it took no part in the war. The spiked helmet, in Sweden called however the *kask*, and the service tunic were both introduced in the Swedish (and Norwegian) armies in 1845, following the example of Prussia. The tunic, as regards the infantry, was piped only on the edges of the cuffs for officers and along the front edge. The shoulder straps, coloured according to the military district to which the regiment belonged, carried the regimental number. The spiked helmet, differing from the Prussian only in its rounded peak, was adorned at the front with a shield bearing the Three Crowns emblem of Sweden, and had a yellow cockade under the right hand rosette of the chinstrap. Note the peculiar copper-kettle carried with the pack.

THE CRIMEAN WAR 1854–1856

The Crimean War was fought between Russia on one side and Turkey, Great Britain, France and Sardinia on the other. The cause was growing tension between Russia and Turkey. Britain became apprehensive that Russia would dominate the Balkans. The main seat of the conflict was the Crimea, where the allies established a bridgehead. After defeating the Russians at Alma in 1854, they surrounded and besieged Sebastopol. Other incidents in the war included the Russian attempt to break out at Balaclava and Inkerman in 1854, and the Allied conquest of Sebastopol in 1855. When peace was concluded in 1856, Russia had to make only small cessions of territory, but her pressure on the Balkans was halted.

301. Great Britain: 17th Lancers. Lancer, 1854

Today, the 17th–21st Lancers. The impact of the Polish lancers' participation in the Napoleonic Wars resulted in the introduction of lancers in the British army in 1816. This regiment, formed as a light dragoon regiment in 1759, was converted into a lancer unit in 1822, and as such took part in the Charge of the Light Brigade at Balaclava in 1854. The regiment had retained the colours it wore as a dragoon unit. Gauntlets were introduced in 1833, and in 1834, the former sabretache with the regimental badge—a death's head and crossbones—was to be discontinued. The jacket had pointed cuffs and white piping to the seams on sleeves and back. The upper portion of the *chapka* or lance-cap was in white—the regimental colour—and was adorned with a black horsehair plume for parades.

302. Russia: Infantry of the Line. Private, 1854

The Russian spiked helmet, which seems to have come in in the infantry in 1844, differed from the Prussian type particularly in not having a border to the peak, and in the flaming bomb, mounted on an extension, forming the point. In 1855 the spiked helmet was replaced by an almost cylindrical shako decorated in front like the former headdress. (The guard, nevertheless, retained the spiked helmet.) In the infantry, uniform coats were worn almost exclusively but on active service they were normally concealed under the greatcoat. The latter were so long that they were usually worn turned up in some way, so as not to prove a hindrance. The footgear was the top boot normally worn by Russian peasants. A curious method of suspending the pack was adopted in 1834, when the straps were arranged so that they could be crossed over on top of the shoulder belts. Such a mounting must have presented a satisfactory appearance on the parade ground, but could hardly have been very practical. The large water-bottle was introduced in 1851. The waterproof container on the pack was for the greatcoat.

303. Great Britain: 89th Regiment of Foot. Man of grenadier company, 1854

Today, *The Royal Irish Fusiliers*. The Crimea revealed many deficiencies in the military systems of the warring powers, and especially in the British army. For instance, the uniforms proved to be quite unsuited to the exigencies of active service. In 1844 the old shako had been replaced by a smaller type with peaks front and back known as the 'Albert'. Otherwise uniforms had remained generally the same. Grenadiers and light companies could still be distinguished by the wings on the shoulders, but various improvements came in during the duration of the war. There were no regrets for the shako when it was replaced by the 'undress cap', which was worn for most of the war. In 1855 a red tunic was worn, without lace trimming but in the existing regimental colours. Eventually a smaller and lighter shako was introduced, but did not prove satisfactory either. The leather equipment remained unchanged throughout (381).

304. Turkey: Artillery. Gunner, 1854

By 1820, the Turkish army had commenced to use European-style uniforms. In the 1840's dark blue uniforms of French style were prescribed for the whole army. The headgear remained the traditional fez however, which was to be retained as long as the Ottoman kingdom existed.

305. Russia: Caucasian Rifle Battalion. Lance-corporal, 1854

Trials of the tunic in Russia had reached a stage at which these were adopted for units with specially arduous or active duties in the field. This battalion was of such a type, and was issued with these tunics in 1848. The battalion colour, raspberry red, was characteristic of Russian rifle battalions. The shoulder straps carried the battalion initials. For Caucasian units the fur cap was of special shape. When the Russian army was re-equipped after the Crimea, the principles were those adopted in this uniform (386).

306. France: 3rd Zouave Regiment. Zouave, 1854

A Zouave battalion consisting of volunteer Parisians and Kabyles was formed in the French forces in North Africa in 1831. In 1852 the French army controlled three Zouave regiments which consisted exclusively of Frenchmen. The uniform was Arabian in style from the commencement, and remained almost unchanged until the Second World War. White gaiters were to be worn over the boots but they seem not to have come in by the Crimean War period. The inside lacing of the boots is noteworthy. The regiments were identifiable by the colour of the 'false' pockets on the tunic—red for the first regiment, white for the second, and yellow for the third.

307. Sardinia: 1st Grenadier Regiment. Corporal, 1855

The two guards regiments comprising the Sardinian grenadier-guard brigade were converted into grenadier regiments in 1850. A new uniform was simultaneously introduced, even more French in style than the former. The regiment could be identified by the grenade on the shako and the lacing on the collar. On active service the shako was worn in a form of waterproof cover. The belt buckle carries the cross from the Savoy arms (402).

308. France: Infantry of the Line. Cantinière, 1854

During the Second Empire period, the French *cantinières*, usually married to N.C.O.s, were dressed in quite becoming garments, although these were worn over trousers and gaiters. The feminine aspect was stressed by bonnets, lace-trimmed collars and skirts of crinoline type. Instead of the large straw hat, made fashionable by the Empress Eugénie, a lighter version of the regimental headgear was worn. At this period the French army evidently wore unusually practical uniforms. The tunic was introduced for the infantry in 1845.

THE FRANCO-AUSTRIAN WAR, 1859

Austrian control over Northern Italy resulted in 1859 in a clash between

Austria and Sardinia. Supported by France, the latter had been secretly working for the unity of Italy. After the French and Sardinian victories at Magenta and Solferino, Austria and France concluded peace, with the former ceding Lombardy to Sardinia. France obtained Nice and Savoy in 1860, in return for recognition of the inclusion of Modena, Parma, Tuscany and a portion of the Papal State in Sardinian territory.

309. France: Imperial Guard, Chasseurs-à-cheval. Trooper, 1858

As under the First Empire, the Imperial Guard during the Second included all branches of the service. This regiment wore virtually the same uniform from its formation until 1870. The plaited cord on the chest was discontinued in 1860, and sabretaches were introduced the same year. The feather and cloth bag on the fur cap were not worn in the field. The officer's dolman was frogged with black cord and lace. The parade uniform was trimmed with silver.

310. Austria: Jaczygier Volunteer Hussars. Lieutenant, 1859

A number of volunteer hussar regiments were formed in Hungary during the war in Northern Italy. They were later included in the Austrian army. The uniform of the Austrian hussars was simplified in 1849. The 'attila', as it was called, with less elaborate frogging and which resembled the service tunic, was adopted instead of the short dolman. Colours, too, were made simpler, the line regiments being given dark or pale blue uniforms, and shakos in the regimental colours. The folk-style felt hat originally worn by the volunteer hussar regiments was replaced when they became part of the army by a small fur cap. The latter was to become standard for all hussar regiments.

311. France: Imperial Guard, Grenadier-à-pied. Grenadier, 1859

Like his great forebear, Napoleon III also had several grenadier regiments in his guard. Their uniforms, established in 1854, were reminiscent of those worn by the grenadiers of the old guard in Napoleon I's time, but were more modern in style. The original dark blue trousers were replaced by red trousers with a narrow dark blue stripe in 1857. The uniform coat, with white lapels, was not conspicuous when worn in the field, because the greatcoat (with tucked up skirts) was the usual wear on active service (355).

312. Austria: Infantry Regiment 'Grosshergoz von Hessen' nr. 14. Private, 1859

The modernization of the Austrian infantry uniforms commenced in 1849 with the introduction of a double-breasted tunic in the same colours as the former coatee. The rounded corners of the Austrian tunic were characteristic. In 1850 a conical shako was authorized, adorned at the front with the double-eagle emblem in brass. When the shako was worn under a cover, the large brass cockade was also covered. During the war in northern Italy, the infantry in the field wore lighter and more convenient linen tunics, called *kittels*, instead of the usual tunic. This was, in fact, a barracks or working garment and not part of active service equipment.

313. Tuscany: Infantry of the Line. Private, 1859

Like the other small Italian principalities under Austrian rule, the uniform of the Tuscan troops was Austrian in style. Up to 1849 the infantry wore white coats, replaced by tunics in that year. The guard battalion wore red trousers. The cavalry wore the same uniform as the infantry, with helmets like those of the Modena dragoons (314).

314. Modena: Dragoon Regiment. Cavalryman, 1859

In the principality of Modena, the dragoons wore a white and blue crest on their helmets on parade. The infantry wore dark blue tunics and grey-blue trousers, with white edging on both. The rifle troops' uniform was confusingly similar to the Austrian (338).

315. Parma: Field Artillery. Officer, 1859

In the principality of Parma, the Austrian element disappeared from the uniforms in 1852 when, simultaneously with tunics, spiked helmets of Prussian style were adopted. The infantry tunics were single-breasted, with pale blue shoulder straps for the first battalion, white for the second, and yellow for the third. The grenadier guards wore red shoulder straps and red horsehair plumes on their spiked helmets. The musketeer guards had black plumes and black leather equipment. The cavalry were uniformed more or less like the artillery, but in 1859 they adopted small shakos.

316. Papal States. Infantry of the Line. Sapper, 1859

Until 1870 the Papal States possessed, in addition to various palace guards, a regular army previously uniformed in virtually Austrian style. From the end of the 1850's, the regular infantry, however, wore a uniform confusingly like that of the French. Only the sappers wore bear-skins. Otherwise the headgear was a small shako (*kepi*) worn in a waterproof cover on field duties.

THE STRUGGLE FOR ITALY'S UNIFICATION 1860–1861

As a direct consequence of the Franco-Austrian War in 1859, the struggle for the unification of Italy began. The guerilla leader, Garibaldi, with his thousand 'red shirts' drove the Neapolitan troops out of Sicily, after which he landed in southern Italy and occupied Naples. A Sardinian-inspired rising in the Papal States the same year led to the kingdom of Sardinia sending troops to 'restore order'. When the Papal army had been routed, the Sardinian army went south where, with Garibaldi's forces, they broke the last resistance of the Neapolitan army. In 1861, Franz II of Naples capitulated in the fortress of Gaeta, and a newly-formed joint parliament proclaimed the Sardinian king Victor Emmanuel 1 as 'King of Italy'.

With the exceptions of Venice and Rome—whose inclusion followed in 1866 and 1870 respectively—the unification of Italy was thus complete.

317. Naples: The Guard of Honour. Officer, 1860

This corps of guards, formed in 1833, consisted of volunteers and served in peace as a royal household guard and in war as a field unit. For a short period after the Napoleonic wars, the Neapolitan uniforms were British in style, but later they followed the French pattern. Thus they were rather old-fashioned. Service jackets, for instance, were still not adopted by 1860. Lapels were not worn on active service, and the shako was worn in a cover, without the plume.

318. Naples: Infantry Carabiniers. Officer, 1860

Many guards units, and others with guards status, were a peculiarity of the Neapolitan forces at this period. This regiment, formed in 1848, had the satisfaction of being the best trained and disciplined in the entire army. The uniform was very like that of the foot guards. The officers had a form of overcoat for wearing both on and off duty, in accordance with *ad hoc* regulations. The collar matched that of the uniform coat. The field cap carried marks of rank in the form of lace, and since there was no such indication on the coat, the cap was readily worn in combination with it. In the last war in which this army was involved, the officers generally wore cap and coat as a field uniform.

319. Naples: Swiss Artillery. Gunner, 1860

The section of the army most loyal to the king consisted of the recruited Swiss troops. At this time there were four Swiss infantry regiments, one rifle battalion and four batteries, the last of these formed in 1850–1851. The uniform of the Swiss artillery was not very different from that of the ordinary artillery. As with Swiss regiments, previously in

French service, the Swiss infantry wore red uniform coats.

320. Naples: 5th Rifle Battalion. Rifleman, 1860

At this period, the Neapolitan infantry of the line wore dark blue coats with collars and cuffs in the regimental colours. The rifle battalions wore green jackets with yellow collars and cuffs. The field uniform, however, as in France, consisted of the greatcoat with turned-back skirts. The shako worn by the rifle troops was like that of the artillery, but with yellow lace. In 1859, in conjunction with new rifles, a new form of leather equipment was introduced, the former shoulder belt being replaced by a waist belt. The cartridge pouch was carried at the back. The small pouch in front was for percussion caps. The white leather equipment worn (instead of black), was an unusual feature. The infantry of the line retained their shoulder belt.

321. Sardinia: Bersaglieri. Private, 1860

From their formation in 1833, the battalions of *bersaglieri* formed the *élite* of the Sardinian, as later of Italian army. Their uniform remained the same in its principal features until the First World War. The broad-brimmed hat with the cock's feather in still worn in peace time, and also with 'battle dress'. The feather plume is also worn with the solar topee and often also with the steel helmet. At this period the officers still wore gilt epaulettes but later they adopted marks of rank on the sleeve. From the time of the Crimean War, the *bersaglieri* battalions, when not wearing the plumed hat or helmet, adopted a form of hat resembling a fez—red with a blue tassel.

322. Sardinia: Field Artillery. Officer, 1860

At this period French influence was still very evident in Sardinian uniforms, but certain details which were to become characteristic of the Italian army were beginning to make their appearance. The traditional identification colours of black and yellow were retained by the artillery. The peacetime uniform was very impressive. Epaulettes and cording were made of yellow thread for the men's uniforms. The blue-grey trousers were for mounted troops, while those on foot wore dark blue. The ranks generally wore a short, dark blue tunic with a single row of buttons as a field dress, with a shako in a cover and field cap of French pattern. The officers wore dark blue tunics with black fur trimming and black hussar frogging.

323. Sicily: Garibaldist, 1860

The irregulars with which Garibaldi overthrew the Bourbon control in Sicily, the renowned 'thousand', were allowed to wear red shirts, whence the name. They retained their shirts until they were disbanded.

324. Sardinia: Engineer Corps. Sapper, 1860

The most distinctive feature of the Sardinian engineer troops was their headgear which, as with the *bersaglieri*, consisted of a wide-brimmed hat, with an ornamental crown like that of a shako.

THE AMERICAN CIVIL WAR 1861–1865

The rivalry between the Southern agricultural and the Northern industrial states in America developed until slavery, the basis of the Southern economy, became an issue leading to civil war in 1861. The war commenced well for the South, with the army of the North beaten at Bull Run and Richmond in 1861 and 1862, and in 1863 at Charlotteville. The battle at Gettysburg the same year was, however, a victory for the North, and a turning point of the war. The resources of the Southern states at this time were virtually exhausted. The following year the Northern armies invaded and in 1865 the last Confederate troops capitulated at Appomattox and Raleigh. The war saved the Union, and advanced the abolition of slavery.

325. The Union: Infantry. Enlisted man, 1861

The regular army uniform was worn by the Northern armies during the civil war. 'Union blue' consisted of a dark blue short blouse and pale blue trousers. The tunic, then called a 'frock coat', was introduced in 1851, but during the war the ranks wore almost exclusively the blouse, which initially came in as a working dress. In 1858, a high-crowned, broad-brimmed soft hat was introduced, likewise the field or forage cap, which latter was most used during the war. The leather equipment, which was the same as had been used in the Mexican War, was blackened in the 1850's.

326. The Union: Cavalry. Sergeant, 1861

The frock coat was introduced for the American cavalry in 1851, but in 1854 a short 'uniform jacket' with lacing was introduced. This was normally combined with epaulettes pressed in brass which were, in fact, adopted by the cavalry as early as 1832 and by the ranks in all branches in 1854. They were seldom worn on active service, however. The soft hat was officially prescribed for the cavalry also, but was not much worn either. During the Civil War, the mounted artillery wore the same uniform as the cavalry, but with all yellow trimming replaced by red. Sleeve marks of rank for N.C.O.s in the form of chevrons in the branch colours were introduced in 1847.

327. The Union: Field Artillery. Captain, 1861

Officers in the Union armies were allowed to wear the same blouse as the ranks, with the appropriate marks of rank, but often they wore the 'frock coat' instead. As worn by lieutenants and captains, this had one row of buttons, and for field officers two rows. The headgear was generally a cap of the same type as was worn by the other ranks, but mounted officers often preferred the 'campaign-hat' as it was called—a variation of the soft hat introduced in 1858. Emblems indicating the branch were worn on both

types, in the form of gold embroidery The ranks also often wore them, but in brass. Since 1835, epaulettes had been replaced in the field by the dummy epaulette straps. These were in the branch colour and carried marks of rank For generals the colour was dark blue for the infantry pale blue, for the cavalry yellow and for the artillery red. The sash was buff for generals, red for other officers, and for the medical branch green.

328. The Union: 11th Indiana Volunteer (Wallace's Zouaves). Man, 1861

Today, the 151st Infantry Regiment (The Indiana National Guard). During the Civil War, both North and South forces were supplemented by militia units, and volunteer corps. Various volunteer units were dressed in more or less fanciful uniforms. The Zouave style was very popular on both sides. The uniform was very closely copied from the French, but certain individual leaders, such as Wallace, had their own idea as to the required dress for active service. In the North the various contrasting uniforms largely disappeared from the battlefields during the course of the first year of war the volunteers adopting 'Union-blue also.

329. The Confederate States: Infantry Enlisted man, 1862

The Southern States adopted army uniforms contrasting as far as possible with those of the Northern army. Grey was chosen as a basic colour. The regulations prescribed a grey tunic with two rows of buttons, and pale blue trousers. Collar and cuffs were in the branch colour, buff for generals, pale blue for infantry yellow for cavalry and red for the artillery. The headgear was a cap of the same style as was worn by the North—originally grey, with trimming in the branch colour, but from 1862 in the branch colour. The leather equipment was the same as was worn by the Union forces. The exceptional marching performances exacted from the Southern infantry soon resulted in the elimination of equipment, only the absolute minimum being carried in a blanket worn over the shoulders. Towards the end of the war, as a result of the shortage of supplies in the South, the sight of an even approximately correctly-uniformed infantryman was very unusual.

330. The Confederate States: Louisiana Tiger Battalion. Zouave, 1862

In the South, also, the volunteer battalions had fanciful names and uniforms. This battalion, which consisted mainly of Irishmen, wore Zouave uniforms paid for by the business men of New Orleans.

331. The Confederate States: South Carolina Volunteers, Hampton's Legion. Trooper, 1861

Hampton's Legion was formed at the outbreak of the war in 1861, being paid for by a single individual as a patriotic gesture. It consisted of infantry, cavalry and artillery. Grey coats were worn by the Southern cavalry as in the North. But the mounted troops wore short jackets for the most part, during the war, because the long ones with skirts were unpopular. Broad-brimmed hats with a waving feather, and some form of trimming on the jacket front were also much in favour among the cavalry.

332. The Confederate States. Horse Artillery. Lieutenant, 1862

The horse artillery of the South also preferred the jacket to the service tunic. The red cap, the pride of the artillery, was worn until the end of the Civil War, even if all other uniform had to be foregone. Marks of rank for the Southern officers consisted of gold tracing in hussar style on the sleeves, as well as gold braid on the collar, with more gold lace on the vertical seam of the cap. Generals wore stars on their collars. The sash was buff for generals, red for the infantry and artillery, yellow for cavalry and green for the medical branch. As in the North, the N.C.O.s wore sleeve chevrons as marks of rank in the branch colour, and, like the officers, matching stripes on the trousers.

THE MEXICAN 'ADVENTURE' 1864–1867

In 1863, using financial disputes as an excuse, Napoleon III sent French troops to occupy the capital of Mexico, Mexico City. With internal clerical-party support, the same year he had the Austrian archduke Maximilian installed as emperor of the newly-proclaimed Mexican dominion. The Emperor arrived in 1864, and was immediately resisted by the large Republican party. When the French troops were withdrawn in 1867, the imperial army was beaten by the Republicans, and the Emperor himself taken prisoner and shot. Mexico was then re-proclaimed a republic.

333. Mexico: Belgian Expeditionary Corps, Rifle Battalion. Cantinière, 1864

To support Emperor Maximilian's Belgian-born consort, Charlotte, a Belgian corps consisting of a grenadier and a rifle battalion accompanied them to Mexico. Their uniforms were very up to date. The hat with the plume of feathers was of Belgian type, while the service jacket was like that worn by the French Imperial Guard (355). The troops wore grey Zouave trousers and matching leggings. Caps of French style were generally worn during the fighting in Mexico, with white covers and solar neck guard (323), and white linen trousers. The ribbon trimming was red for grenadiers and white for staff personnel. For daily duty the officers wore hussar trimming of black silk, with gold for ceremonials. The institution of the cantinière had developed in Belgium as in France, and in this instance the uniforms were established by regulation.

334. Mexico: Austrian Volunteer Brigade, Rifle Battalion. 1st Lieutenant, 1864

To support Maximilian, an Austrian brigade consisting of all branches of the army accompanied him to Mexico. The brigade was uniformed in up-to-date style. All dismounted troops wore a similar uniform, and were identifiable only by the feathers in their hats. These were red for the artillery and white for pioneers. The ranks had no special neck-wear, their tunics being fastened at the neck with a turn-down collar. The cavalry consisted of hussars and lancers, both in green.

335. Mexico: Turkish Auxiliary Battalion. Lieutenant, 1864

The Turkish support for Maximilian consisted of an Egyptian battalion. The uniform was the normal Egyptian dress, apart from the colour. In hot weather, white linen uniforms were worn in the same style. For ceremonial the officers wore an all-red uniform with a great deal of gold lace. Epaulettes were worn for parade and ceremonial duty.

336. Mexico: Imperial Palace Guard. Sergeant, 1865

The uniforms of this guard corps were established in 1865. The one used for ceremonial guard duty, dismounted, as shown, was certainly inspired by various European guards uniforms, although it shows signs of the emperor's individual taste. The ceremonial weapon and the colour of the tunic resulted in a certain Austrian appearance. The white breeches, gauntlets and high boots were worn in Prussia and Russia as well as in Austria. Russia seems to have provided the inspiration for the braiding on the jacket and helmet. The uniform included the Mexican national colour in the green stripe in the braiding. As in Prussia and Russia, the helmet carried the armorial eagle. The ornamentation on the shoulders and the fringes below—more especially the absence of a high military collar—probably betray the emperor's own taste. The corresponding officer's uniform had a wide edging of leaf-embroidery instead of lace, and plaited shoulder pieces and frogging instead of the ornamentation and fringes. Daily uniform consisted of a long jacket of civilian cut and long trousers, both in green material with red trimming, and a white cap of French style.

THE SECOND SCHLESWIG WAR 1864

The Second Schleswig War was caused by Prussia but formally declared by the German Confederation, with the result that Prussia and Austria had to go to war to prevent the incorporation of Schleswig-Holstein in Denmark. The official cause of the war was the 'November Constitution' which stated that the duchy of Schleswig was to be incorporated in the kingdom, contradicting earlier agreements. The decisive events of the war were the occupation of the Dannewerk fortifications, the storming of the Düppel fortifications and the conquest of Als. The Danes conducted themselves well under these circumstances, but better arms and leadership tipped the scales in Prussia's favour. The outcome was that Denmark was forced to cede the duchies of Schleswig, Holstein and Lauenberg to Prussia and Austria.

337. Prussia: Westphalian Field Artillery Regiment nr. 7. Gunner, 1864

Uniforms of the Prussian artillery generally followed the pattern of the infantry. Overcoats were introduced in 1807, and changed little subsequently. Collars were high, with a black patch with a red border for the artillery, and the same on the service jacket. In this instance the patch was hidden by the cover worn by the field troops in 1864, attached to the lower edge of the collar. In spite of the experience of the 1st Schleswig war, the Prussians retained the short boots adopted in 1819. When the long trousers were worn inside the boots in bad weather, they were tucked inside the socks also. This was hardly satisfactory, since damp and dirt came in over the 'floppy' tops of the boots, and the various colours and lengths of the long socks were unsightly.

338. Austria: Feld-Jäger Bataillon nr. 9. Rifleman, 1864

A new tunic was introduced in the Austrian army in 1861. In design it was well ahead of its time, in having a turn-down collar and convenient cut (345). It had only a single row of buttons and no edging for the other ranks, but was otherwise in the same colours as before—dark greenish-grey with pale green collar and cuffs for the *Jäger* troops. The turn-down collar of the greatcoat was fitted with a patch of the same colour as the collar of the service jacket. The earlier division of the footwear into shoe and legging was retained. The leggings were consequently designed so that the trousers could be tucked into them in the field. Note that the front of the greatcoat is turned inwards and fastened up.

339. Denmark: 11th Infantry Regiment. Lance-corporal, 1864

Today, the *Falster Infantry Regiment*. At the beginning of the war against Prussia and Austria, the Danish battalions were converted into regiments. Their uniforms were based on the experience of the First Schleswig War. Nevertheless, certain details of equipment were improved. For instance a larger and stouter greatcoat was introduced in 1859, and the leather equipment was improved in 1855 and 1859. In 1852 the shako was reintroduced and in 1858 a new model, conical and with peaks front and back, was introduced. But only the 18th Regiment wore the shako during the war, the others wearing the field cap, 1858 model. By 1854 longer boots which had begun to come in during the First Schleswig War, were made standard, so that under bad conditions the trousers could be tucked inside or turned up. During the war, neckerchiefs of every conceivable colour were permitted. Woollen gloves were standardized in 1853. The curved pipe with wooden bowl, the so-called 'service' or 'field' pipe, seems to have been obligatory for both German and Danish troops, officers and ranks. Normally the tobacco pouch was hitched over one of the buttons, likewise the pipe when not in use. Regimental mascots, which shared the campaign medals, were known from the British army, among others. The only instance in the Danish army, however,

was this regimental dog Flora, who went into battle and was wounded in 1864. After the war Flora was awarded a medal to be worn on her collar until her death. The Falster Infantry Regiment still remembers its regimental dog.

340. Denmark: 6th Dragoon Regiment. Dragoon, 1864

Today, the *Jutland Dragoon Regiment*. In 1854 it was decided that the service tunic of the Danish dragoons was to be pale blue, instead of the dark blue of 1848, and with all metal items white. At the same time the helmet mainly used until the modern period was introduced. The leather equipment remained white. The cavalry greatcoat was wide enough to be worn over the leather equipment, and, when mounted, always with the front undone and the slit buttoned up, so that it lay like a blanket over the horse's back. When the Danish cavalry coat was worn thus, it was said to be impenetrable, consequently the Prussian and Austrian cavalry were instructed to thrust and not to cut when attacking the Danish dragoons.

THE AUSTRO-PRUSSIAN WAR 1866

The rivalry between Austria and Prussia concerning the supremacy in Germany resulted in war in 1866. For the Austrians, fought the kingdoms of Bavaria, Hanover, Saxony and Württemberg, the duchies of Baden, Hesse Darmstadt, Hesse-Kassel and Nassau, plus the free city of Frankfurt-am-Main. On the Prussian side were the duchies of Brunswick, Mecklenburg-Schwerin, Mecklenburg-Strelitz, Oldenburg and the free city of Hamburg. Prussia had also allied herself to Austria's traditional enemy, Italy. Austria thus had to fight on two fronts, and won brilliant victories in Italy, but suffered a resounding defeat at Prussian hands in the main seat of the war in the north, at Königgrätz (Sadowa). At the conclusion of hostilities Austria agreed to the dissolution of the German Confederation and to her own exclusion from the North German Confederation under German leadership. Prussia annexed the kingdom of Hanover, Hesse-Kassel and Nassau, the duchies of Schleswig, Holstein and Lauenberg, and the free city of Frankfurt-am-Main, while Italy received Venice in return.

341. Prussia: 3rd Garde-Regiment zu Fuss. 1st Lieutenant, 1866

Since their introduction in 1842, the uniform coat and the spiked helmet underwent various minor changes in the Prussian army. The spiked helmet became smaller, and in 1867 a still shorter design, with rounded peak, was introduced. During the war against Denmark the officers, so as not to render themselves conspicuous, abandoned their epaulettes. This resulted in certain problems of leadership recognition so that what were called *feldachselstück* (i.e. 'field shoulder pieces') were introduced at the beginning of the war, and were later officially adopted for field duty in peacetime also. Like their men, the officers wore long trousers tucked into their boots in the field. This regiment, formed in 1860, wore white horsehair plumes in their spiked helmets for parades. The other ranks wore yellow shoulder straps without numbers (397).

342. Prussia: 2nd Brandenburg Lancers, nr. 11. Trumpeter, 1866

In 1914, *Lancer Regiment Graf Haeseler* (*2nd Brandenburg*), *nr*. 11. The Prussian lancers first adopted the tunic in 1853, in the special design called the *ulanka*. Sleeves and back had a coloured piping on the seams, and lapels of the same colour as the collar were buttoned to the tunic for parades. Epaulettes were introduced for the ranks in 1824, and in 1843 a shorter *chapka* was prescribed. Since the upper portion was of fabric, in this instance yellow, it was worn in a cover in the field. The retaining cords were not worn when the *chapka* was covered. In 1867 a still shorter design was introduced in leather throughout. The long trousers with leather lining were replaced in 1870 by tighter riding breeches and high boots (405).

343. Mecklenburg-Schwerin: 4th Infantry Battalion. Sergeant, 1866

In 1914, *Archducal Mecklenburg Fusilier Regiment, nr. 90, 'Kaiser Wilhelm'*. The introduction of the spiked helmet in 1842 provided Prussia with a military headgear that was to become the symbol of all things Prussian. In the German states it also represented influences friendly to Prussia, so that the adoption or abolition of the cap took place in step with Prussian relations. In the archduchy of Mecklenburg-Schwerin, which had copied the Prussian style since the Napoleonic wars, the tunic and spiked helmet were introduced in 1848. At the commencement of the 1860's, however, there was a change: the spiked helmet was replaced by one of the type adopted for the Russian infantry in 1862. For parades and ceremonial occasions the helmet was fitted with a metal plate and a black plume. When the Mecklenburg troops were included as a contingent in a Prussian army corps, their uniform was adapted to the Prussian (397).

344. Hamburg: Contingent Cavalry. Dragoon, 1866

Since Napoleon's time, the troops of the free city of Hamburg wore green uniforms with red distinctions. During the 1840's, tunics and spiked helmets were introduced on the Prussian example. For the dragoons the steel type of spiked helmet worn by the Prussian cuirassiers was chosen. Although it was later discontinued for the infantry, this helmet was worn by the Hamburg dragoons until they were included in the Prussian cavalry in 1867.

345. Austria: Field Artillery. Lieutenant, 1866

The traditional colours of the Austrian artillery, brown and red (18) were retained in the service tunics. In 1860 a special shako was prescribed for the artillery, characterized especially by the plume which was always worn tied on the left. When the shako was worn uncovered, the plume was retained in place by means of a gilded chain. The gold braided shoulder-belt for officers was also introduced in 1860. Pale blue trousers properly belonged to the uniform, but officers were allowed to wear grey trousers with leather attachments in the field. Up to 1849, only field officers as such were distinguished by braiding, but that year, proper marks of rank in the form of stars on the collar, combined with braiding, were introduced for them.

346. Saxony: 4th Infanterie (Leib) Brigade. Private, 1866

In 1914, 1st (*Leib*) Grenadier Regiment nr. 100. In 1849 the Saxon infantry were formed in brigades, and the battalions from then on were numbered. The spiked helmet was not worn in Saxony after 1866. When the service tunic was introduced in 1849, the conical shako introduced in 1846 was retained. The colours of the service tunic were changed in 1862 from green to pale blue. Collar, cuffs and pipings were coloured according to the brigade: red for the 1st, yellow for the 2nd, black for the 3rd and white for the 4th, all with red edging. The leather equipment, which was black throughout the infantry, was changed to the Prussian pattern after 1849. When the Saxons joined the North German Confederation in 1867, the army uniform was adapted to the Prussian, so that the spiked helmet and dark blue tunic were introduced.

347. Hanover: 6th Infantry Regiment. Private, 1866

The Hanoverian army, earlier uniformed on the British model, adopted the Prussian style in 1837. Tunics and spiked helmets were prescribed in 1849. However, the latter was once more dropped in 1858, and a *kepi* (shako) very close to the Austrian model was introduced. This was adorned with the leaping horse of Hanover in front, in white metal, and with a crowned wreath in brass. All infantry regiments wore lace; the guards regiment white, and cuffs without flaps. Pairs of regiments wore red, yellow or pale blue shoulder flaps with the regimental number. Leather leggings were worn in place of long boots. The only British detail worn was the barrel-shaped water bottle, which bore the mark of the unit painted on it in white.

348. Bavaria: 2nd Cuirassiers. Trooper, 1866

In 1914, *Royal Bavarian 2nd Heavy Cavalry Regiment, the Archduke Franz Ferdinand of Austria-Este*. Tunics, in most cases in their former colours, were introduced in the Bavarian army in 1848. The cuirassier helmet was introduced in 1815, and in this instance with a fur trimming to the crown which was done away with in 1859. Instead of leather-inset trousers, long leggings resembling boots were worn. In 1875 the cuirass was abolished, and in 1879 the cuirassier regiments were converted to heavy cavalry, and equipped with spiked helmets.

THE FRANCO-PRUSSIAN WAR 1870–1871

The cause of the Franco-Prussian War was French opposition to Prussian dominance after the victory over Austria in 1866 and to Bismarck's attempts to unite Germany. The war was brought nearer partly as a result of the 'Ems despatch' concerning the candidature of the house of Hohenzollern to the throne of Spain. France declared war. Contrary to French expectations, the South German states supported Prussia, while the hoped-for allies, such as Italy and Austria, opted for neutrality. The up-to-date equipment of the Prussian troops, and the brilliant planning of the general staff, combined with French lack of initiative and resolution in leadership, resulted in a series of German victories. The French Rhine army was defeated and confined in the fortress of Metz in August, 1870. The relief army was surrounded and surrendered at Sedan in September the same year, while the French army of the Loire was also defeated. Napoleon III was among the prisoners taken at Sedan. Metz capitulated in October 1870 and Paris in January 1871. In France the defeat resulted in the end of rule by the

Emperor and the declaration of the republic. Germany was welded together as a united kingdom, with the king of Prussia as ruler. When peace was concluded in 1871, France ceded Alsace and part of Lorraine to Germany, and agreed to pay an indemnity of five billion Francs.

349. Prussia: Magdeburg Cuirassier Regiment nr. 7. Trooper, 1870

In 1914, *Cuirassier Regiment von Seydlitz (Magdeburg) nr. 7*. When tunics and spiked helmets were introduced in the Prussian army in 1842, the cuirassiers received their special issue. The long tunic, called the *koller*, was fastened up the front. The arm-hole and seams on sleeves and back were trimmed in the regimental colour. The braiding was in gold or silver for the officers. Individual regiments had spiked helmets of gilded metal with white-metal ornamentation. Cuirasses, taken from captured French stocks, were introduced in 1814. In 1865 the tight white trousers and the 'old Brandenburg' type top boots were coming in. Gauntlets had been worn for parades since 1842. The cuirass was retained for parade duty only in 1888. Apart from minor changes in helmet and boots, the uniform was worn unchanged until 1914.

350. Prussia: 1st Silesian Rifle Battalion nr. 5. Rifleman, 1870

In 1914, *Jäger Battalion von Neumann (1 Silesian) nr. 5*. From an early period the Prussian jägers had worn green and red, as in other armies. Since 1817 the shoulder straps had been red with the unit number. In 1842 tunics and spiked helmets were introduced, but in 1854 the helmet was replaced by a conical shako. A black plume was worn with the shako, but had been reserved for ceremonial occasions since 1856. The rifleman's pack was called a *dachs* (badger) because it was covered in badger skin so arranged that the head was central at the top, a reminder of the ancestry of the pack in the game-bag. Since the modern mode of fighting normally required shooting

from the prone position, it proved impractical to carry the greatcoat over the shoulders during the war against France. It was thus decided in 1889 that in future it would be securely attached round three sides of the pack.

351. Bavaria: 2nd Lancers. Lancer, 1870

In 1914, *The Royal Bavarian 2nd Lancer Regiment, the König*. In 1822 the Bavarian lancers were discontinued, but in 1863 two such regiments were re-established. They were dressed in Prussian style, wearing lapels buttoned to the tunic for parades. The term *ulanka* was not used in Bavaria. The 'spencer', as it was called, was worn in the field—a short jacket in the same colour as the tunic and with epaulettes from the latter. The *chapka* was crimson at the top, with a white plume for parades. The carrying of haversack and waterbottle by the cavalryman, and not attached to the horse, was at this time very unusual.

352. Bavaria: 5th Infantry Regiment. Private, 1870

In 1914, *Royal Bavarian 5th Infantry Regiment, 'Grandduke Ernst Ludwig of Hesse'*. Regimental facings, abolished in the Bavarian army in 1814, were re-introduced in 1826 and transferred to the service tunics when these came in in 1848. The crested helmet, in shape now *Hesse'*. Regimental facings, abolished in the Bavarian army in 1814, were re-introduced in 1826 and transferred to the service tunics when these came in in 1848. The crested helmet, in shape now influenced by the spiked helmet, had its neck-protection and the metal portions cut down. At the front it carried the crowned royal cypher. The former white crossed shoulder belts were replaced in 1860 by black leather equipment with a waist belt. Though, after 1870, the Bavarian troops maintained an independent position in relation to the German army, their uniforms and equipment nevertheless were later formed on the German model. In 1873 tunics of Prussian style were authorized, with red collars throughout. In 1886 the spiked helmet was introduced. The pale blue basic colour of the uniform was, however, retained until the field grey uniform came in.

353. France: Chasseurs-à-pied. Lance-corporal, 1870

The uniforms of the French chasseurs were very similar to those of the line infantry, except for the colours of trousers and cap, and the shape of the cuffs. The original tunic was relatively long. In 1860, however, a very short tunic and Zouave trousers were introduced, but these were replaced in 1868 by a double-breasted tunic of moderate cut and trousers more normal width and length. Meanwhile a conical, cloth-covered shako was introduced, but during the war against Germany the field cap was worn almost exclusively. The line infantry, with red trousers and red caps with a dark blue border at the base, wore the dark blue overcoat with skirts turned up and red epaulettes almost exclusively during the war. The epaulettes were standardized for the entire line infantry in 1867, when the division into grenadiers, fusiliers, etc., was done away with. Note the two mess-tins on the pack; the small one carried above belongs to the soldier; the larger was called the section mess-tin.

354. France: Cuirassiers. Trooper, 1870

The classic French cuirassier helmet, famous during the Napoleonic wars, was replaced in 1816 by a type having a worsted crest instead of a hairplume on the 'comb'. In 1845, however, the former model was reintroduced. The guard cuirassiers, formed in 1854, were issued with service tunics in 1856, and in 1860 all cuirassiers of the line were equipped with these. The regiments were differentiated only by the numbers on their buttons. The guard cuirassiers wore tight red trousers and high boots during the Franco-Prussian war. All cuirassier officers wore silver epaulettes and wide, dark-blue stripes on their trousers.

355. France: Imperial Guard, Grenadiers-à-pied. Grenadier, 1870

In 1860–1866, the uniforms of the French dismounted guards entirely changed its character. The tunic now introduced was somewhat longer than that used by the line regiments. As regards leather equipment, only the belt was now white. Besides the small pouch in front, a larger one was carried on the back, its flap being adorned with an eagle and four flaming grenades in brass. For guard duty, parades, and daily duty, the bearskin was worn (311). On the outbreak of war in 1870, the grenadiers took the field in their bearskins, but it was soon decided that they were to be returned to depot and replaced by the recently introduced field-cap similar to that used by the regular regiments. Since the field cap never reached the guards units, the grenadiers wore what was called the 'quarter-cap' throughout the war. Only officers wore the field cap, combined with a service tunic without lace. It was considered very fashionable during the war to wear a flannel sash round the waist, over the short tunic or jacket, as was the custom among the troops in North Africa. The colours of the sash could vary but pale blue, red or dark blue were most general.

356. France: Field Artillery. Gunner, 1870

The tunic had still not been introduced for the French artillery at this time. Coatee and dolman (for the guards) were still regulation. During the Franco-Prussian war the ranks nevertheless wore almost exclusively the short drill jacket, with which the guards wore the fur cap in hussar style.

357. France: 2nd Hussars. Corporal, 1870

At this time the French hussars still wore the old heavily frogged dolman. In 1869 it seems that it was decided in future all regiments were to wear pale blue jackets; these were, nevertheless, introduced only in the 1st and 8th regiments. The pride of these units was the brown dolman worn only by this regiment in France, but which had also been worn in other armies (251). The pelisse was abolished in 1862. For parades a red bag was worn on the fur cap. In the field, officers wore a small shako in a black cover, and black frogging and braiding on their dolmans.

358. France: Chasseurs d'Afrique. Trooper, 1870

The chasseurs d'Afrique, formed during the French North African campaign in 1831, originally wore a form of lancer uniform. Lances and *chapkas* were done away with in 1833, after which date the red field cap became the standard wear. It was often worn in a white cover with a neck-flap. In 1862 the tunic was replaced by a dolman, but in the field the ranks wore a drill tunic combined with a wide red sash.

359. France: Garde Mobile. Battalion commander, 1870

The Garde Mobile, formed in 1868 from troops not in the regular army, were commanded partly by retired officers. The uniform was simple, but similar to that of the infantry. The other ranks wore the same uniform as the officers but with white gaiters and of course without gold braiding on the cap and cuffs. Equipment was the same as that of the regular infantry.

360. France: Naval Battalion. Lance-corporal, 1870

To reinforce the army during the war against Germany, the French fleet landed troops and guns which were used in the defence of fortified positions especially. The seaman's uniform subsequently became similar to that worn today. The seaman's cap, 1858 model, was properly a working cap so it was not fitted with the name-band indicating the ship. The parade dress consisted partly of a blue seaman's collar worn over the large jacket. The seamen were equipped like the infantry. The sleeveless leather jerkin was much used during the winter of 1870–1871.

361. Baden: 2nd Dragoon Regiment. Dragoon, 1870

Before the Baden troops were included in the Prussian army in 1870 their uniforms were fully Prussian, apart from the ornament on the spiked helmet (in this instance a griffin holding the Baden armorial shield) and the cockade. On inclusion in the Prussian army the Baden helmet decoration was retained. Service tunic and spiked helmet were introduced in Baden in 1848. At first the helmet was fitted with the ball instead of the point, but the latter, as used in Prussia, came in in 1850. The tight riding breeches, with no coloured trimming and the high boots, were first prescribed in 1870.

362. Brunswick: Hussar Regiment nr. 17 Lieutenant, 1871

This regiment was formed in 1809, as a unit in the Black Corps (258). With the introduction of the attila, in 1850, the basic colour, dark blue since 1830, once more became black as a reminder of the earlier connection. The uniform style was reminiscent of the Prussian, but nevertheless diverged from it in detail. Up to 1871 the shoulder distinctions were black and the bag of the cap worn falling on the right. The metal band on the fur cap introduced in 1867 carried the inscription 'Peninsula–Sicily–Waterloo' as a memorial of the regiment's service during the Napoleonic wars. In 1883 the cap was fitted with a death's head in white metal, as worn in 1809. In 1886 the Brunswick troops were included in the Prussian army.

363. Württemberg: 4th Infantry Regiment. Private, 1870

In 1914, *Fusilier Regiment Kaiser Franz Joseph of Austria, King of Hungary (4th Württemberg) nr. 122.* The Württemberg infantry wore medium blue tunics, as introduced in 1849, during the war against Prussia in 1886. The uniform worn during the war against France in 1870 was authorized in 1864 but first adopted after 1866. A reinforced cap with a front plate was worn for parades. The regiments could be identified by the

coloured patches on their collars, white
for the 1st; black for the 2nd; orange for
the 3rd; green for the 4th; pale blue for
the 5th; blue for the 6th; dark red for the
7th and yellow for the 8th. The shoulder
straps bore the number of the company.
1871 saw the introduction of uniforms
with spiked helmets and equipment on
the Prussian model, but the single-
breasted tunic was not introduced until
1892.

364. Hessen-Darmstadt: Pioneer Company. Pioneer, 1870

In 1914, the *Infanterie-Leib-Regiment
Grosshezogin* (3 *Grossherz Hess*) *nr.* 117.
The uniforms worn by the Hesse infantry
in 1870 had been introduced as early as
1849. The cut followed the general line
of development. The habit of wearing
the trousers inside the boots had resulted
in longer boots, first in Prussia, and later
in the other German states. The Hesse
infantry also wore bright red pipings on
their tunics. The collar carried two bars
of white lace in all regiments, and the
regimental colours were red for the 1st
regiment, white for the 2nd, pale blue for
the 3rd and yellow for the 4th. In 1871
the Hesse troops were included as a contingent of a Prussian army corps, and in
1872 the uniform changed to conform in
full to the Prussian system. This pioneer
company, which was included the same
year in the above regiment, as its 9th
company, subsequently wore a pioneer
sign on its helmets as a reminder of its
origin.

COLONIAL TROOPS 1870–1960

The European colonial powers were continually compelled to maintain troops in
their oversea possessions, for the main-
tenance of law and order and for defence.
It was usual with most of the powers to
form units of loyal native-born inhabi-
tants to reinforce the garrisons of regular
troops.

365. French North Africa: Spahi, 1898

Among the troops maintained in North
Africa by France over the years were the
Zouaves (306); the *turcos* or Algerian
tinailleurs, with all pale blue Zouave
uniform and yellow lace; the Foreign
Legion (463) and the African light infantry, both of which were uniformed
like the line infantry. Among the cavalry
there were the *Chasseurs d'Afrique* (358)
and the Spahis. The latter, formed in
1834, were recruited among the native
population and commanded by French
officers. The uniforms, based on the
dress of the desert tribes, changed little
from the commencement up to the
Second World War. The French officers,
however, wore European uniforms with
red service tunics and with them very
often the Arabian *haik* (burnous).

366. Italian Somaliland: Askari, 1900

At this period the Italians in Somaliland
maintained a force consisting of African
rifles (468) and Askaris, which consisted
respectively of Europeans and of natives,
under the command of Italian officers.
The Askaris wore white, with red fezzes,
and dark blue jackets. In the Italian
colonies the fez had risen to an exceptional height, and carried a tassel in the
colour of the unit. The sash, originally
multicoloured, was at this time plain red.

367. German South-West Africa: Protectorate Troops. Trooper, 1899

At this time Germany maintained a force
consisting wholly of Europeans in South-
West Africa. The uniform, established in
1896, was both practical and had a
certain boldness and dash about it.
Besides the grey uniform, which was
worn at home and during the cooler
season in Africa, the riflemen wore khaki
drill uniforms with—for officers—a white
formal uniform for the summer. In East
Africa and the Cameroons, where the
German troops consisted of natives
under German officers, only khaki was
worn, but with grey and white uniforms
for the officers. In East Africa the grey
uniform had white pipings and in the
Cameroons, red.

368. The Congo: Army Force. 1st Lieutenant, 1890

At this time the Congo maintained a small force consisting of native volunteers and conscripts under European officers. The troops' uniforms were dark blue with red fezzes and red sashes. The officers' uniform was very civilian in style. Instead of the tropical helmet, a peaked cap with white or blue crown could be worn. The active service uniform for officers was white linen throughout.

369. British India: 15th Ludhiana Sikhs. Sepoy, 1888

In 1947, 2nd Battalion, 11th Sikh Regiment. When the East India Company handed over India to the British crown in 1858, the company's troops entered the British service. Their uniforms had for long been very British in style, under the influence of the British troops stationed in India since 1754. With the army organization of 1860, there was a marked tendency to adapt the uniform more closely to actual conditions than had been the case hitherto. A curious arrangement was introduced on the front of the red tunic, giving the impression that it was worn over a coloured waistcoat. Later, a high collar in the same colour as the central panel was introduced. The tying of the turban varied not only according to race and creed, but also according to fashion. This regiment traditionally wore a steel ring on the turban. Originally this was a throwing weapon, a form of discus, the outer edge was ground sharp. 'Sikh' indicates a member of a religious community, and although Sikhs belong to most of the many Indian castes, they all observe the same customs. These are outwardly manifested in that a Sikh may not cut his hair or beard, so the sepoys in the Sikh regiments wear their beards rolled up for the sake of neatness.

370. British India: 27th Light Cavalry. Native officer, 1906

In 1947, 16th Light Cavalry. In 1863 the Indian cavalry adopted uniforms of a type that generally reflected more mature characteristics. The long tunic or alkalak, later called a kurtha, was in the traditional colour for the regiment, in this instance 'French grey', worn by the cavalry in Madras. The sash, or cummerbund, was more striking for the ranks than for the officers. The turban, or lungi, was wound on a pointed cap called a kullah. Chain mail was worn on the shoulders as a protection from sabre cuts, with the badges of rank on it. The belt buckle and buttons carried crossed lances, since earlier the regiment belonged to that branch. Similarly, the regiment's British officers wore a lancer's tunic in French grey, with a plastron in buff. In certain regiments British officers also wore Indian uniforms when serving with their men.

371. French Indo-China: Annamite Sharpshooters. Lance-corporal, 1889

At this time France maintained a force in Indo-China consisting of colonial troops and natives under French officers. For the Annamite sharpshooters, the native costume was made into a uniform by the addition of a tunic and the necessary leather equipment. The officers wore European uniforms and white tropical helmets.

372. Dutch East Indies: Colonial Army. Infantry man, 1900

Today, the Van Heutz Regiment. The Netherlands maintained a significant colonial army in the East Indies at this time. It consisted of natives under Netherlands officers. At first it wore uniforms like those of the motherland but in the 1870's a special dress was adopted. The hussar frogging on the breast was attached by means of buttons and was worn only on ceremonial or state occasions. The helmet, made in the same fashion as a tropical helmet, carried the Netherlands arms within the star at the front, on an orange-coloured cockade. The point could be unscrewed, and was worn only for parades.

373. Australia: New South Wales Lancers. Trooper, 1900

Although each of the Australian colonies had its own army at this period, there were nevertheless certain common characteristics among them. Grey, brown and khaki were dominant. The bush-hat became characteristic of the Australians and has remained so. This regiment's uniform, apart from the headgear, basic colour and colour of gloves and boots, was very like the British lancers ceremonial uniform of the same period.

374. New Zealand: Canterbury Volunteer Cavalry. Trooper, 1875

Apart from the regular British troops, at this time there were several military units and volunteer corps in New Zealand under British control. This corps was formed in 1864 and was very well uniformed and drilled. The uniform, as was often the case in volunteer corps, was a variation of that worn by the regulars.

375. The Fiji Islands: Artillery. Sergeant, 1957

The former *gendarmerie* in the Fiji Islands was changed during World War Two into a defence force comprising all branches. The *gendarmerie* had worn dark blue coats, but the defence force adopted red coats for special duties after the war. The loincloth, or *sulu*, was part of the native dress. No headgear was worn, but instead the native hair-style. This now seems fairly certain to become obsolete, but there is still no standard headgear. These remarks also apply to foot coverings.

376. Samoa (U.S.A.): Governor's Bodyguard. Private, 1943

During the Second World War, America maintained a small native corps in Samoa, in addition to their regular American and native troops. It had police and *gendarmerie* duties, as well as forming a governor's bodyguard. Formed soon after the turn of the century, it was called the *Fita Fita*, or 'brave ones'. The uniform remained unchanged from the outset. The cap, called a turban, the loincloth, or *lava lava*, and the sash were all modelled on the native costume. In addition to the white parade-loincloth, a blue one with white stripes was also worn. Marks of ranks, if any, were worn on the edge of the loincloth, near the upper stripe.

377. Canada: Infantry Officer, 1870

Uniform in the Canadian army was exactly like the British uniform at this time. The climate required special winter items nevertheless, as worn by this officer. The high boots were lined with felt or fur. The fur-collared coat was fastened with hussar frogging. The same system is still used for certain details of winter dress in the Canadian army.

378. Canada: Governor-General's Bodyguard. Trooper, 1898

Today, the *Governor-General's Horse-Guards*. Permission given earlier in the nineteenth century to wear uniforms like those of the British regular army was exploited to the full in Canada. Thus there were units in dragoon-guard, hussar, Highland and rifle-corps uniforms. This guards corps was based on the first of these, and was formed in 1855.

379. British West Indies: West India Regiment. Lance-corporal, 1926

This regiment was formed in 1795, and was dressed until 1859 like the British regular regiments. The French style of uniform which influenced the British style during the Crimea period certainly inspired the Zouave-type uniform worn almost unchanged from this date until 1926. The turban, like the red waistcoat, was worn only for guard and parade duty. The daily headwear was a soft fez.

380. Danish West Indies: Police Corps on St. Thomas. Man, 1916

At this period Denmark maintained a *gendarmerie* in the West Indies consisting of volunteers from the mother country, and a civic guard recruited locally. The *gendarmerie* was dressed in pale blue uniform; the guard in khaki uniforms made of linen. The star on the tropical helmet carried a shield with the Danish arms; while the armorial leaves and hearts were also to be found on a white ground in the brass buckle of the belt. The officers wore marks of rank on their sleeves consisting of gold cord and wide red stripes on their trousers.

THE BOER WARS 1880–1881 and 1899–1902

Despite the fact that Great Britain had earlier recognized the Boer Republics of Orange and the Transvaal, towards the close of the nineteenth century the situation deteriorated and war broke out. The first Boer War, during 1880 and 1881, went badly for the British. In the second, during 1899–1902, the Boer army administered a series of defeats involving considerable losses, but Britain's greater resources turned the war in her favour. The most famous of the Boer victories was Magersfontein in 1899, while the British defence of Ladysmith (1899–1900) is equally renowned. In the outcome, Orange and the Transvaal were included in Cape Colony.

381. Great Britain: 58th (Rutlandshire) Foot. Private, 1880

Today, the *2nd East Anglian Regiment* (*The Duchess of Gloucester's Own Royal Lincolnshire and Northamptonshire*). By the middle of the nineteenth century, the British troops in India in wartime began to dye the standard white linen dress. This was considered a temporary measure only, and when peace was restored the white uniforms were again adopted. Steps were taken to lighten the uniform by substituting a 'frock' of lighter material for the cloth tunic. Leggings were introduced in 1859, and a new type of pack in 1868. After the Crimean War there were several changes of shako following the French pattern but after the defeat of France in the Franco-Prussian War, a Germanic type was considered and in 1878 a form of spiked helmet was introduced; a white version for use by the troops at oversea stations (401).

382. The Boer Republic: Boer Army. Sharpshooter, 1880–1902

The Boer army consisted of a muster of all armed men, assembling in their ordinary clothing. They were accustomed to moving in open country and had no difficulty in operating with little equipment and no supply lines. Since they were all formidable riders and sharpshooters, they were dangerous rivals even for well-trained British troops. Their dress was so inconspicuous and their use of cover so ingenious that they were able to engage the British long before the latter could catch sight of them. The Boer War finally convinced military authorities everywhere of the need to dress soldiers on active service in uniforms matching the terrain.

383. Great Britain: The Gordon Highlanders. Private, 1900

Under the reforms of 1881, British infantry regiments were to have names instead of numbers. The question of uniforms was also dealt with. Thus the troops in India were already issued with khaki-coloured linen uniforms in 1880. Troops posted to South Africa at this time were also equipped with khaki uniforms, but at home the red uniform was still obligatory. The tropical helmet, originating in fact in India, was also issued to the troops who went to South Africa. Originally it was white, and the khaki covers were not sufficiently available, so the troops had to colour their helmets themselves. An improved set of leather equipment was introduced in 1888. It remained white in colour, and so had to be darkened for use during the Boer War.

384. Great Britain: City Imperial Volunteers. Volunteer, 1900

In Great Britain voluntary enlistment was maintained in the regular army until the First World War. Besides the regular troops, there were a number of military units formed by conscription and various volunteer corps. During the Boer War many volunteered for service oversea. Most of them were enrolled in the regular battalions, but certain regiments consisted exclusively of volunteers like the 'City Imperial Volunteers'. After 1886 khaki was prescribed for active service abroad. Since there was insufficient linen, khaki uniforms made of woollen cloth were authorized in 1900. Meanwhile leggings were replaced by puttees, which originated in India. The wide-brimmed soft hat or slouch hat, later called the bush hat, was adopted by nearly all volunteers from the colonies. From 1901 they were also issued to regulars, instead of the tropical helmet (412).

THE RUSSO-JAPANESE WAR 1904–1905

Russian expansion in the Far East, and especially her occupation of Manchuria and leasing of Port Arthur, led to war with Japan in 1904. The Japanese fleet struck pre-emptively at the Russian Mediterranean squadron in Port Arthur, and a Japanese army cut off the garrison from the land side. Port Arthur capitulated in 1905, and the same year Russian forces in the Far East—already defeated by the Japanese at Liaojang—suffered a further defeat at Mukden. The Russian Baltic Fleet, which had joined the remainder of the Mediterranean Fleet in the Far East, was decisively defeated by the Japanese in the Tushima strait later the same year. The war ended with a considerable loss of prestige by the Russians, while the Japanese gained a foothold on the Asiatic mainland.

385. Japan: Guard Infantry. Private, 1904

In the 1870's, Japan's Samurai army was replaced by an army formed and dressed on the European model. The units which operated in 1904, dressed in the dark blue uniforms introduced under the 1879 order, and which were still in use in the greater portion of the army, now soon adopted khaki working dress instead. In cold weather this linen dress was worn outside a cloth uniform. The working dress had no buttons, but was fastened by means of hooks or tapes. The white

leggings, properly part of the dark blue uniform, were not darkened. In the winter of 1904–5, the army in the field adopted khaki uniforms made of cloth (488).

386. Russia: Infantry of the Line. Private, 1904

The pan-Slavic tendency in Russian politics after 1881 manifested itself also in army uniforms. Apart from individual guards regiments in 1882, the entire Russian army officially adopted uniforms in a form of old Russian or Slavonic style. The tunic was replaced by a caftan, as it was called, cut looser and with no buttons showing. At the front it took the form of a double-breasted tunic, at first with hooks, later with concealed buttons, and with a plain back without slits or buttons. The headgear was a low fur cap for parades, and for normal and active service wear, a *fouraschka* or cap with no peak for the ranks. The identification colours remained unchanged. The pack arrangements were also changed in 1882, with the knapsack being replaced by a kit-bag (or rucksack) worn over the right shoulder, the rolled greatcoat being worn over the left side. Tent-pegs and the like were fastened to the coat on the back, with the ends of the coat tucked down into the copper cooking vessel. In summer a *kittel* replaced the *kaftan*, that is, a Russian blouse, made of white linen with coloured shoulder straps made of cloth. Such a dress, smart and comfortable in peacetime, betrayed its wearer at a distance in war, so that the troops at the front had to colour their *kittels*. The Far Eastern war thus tended to promote further the adoption of camouflage-uniforms in most armies (413).

387. Japan: Imperial Navy. Commander, 1905

With the Europeanization of the army in the 1870's, a similar tendency commenced in the fleet. American influence was apparent in the naval officers' uniforms, as well as British. Thus the 'service-coat' introduced into the American forces in 1877 was also adopted by

Japan, where it became very well liked. Rank was indicated by the plain black stripes on the sleeves.

388. Russia: Imperial Navy. Commander, 1905

Peter the Great introduced dark green uniforms for his naval officers. Later it became customary to wear as dark a uniform as possible, thus by the end of the nineteenth century the Russian naval officers' uniform was black, although the earlier regulation was still in force. Braiding on the sleeves was unknown in the Russian navy. Epaulettes were worn for ceremonial purposes, and marks of rank on the shoulders for normal duty; the latter were called *pogoni* and followed the army system. In summer, white tunics with high collars, a row of gilded buttons, and *pogoni* could be worn.

THE BALKAN WARS 1912–1913

The desire of the Balkan states to expand at the expense of the European portion of Turkey led in 1912 to the First Balkan War, fought between Montenegro, Bulgaria, Greece and Serbia, allied against Turkey. Turkey was defeated on all fronts. The principal events were the Greek conquest of Salonica and Janina, and the Bulgarian and Serbian conquest of Adrianople. The partition of the conquered Turkish territory at the peace of 1913 led to the Second Balkan War the same year, between Bulgaria and the former allies, joined by Russia. Turkey took the opportunity of re-occupying Adrianople. Bulgaria, faced by superior forces, relinquished part of the conquered Turkish territory to Greece and Serbia, while Turkey retained Adrianople. Another consequence of this conflict was Albania's assumption of independence.

389. Bulgaria: Field Artillery. Captain, 1913

The Bulgarian army wore uniforms of markedly Russian style from the outset. In 1880 a tunic without buttons like the Russian 1882 model was worn, with a low fur cap. Tunics were introduced for officers about 1900, with buttons like those prescribed for the Russian dragoons in 1897. Meanwhile it was decided that in future fur caps were to be worn only in peacetime. The basic colour was the Russian, i.e. green; the cavalry alone wearing blue. Marks of rank for officers were epaulettes for ceremonial and *pogoni* for daily duty, as in Russia. White tunics or *kittels*, and white caps were widely worn during the summer months (422).

390. Serbia: Cavalry. Trooper, 1913

From about the middle of the 1890's, the Serbian army wore uniforms of French pattern. Under pan-Slavic influence, kaftans of Russian style were subsequently introduced. The traditional colours were retained, but the kaftan was not equipped with trimming in the branch colour until 1901. Low fur caps were also now introduced. Besides Russian-style peaked caps for officers, an Austrian-style field cap was also adopted for the other ranks (416).

391. Greece: Infantry. Private, 1913

When George I succeeded to the Greek throne in 1863, army uniforms were changed, a partly Danish style being adopted. The artillery wore dark blue trousers and collars of the same colour, with a red edge. The artillery officers wore double-breasted tunics. The engineer troops wore crimson collars and edging. The small pompon worn only on parade, was red for the artillery and blue for the engineers. The cavalry wore green hussar uniform with white frogging and crimson collars and cuffs (482).

392. Greece: The Royal Guard. Evzone, 1913

George I formed his bodyguard of riflemen, the *evzones* as they were called. They wore national dress for parades and guard-duty, of which the outstanding feature is the *fustanella* or bulging skirt made of white linen. The national dress also included a short white cloth coat, covered almost wholly with black cord embroidery. For daily duty and active service, the coat and skirt were replaced by a blue tunic with long white hose. Both uniforms were worn virtually unchanged on guard duty.

393. Rumania: 3rd Rifle Battalion. Rifleman, 1913

When the principality of Rumania became a kingdom in 1891, French uniform styles became dominant. There were, however, certain peculiarities, such as the uniforms of the rifle troops, which was presumably inspired by the uniforms worn earlier by the Wallachian frontier corps. The line infantry wore dark blue uniforms, while the cavalry were uniformed like hussars, in red or dark blue (424).

394. Albania: Officer, 1913

The principality of Albania followed the custom in the Balkans and Eastern Europe of giving uniforms a national character by including elements of the national dress. Though the influence of Austria is apparent in the braiding to indicate rank, on collar and cuffs, the plaiting on the shoulders is closest to the German style. The round fur cap was Russian in style.

395. Montenegro: Corporal of the Reserve, 1913

At this time the Montenegrin army was dressed exclusively in national costume, for the simple reason that no other uniform was issued. But the latter was so distinctive and individual that it formed a very satisfying and colourful, if primitive uniform. It was worn by both officers and men, but for the former it was more decorative and included black riding boots instead of shoes. The soldier carried his own armoury in his sash, consisting normally of a brace of muzzle-loading pistols and some knives. Only the rifle was issued. This, with the cap-badge, identified its bearer as a soldier. The degree of elaboration of the badge also provided indication of rank (421).

396. Turkey: Brigadier-General, 1913

French influence on the uniform of the Turkish army, manifested partly in wider use of Zouave style uniforms, was checked about the middle of the 1870's, when a more German style of uniforms came in. The long coat, which all officers could wear when at the head of their troops, was very popular. Generals wore special gold braiding on its sleeves, as a mark of rank, which was indicated by the number of angled stripes (420).

TROOPS OF THE GREAT POWERS AT THE OUTBREAK OF THE FIRST WORLD WAR 1914

The year 1914 forms a dividing line in the world of uniforms. Certainly the necessity to dress armies in terrain-coloured uniforms was already well-understood in most countries and such uniforms were ready for use in the stores. But the old uniforms, rich in tradition, like old soldiers, tended never to die. Though for the last time, armies still wore the red, blue, green or white uniforms with bright buttons and shining helmets when being inspected by emperors, kings and generals, themselves in resplendent uniforms with waving plumes. The outbreak of the First World War in August, 1914, brought in the use of field-grey and khaki more rapidly than was expected.

397. Germany (Mecklenburg-Strelitz): Grenadier Regiment nr. 89. Grenadier, 1914

The many German troop contingents were welded together to form an army for the first time after 1871. Arms and equipment were standardized, as was the uniform—on the Prussian pattern. Nevertheless certain regiments in the various contingents were allowed to retain small details persisting from earlier customs. In 1897 the red, white and black national cockade became a general emblem, worn on the right side of the helmet, while the regional cockade was worn on the left. In nearly all contingents individual regiments were specially distinguished, as were the guards, by lace on cuffs and collar, and, for parades, by horsehair plumes on the helmet. A new distinction for marksmen was introduced in 1894, taking the form of a plaited cord on the right shoulder, issued in four classes (406) according to ability.

398. Austria-Hungary: Infantry Regiment 'King of Denmark', nr. 75. Private, 1914

The reorganization of the Austrian army after the debacle of 1866 also led to changes in uniforms. The most comprehensive change was certainly the introduction of the dark blue service tunic in 1868. The retention of the old system of identification of the regiments by means of special collar-and-cuff colours, plus button-colour, was peculiar to the Austrian army at this time. To distinguish the many regiments comprising the infantry in 1914, many different shades were required: among the most unusual may be mentioned amaranth red, crayfish red, rose-red, seaweed green, popinjay green, apple-green, ash-grey, orange-yellow, sulphur yellow, etc. The old imperial sign, a green sprig of leaves in the cap, was still worn for parades. The Austrian badge of merit for marksmanship had only one class, and was worn on the left side. Christian IX and Frederick VIII of Denmark were honorary colonels of this regiment (419).

399. Russia: Preobraschenski Guards. Guardsman, 1914

Since the war with Japan had shown that the 1882 model uniform was not particularly suitable under field conditions, a new peacetime uniform and a new battle uniform were introduced in Russia. Tunics with buttons had already been introduced in the cavalry. In 1910 the infantry had them too, while the cavalry adopted once more the former dragoon, hussar and lancer uniforms. The guards infantry returned to the pre-1882 uniforms, but could not, accustom themselves to the reintroduction of the spiked helmet worn by the guard at that

period: instead, a shako called the *kiver*, Napoleonic in style, was adopted. The white border worn on lapels and cuffs by the regiments of the 1st Guards Infantry Division was originally granted to this regiment to commemorate sea service with the fleet in Peter the Great's time. The uniforms of the 2nd Guards Infantry Division had no white edges while for the 3rd all red trimming was replaced by yellow, to mark the fact that the division consisted of Lithuanian and Polish regiments. All guards regiments wore red shoulder straps. The marksmanship distinction, awarded to the individual or to the unit, consisted from the commencement of silver medallions and badges, worn attached to a silver chain at the fastening of the uniform (413).

400. France: 5th Line Regiment. Infantry man, 1914

Although the French infantry generally wore greatcoats both summer and winter, the tunic was a ceremonial item worn for parades, inspections and on leave. Despite various detail changes, the appearance of the French infantry remained as it had been during the war against Germany in 1870. The shako was abolished in 1884, and a reinforced cap, the *kepi* with a pompon was worn instead on parade. The tunic was made single-breasted in 1899, while no epaulettes were worn on active service after 1872. The French distinction for marksmanship was a hunting horn made of red fabric or gold embroidery worn on the left upper sleeve (409).

401. Great Britain: The Buffs (East Kent Regiment). Private, 1914

Today, *The Queen's Regiment*. In Great Britain, Canada, and to some extent also in India, the red uniform was still worn for parade and ceremonial duties and for off-duty wear. The spiked helmet, introduced in 1878, was worn only on duty and differed from continental patterns in being made like a tropical helmet, and with cloth covering. As regards style, the point was shorter and thinner and the crown higher than on the German helmet. In 1881 it was laid down that the English regiments were to wear white collars and cuffs, the Scottish yellow and the Irish green, while royal regiments were allocated dark blue. Later various regiments were allowed to wear the time-honoured colours, the Buffs among them. The regiments could also be identified by badges on the collar and in the star plate on the front of the helmet. After 1902, the red tunic had brass buttons and white piping down the front, with pointed cuffs, and after 1913, shoulder straps in the regimental colour. The marksmanship badge was a pair of crossed rifles embroidered on the left sleeve. In 1906, Frederick VIII of Denmark was appointed honorary colonel of the Buffs, an honour conferred ever since on the Danish kings (412).

402. Italy: Grenadiers of Sardinia. Grenadier, 1914

When Italy was united in 1861, the use of the Sardinian uniform was extended to the national army, but with the addition of the red, white and green national cockade. In 1871 the first uniforms specially provided for the Italian army were introduced. Noteworthy is the five-pointed 'active service' star worn by all soldiers as a distinction on the collar. The field dress for the infantry consisted of the greatcoat with the skirts turned up. Normally the shako was worn in a white cover. In 1903 the service tunic incorporated a rounded collar, and the leather equipment was black. The grenadiers wore flaming grenades on their shoulders and the other regiments their number.

403. U.S.A.: Infantry. Enlisted man, 1914

In 1881, spiked helmets of British pattern were introduced into the American army. The branch colour of the infantry, hitherto pale blue, became white in 1884. In 1902, however, the whole uniforming was remodelled. Blue was kept for garrison service and ceremonial duties. The spiked helmet was abolished, and ceremonial cords and tassels worn at the breast was introduced. The branch colour

of the infantry once more became pale blue. The leather equipment, worn also with the field-dress, was brown, but the waist-belt only was worn with the blue uniform. Cap and collar carried branch badges made of brass, consisting for the infantry of crossed rifles, with the regimental number and company initial. Regular units also wore the Union initials 'U.S.' on the collar. The tunic had no piping down the front. The American distinction for marksmanship, issued in various classes, consisted of a cross, like the cross of an order, worn on the left breast (434).

404. China: Infantry of the Line. Private, 1914

There were no uniforms in the European sense of the word in China before the Boxer Rising in 1900–1901. There was an attempt to introduce them under some regulations of 1902, but the first systematization of the Chinese army uniforms seems to have been in 1910. The guard division wore a pale grey uniform of German style, while the remainder of the army wore dark blue in winter and for ceremonial, and khaki for summer and field duty. The leather equipment, worn with both, was brown. The branch was indicated by the colour of the shoulder straps; red for infantry, white for cavalry, yellow for artillery, blue for pioneer troops and dark brown for commissariat.

FIRST WORLD WAR 1914–1918

The Great War took place between the 'Central Powers'—Germany and Austria-Hungary, supported by Bulgaria and Turkey—and the 'Entente'—France, Russia, Great Britain, Belgium, Montenegro and Serbia. The Entente was later supported by Italy, Rumania and the United States. The immediate reason for the war was the murder of the Austrian Archduke Franz Ferdinand in Sarajevo, in June 1914, for which Austria held Serbia responsible. Treaty obligations resulted in the mobilization of the great powers in August 1914 and subsequently.

Germany attempted a deep penetration of France, after a *blitzkrieg* through neutral Belgium, but was brought to a halt on the Marne, after which the Western Front took shape.

On the Eastern Front, Germany proved superior to Russia, and later crushed Rumania. Austria-Hungary was less successful, but managed to defeat Serbia, before conducting a severe struggle against Italy in the Alps. Great Britain won supremacy on the seas, and established a blockade of Germany but the latter's retaliation by means of unrestricted U-boat warfare resulted in the U.S.A.'s entry into the war in 1917. Victories in the East were of no avail and, her allies defeated, Germany had to sue for peace in 1918. When peace was concluded in 1919, Germany had to reduce her forces to 100,000 men, surrender her fleet and pay reparations for the war. In addition to her colonies, she had to cede Alsace-Lorraine to France, Poznan, West Prussia and Upper Silesia to Poland; Memel to Lithuania, Eupen and Malmedy to Belgium, and North-Schleswig to Denmark, while Danzig was made a free city. The repercussions on Austria-Hungary were the separation of Hungary from Austria; the formation of Czecho-Slovakia, and the extension of Serbia into Jugoslavia. All in all, the result of the First World War was to make Europe richer by seven states and poorer by three empires.

405. Germany: (Prussia): Lancer Regiment 'Hennigs von Treffenfeld', nr. 16. Lancer, 1914

After many years of research the outlines of an army field-uniform were established in Germany in 1907, and patterns produced. First to be changed were the basic colours of the uniform and equipment. Then the cut was made less close-fitting and uncomfortable, and the jackets were given pockets at the sides. The *ulanka*, prescribed in 1908, was given shoulder straps like epaulettes, and pipings like the peace-time uniform. In 1911, the cavalry throughout adopted cartridge pouches with similar means of suspension to that used by the infantry.

406. Germany: 10th Württemberg Infantry Regiment nr. 180. Private, 1914

There were such adequate stocks of field-grey uniforms in Germany in 1910 that issue commenced, but it was decided, nevertheless, that for the time being field-grey was to be used only in war and large-scale manoeuvres. The cover for the headgear had been introduced in 1892, and in 1897 regimental numbers were fitted to it. Leather equipment had to be blackened in time of war. Cartridge pouches of a new type were introduced in 1911. All buttons were oxidized and adorned with a crown. There was no spit-and-polish for metal items of any kind in wartime (429).

407. Germany (Prussia): 1st Guard Field Artillery Regiment. Captain, 1914

Regulations governing the German field uniforms emphasized that the uniforms of the officers were to be of more or less the same colour as those worn by the men. Units wearing lace on previous uniforms also adopted it for field uniforms. For officers it was made of dull silver thread. Eventually lace at the cuffs was accompanied by a coloured edge at the bottom. Field distinctions for captains and lieutenants were made of dull silver cord after 1888. In 1896 a waist-belt with sash-band was introduced for officers. Blackened scabbards were worn after 1905. Leggings and laced boots, used from 1908, were of the latest type in the German army in 1914.

408. Germany: Machine-gun Section nr. 11. Man, 1914

The German machine-gun sections, formed in 1901, were issued with a work-manlike uniform from the outset. The material was grey-green, as for the field uniforms of the jäger troops. Leather equipment was brown, as worn in peace-time. Brass was not polished in the field. This soldier is an auxiliary attached to a machine-gun crew: for the sake of clarity the gunner is not shown. At the outbreak of war in 1914, the entire German army was equipped with terrain-

matching uniforms, but they were evidently based on traditional designs. So
the hussars wore field-grey *attilas* but, as
with uniforms in general, they were very
well adapted for field purposes. Officers,
however, were still too conspicuous for
comfort, as a result of their sabres, their
sash-band-covered belts, and their decorations. Sabres were abolished soon
after the war started, the elaborate belts
were replaced by brown ones, and decorations were blackened.

409. France: 145th Regiment of the Line. Soldier, 1914

Trials of various types and colours of
field uniforms in France in 1912 led to
the adoption of a reseda-green field
uniform which was received with such
disfavour that its introduction was suspended. After 1905 there was an experimental abandonment of greatcoats for
large-scale manoeuvres, but it was not
made permanent. Apart from the introduction of the infantry trenching tool
there had been little change in equipment
since 1870 (353). When the French infantry went up to the line in 1914, the
red caps were universally worn with grey
or grey-blue covers (430).

410. France: 13th Cuirassiers. Lieutenant, 1914

Although the Prussian cuirassiers wore
their cuirasses only on parade after 1888,
their French counterparts took the field
wearing them in 1914. Covers for helmets and cuirasses were decided by the
regiment, so they varied in colour from
unit to unit. A new model helmet with
stronger neck protection had been introduced in 1872. Long, leather-trimmed
trousers were worn into the 1900's, but
in 1914 the other ranks wore breeches
and boot-like leggings.

411. Belgium: The Carabiniers. Private, 1914

At the outbreak of war in 1914, Belgium
was involved in army reorganization,
which certainly included changes of uniform. Field uniforms were being considered, but the army still wore the

uniforms introduced in the 1850's. The
regiment illustrated was an *élite* unit in
jäger uniform, distinguished by the round
hat worn since 1837. It was adorned with
the Belgian cockade and a green *pompon*
on the left, but was worn in a waterproof
cover in wartime. In 1915 khaki was
introduced on the British pattern for the
whole army, with high collars and
patches, while the trousers were still
worn with short leather leggings. Steel
helmets of French type, khaki-coloured
(430) and brown leather equipment,
were subsequently adopted. Collar patches were red for infantry, white for
cavalry (alternatively yellow or pink),
dark blue for the artillery, with red edges,
and black for the engineers (452).

412. Great Britain: The Royal Fusiliers. Private, 1914

In 1902 khaki (or service drab) was
standardized for the British army for all
duties except ceremonial. The British
Expeditionary Force was thus well
equipped at the outbreak of war in 1914.
The cap introduced in 1905 bore the
regimental badge, and the shoulder
straps the name or initials in brass letters.
Brown leather equipment, which had
replaced white for field duty, was replaced in 1908 with woven material,
'webbing', which later became universal
throughout the world (432).

413. Russia: 180th Windau Infantry Regiment. Private, 1914

The uniform introduced in Russia, based
on the experience of the war against
Japan during 1904–1905, used a form of
khaki material into which, for camouflage, had been introduced yarn in the
main colours of the spectrum. The
equipment was brown, or made of grey-
green material. The greatcoat was unchanged, like the mode of wearing the
equipment (386). A tall grey fur cap was
introduced for winter use, called the
papacha. The shoulder straps of the field
uniform, which were reversible, were
coloured on one side and sombre on the
other. On the sombre side were the
indications of unit: in yellow for the

infantry, raspberry-pink for sharpshooter battalions, bright red for the artillery and brown for the pioneers.

414. Russia: Chóper Regiment, Kuban Cossacks. Captain, 1914

Throughout, the Cossack armies wore field uniforms like the normal cavalry (415) with dark blue distinctions on the shoulder straps. An exception, however, was the Caucasian Cossack army, whose picturesque uniform nevertheless embodied colours suitable for modern field duty. The prominent containers on the breast of *Czerkeska* is a reminder of the period when the cossacks were armed with muzzle-loaders. Each compartment then contained a measure of powder for a single loading (8–9). When breech-loading weapons came in, the holders were retained as an integral part of the outfit, but they contained small rods with richly ornamented silver ferrules, matching the silver-mounted weapon. For normal wear the rods had white ferrules at one end and black at the other. The black could be turned upwards in war-time. Spurs were not worn by the cossacks. These Caucasians wore very soft boots without heels.

415. Russia: Guard Horse Artillery. Gunner, 1914

All Russian cavalry units retained their grey-blue trousers with coloured trimming. The *kittel*, or Russian 'blouse', was still worn in summer, but was now more sombre in colour, for both mounted and unmounted troops. Since the *kittel* did not carry the small coloured identification mark worn by the guard on conventional cloth uniforms, and the shoulder straps had no marks of unit, the guards wore the latter with the red side out, even in the field. Officers' shoulder straps with gold or silver braid were soon replaced by shoulder boards with grey or grey-green braiding. Steel helmets of French type were introduced during the war, but did not gain wide acceptance.

416. Serbia: 20th Infantry Regiment. Private, 1914

In Serbia the first khaki came in in 1912, and by 1914 most of the army were wearing it. According to regulation leather equipment was to be brown, but large stocks of black had to be used up first. During the war the *opanker*, the national peasant footwear, was largely worn, especially by the drafted troops. The colours of the officers' uniforms were in full colour. The branch colours of the collars were dark blue for cavalry, black for artillery, and cherry-red for the engineers (481).

417. Austria-Hungary: Tiroler Kaiserjäger Regiment nr. 4. 1st Lieutenant, 1914

When the Austrian infantry went over to dark blue uniforms in 1868, in addition to the tunics, 'blouses' were prescribed, with covered buttons, breast and side pockets and collar patches. In 1909 a field uniform of blouse-cut was introduced. The basic colour was the 'pike' grey already long in use in Austria. The collar patches remained in the old regimental colours, and still carried marks of ranks. The buckle of the officer's belt still carried the imperial eagle, but in the field it was concealed by the sash, still worn, like the green sprig in the cap. Sash and sabre were soon dropped after the outbreak of war.

418. Austria-Hungary: Dragoon Regiment nr. 15. Dragoon, 1914

When, in 1868, the Austrian infantry adopted dark blue as regulation, the dragoons and lancers wore pale blue with red riding breeches; the hussars dark blue or pale blue *attilas*, and tight red trousers. Even in 1914, field uniforms for the cavalry were too basic a change to be tolerated. Soon after the outbreak of war the headgear was fitted with a grey cover, or the dragoon helmets were sometimes painted grey. At the close of 1914 the red trousers were replaced by grey, and subsequently 'pike' grey blouses cut like the infantry's were adopted. Although the value of the pelisse was highly questionable, it was—in 'pike' grey material—worn throughout the war.

419. Austria-Hungary: Infantry Regiment nr. 102. Private, 1914

The uniform of the troops in the Austrian infantry differed from the officers' at this time in having long trousers with short cloth leggings. Hungarian regiments still wore tight trousers with frogging. The Bosnian regiments wore trousers of special cut, and fezzes (477). The Alpine *jäger* troops, distinguished by an *edelweiss* emblem on the collar patch, and a capercaillie feather on the field cap, wore climbing boots and stout sports stockings with 'plus-fours'. (431).

420. Turkey: General, 1914

Field uniforms were introduced in Turkey in 1909. They were to have been khaki, but the shades varied from greenish to brownish. The ranks wore a cap reminiscent of a tropical helmet, while officers throughout adopted the fur cap prescribed for the cavalry. The trimming on collar and cuffs, and on the cap crown, was olive-green for sharpshooters, pale grey for cavalry, dark blue for the artillery and pale blue for the engineers. The infantry had no trimming and wore a khaki crown. Generals alone enjoyed wide stripes on their trousers.

421. Montenegro: Infantry. Private, 1915

In 1910 uniforms were introduced for the Montenegrin army. For the ranks the small round cap and the unusual trouser style were retained. A khaki sash was prescribed to go with the blouse, but the choice of pack was left to the individual. Officers adopted uniforms cut like the Russian, with gold epaulettes or shoulder tabs with gold braid for field use. Badges of rank in the form of emblems on the headgear were retained. N.C.O.s were distinguishable also by an edging on their shoulder straps. This was red for the infantry, pale blue for machine-gun troops, yellow for artillery and green for engineers.

422. Bulgaria: Infantry Regiment nr. 40. Private, 1915

Even before the introduction of a field uniform was decided upon in Bulgaria in 1908, the dark green uniforms originally standard in the army were worn only on parades. For all other duties, uniforms of locally produced woollen fabric with a brownish tint were worn. The field uniform prescribed in 1908 was to have been like the Russian, but in 1915 it was being worn by the officers only. The brownish uniform of the rankers—with a slight alteration of shade—proved suitable for use as a field uniform, and was retained until the Second World War. In 1915 trousers were generally of the national folk style, and a large part of the army wore the *opankers*.

423. Italy: 94th Infantry Regiment. Soldier, 1915

On the entry of Italy into the war in 1915 the field uniform worn experimentally since 1908 became regulation. The coloured patches on the collar, introduced in 1903 were retained. The cap carried the badge of the branch, and the regimental number; black for the ranks and silver for the officers. The officers also wore silver or pale grey lace on the cap according to rank, and wore 'rank' stars in silver on their cuffs. The cavalry generally wore grey-green tropical helmets. The artillery and the engineer troops had black collars with yellow and red edging respectively. During the war, steel helmets of the French pattern were used (459).

424. Rumania: 44th Infantry Regiment. Private, 1916

Trials of a grey-green field uniform were commenced in Rumania in 1912, but under the last arrangement, of 1916, blue-grey was chosen. The leather equipment was not to be blacked, and when a new type of cartridge pouch came in, brown was chosen, the older leather equipment remaining black. The branch of the service was indicated by the distinctions of cap, collar and shoulder straps, and by the collar patches. *Jäger* troops adopted green trimming, with a green hunting horn emblem instead of a patch. The artillery wore black piping and patches, the engineers likewise, except that their patches were edged in red and the commissariat red piping with plain black patches. In 1916 steel helmets of French pattern (475) were adopted.

425. Germany: Imperial Navy. U-boat sailor, 1915

Characteristic of the German Navy from the Great War period until the present has been the wide cap crown, raised at the front, and the long neck ribbons. A black leather uniform was standard for U-boat crews. On their leather tunics the officers wore marks of rank at the shoulder, while the N.C.O.s wore them on the left arm.

426. Great Britain: Royal Navy. Petty Officer, 1st Class, 1915

Standardized uniforms for the ordinary seamen were established in the British Navy as late as 1857. The seaman's cap and the collar with the three white lines were established at the same time. In 1880 the wearing of both blue and white blouses outside the trousers was permitted. In 1906 it was ordered that marks of rank, etc., on the jacket were to be in gold, with red for normal duty only. The badge on the sleeve of course indicates rank, and the chevrons are long-service (8 years) badges. Bell-bottomed trousers were peculiar to the British Navy at this time, but have since been adopted by all navies.

427. Germany: Air Battalion nr. 2. Lieutenant, 1916

Military aviation in Germany was at first dominated by the dirigible airship (the zeppelin) and research with military aircraft did not begin until 1912 on any scale. The air battalions were formed in 1913. Earlier than expected, the First World War necessitated completion of an already commenced modification in the German army uniforms. In 1915 the 'blue' coloured uniform was condemned to total abolition. In its place came service jackets and the like made of field-grey material, with the same collars, cuffs, edging and polished buttons as on the 'blue' uniform. Helmets without covering were also worn. The 1915 field uniform consisted of a very simple 'blouse' of which the principal characteristic was an edging in the branch colour on the shoulder tabs. The units formerly wearing lace now wore it in grey, but on the collar only. Regulation for officers in the field was the brown officer's belt, and black footwear. At this stage of the war the field cap still had its coloured trimming, but towards the end it was changed to field-grey. The lieutenant shown is decorated with the Iron Cross, 2nd Class (the ribbon on the closing of the tunic), and is wearing his pilot's badge on his breast. (See also 429 and 445.)

428. Great Britain: Royal Flying Corps. Sergeant, 1915

The R.F.C. was formed in 1912, and comprised an army unit, the Military Wing, and a naval unit, the Naval Wing, which latter was hived off late in 1914 as the Royal Naval Air Service. The normal service uniform was established in 1913. The tunic had concealed buttons and was double-breasted. The corps wore khaki for the duration. In 1918 a pale blue uniform for the newly-formed, independent R.A.F. (461) was chosen.

429. Germany: Infantry. Private, 1917

The 1915 model service or field tunic replaced the 1910 model in the German army. The trousers were now slate-grey and without trimming and the boots blacked. Puttees were widely used in trench warfare as a result of enemy influence. The spike on the helmet was not worn at the front after 1915, and the number on the cover was dark green, or was done away with altogether. Meanwhile the leather helmet and its substitutes, the felt or sheet-iron helmet proved inadequate protection against shrapnel. In trench warfare, moreover, edged infantry trenching-tools were used as weapons, so in 1915 a steel helmet was issued.

Within a short time, and though not in fact officially introduced, it was being worn by the entire army in the field. Leather equipment was once more blacked, almost certainly because the brown was difficult to maintain. Trench warfare resulted in various changes in the equipment, and increased demand for ammunition led to extra cartridge belts, worn round the neck or over the shoulders. The introduction of poison gas in 1915 required further equipment, i.e. the gas mask (446).

430. France: Infantry. Private, 1917

The stern realities of war compelled the French authorities to introduce a field uniform to replace the blue and red before the end of 1914. The cut of the uniform worn by the ranks was not significantly changed, however. The colour was blue-grey, or horizon-blue, a shade already tested before 1912, and now chosen almost certainly as providing the most evident contrast to the German field-grey. Puttees were introduced instead of leather leggings. The leather equipment was intended to be brown, but black remained in use for a considerable period (437). In 1915 a steel helmet was introduced, for which the model was undoubtedly the Parisian fire-brigade helmet, with an ancestry extending back to the engineers of the Imperial Guard in Napoleon's time. The horizon-blue uniform never came into full use with the chasseur troops, who all wore blue uniforms and blacked steel helmets until the end of the war. Colonial troops, the Zouaves included, wore khaki uniforms (456).

431. Austria-Hungary: Infantry. Private, 1917

Production of field uniforms made of German material or in the German colour had commenced by 1915 in Austria. The Austrian style was maintained, but in 1917 the tunic was fitted with a turn-down collar with the regimental colour reduced to a small stripe on either side of it. A waterproof 'target' on the shoulder straps carried the regi-

mental number. After the war the Austrian uniforms were more like the German, but in 1933 the army once more adopted uniforms of traditional Austrian style.

432. Great Britain: Infantry. Private, 1917

The most important change in the British uniforms since the outbreak of war in 1914 was the introduction of the steel helmet in 1915. Trench warfare in the British, as in other armies, led to the use of various forms of gumboots, raincoats, fur or leather jackets, and woollen or waterproof hats (462).

433. France: General of Brigade, 1917

The officer's version of the French horizon-blue uniform had a certain British look, with its external pockets. The horizon-blue cap carried no marks of rank, so officers generally wore a coloured cap with indication of rank in gold or silver cord. At the beginning of the war, officers' marks of rank had been generally gold or silver braiding on the lower portion of the sleeve. Only cavalry officers wore epaulettes. Since braid 'rings' proved themselves too conspicuous, they were reduced, on the horizon-blue uniform, to short braid pieces over the cuff on the outside. Since 1871, generals were distinguished by stars on the lower sleeve, when epaulettes were not worn. This system was retained for the horizon-blue uniform, and the stars were introduced also on the cap. Dark blue double stripes on the trousers were also regulation for generals, but they were not in fact invariably worn.

434. U.S.A.: Infantry. Lieutenant-Colonel, 1918

Khaki uniforms in wartime had begun to be used in the American army since 1898, and in 1902 the 'olive-drab' field and service uniform was prescribed. Officers wore the same distinctions as on the blue service uniform on their high collars, but they were now made of bronze-finished metal. Marks of rank were introduced directly onto the shoulder straps. When America entered the First World War in 1917, gas-masks, British type steel helmets and a field cap —called the 'oversea cap'—were introduced. The latter item was edged in the branch colour, and carried badges of rank on the side. Officers adopted the British belt, and the swagger cane, the latter being the dominant fashion after the disappearance of the sabre.

435. Great Britain: Cavalry. Major, 1917

The introduction of the khaki uniform involved the adoption of a tunic with lapels and collar in civilian style, which was available in time for the First World War, and which became the prevailing military fashion. Meanwhile the British officers' belt was copied all over the world. This, the Sam Browne, was called after General Samuel Browne who designed it in the 1860's, and it was accepted during the 1880's for use in connection with functional service dress. The belt was admirably suited for use with all kinds of equipment. When full equipment was carried, both supporting straps could be used (like braces) while on other occasions one strap could be worn over the right shoulder. This latter mode became a form of international characteristic indicating commissioned rank after the First World War (452, 481 and 483). During the war the badges of rank were worn on the lower sleeve, but after the war they were returned officially to the shoulders. Although the cavalry served almost exclusively on foot and in the trenches, i.e. as infantry, they could not be persuaded to abandon their spurs (483).

436. U.S.A.: Infantry. Enlisted man, 1918

The collar badges on the American ranker's uniform consisted of discs of oxidized bronze. The right-hand disc carried the initials 'U.S.', and the left the branch badge, both in relief. With this uniform a cap was prescribed, as worn with the blue uniform (403), but also the 'campaign hat' or 'field hat' (327)—the broad-brimmed felt hat used

since the Civil War. The latter had a cord round the crown in the branch colour, or in gold for officers. Up to 1912 there was only a single fold in the hat, but the four dimples called the 'Montana peak' were introduced that year as well as a stiff brim. At the front the hat was replaced by the 'oversea cap'.

THE WARS OF LIBERATION IN EASTERN EUROPE 1918–1922

The collapse of the three great empires during and after the First World War resulted in the liberation of a number of peoples, and the formation of various independent states. For Russia and Austria, this break-up meant the establishment of Poland and Czecho-Slovakia respectively, as independent countries. Conflict over the Ukraine resulted in war between Poland and the Soviet Union in 1920. Among the consequences of the October Revolution were proclamations of independence by the border states, Esthonia, Latvia, Lithuania and Finland. These countries conducted freedom wars against internal enemies, and against the White Russian army and the Red Army, which lasted more or less until 1922.

437. Poland: The Polish Legion in France. Rifleman, 1919

Polish units were formed in France, Russia and Austria during the First World War with the aim, as far as possible, of fighting for the restoration of Polish independence. This legion wore French horizon-blue uniforms. The four-cornered hat with the white eagle indicated nationality. The shoulder straps also carried the white eagle. Only rifle troops wore green piping, the others having dark blue (449).

438. Czechoslovakia: The Czech Legion in Russia. Cavalry corporal, 1919

Czech deserters and prisoners-of-war were formed into legions in France and Russia during the First World War and fought on several fronts against the Central Powers. This legion wore uniforms made of Russian material. The cavalry adopted red trousers like those worn by Russian hussars before the war, with fur caps of the same type as were worn by the cavalry between 1882 and 1910. Badges of rank were worn enclosed in the shield on the sleeve. The collar patches were crimson for the infantry and bright red for the artillery.

439. The Soviet Union: Red Army. Artillery man, 1919

As a first and interim uniform the Red Army wore red armbands with black inscription as an identification. The red star cockade was regularized in 1918. When, in 1919, the first real uniforms were introduced as great a contrast as possible to the earlier Russian uniforms was sought. The conspicuous pointed cap was of cloth, and the edge could be let down to fasten under the chin, so that the whole formed a complete head-covering (469).

440. The Soviet Union: Red Army. Infantry man, 1919

The blouse-like tunic introduced for the Red Army in 1919 was trimmed in the branch colour. The big star on the cap, on which were the red star and hammer and sickle, was also in this colour. These branch colours were raspberry-red for the infantry, orange for artillery, medium blue for cavalry, black for engineers and pale blue for airmen. Badges of rank, introduced in 1919, consisted of a system of triangles or rectangles arranged on the lower sleeve. In 1922 badges of rank were placed in a patch on the left lower sleeve, above which was a branch badge made of cloth, which latter had been granted in 1920 (470).

441. Finland: White Guard. Private, 1922

The dress of the Finnish army during the freedom war was only provisional, but in 1918 work on the establishment of a uniform for the defence force was begun. In 1919 the main characteristics of the uniform were established, and with the regulations of 1922 the uniforms assumed their final form. These combined functionalism with a neat appearance. With the exception of the cavalry, who had a separate uniform, the main indication of the branch and regiment was the shape of the cuff combined with the shoulder strap piping colour and badge. The badge of this corps of guards was a heraldic vessel. The grey buttons were decorated with the Finnish lion also contained in a wreath on the belt buckle. The steel helmet was of German type, and a fur cap was official for winter wear. The marks of rank for officers were in the form of heraldic roses on the collar. The white brassard with the Finnish arms was only worn for special parade days.

442. Esthonia: Cavalry man, 1922

During the freedom war, the Esthonian uniforms were very varied. Black collars appear to have constituted a form of identification in this period, and were also continued on the uniforms later established. Curiously enough, the cavalry adopted a hussar uniform so like the Russian 1910-style that it seems as though old Russian garments were taken over. Only the cap was of separate conception. Generally speaking the army wore khaki, with steel helmets of the German type.

443. Latvia: Infantry man, 1923

The usual indication of the Latvian army during the liberation war, a red collar patch with a white oblique bar, was transferred to the uniform finally established later. Except that now the patch, as with the upper portion of the cap, was in the branch colour—blue for artillery, orange for cavalry, black for pioneer troops and green for supply. Badges of rank were also worn on the collar patches. The steel helmet was of the French type.

444. Lithuania: Engineer troops. 1st Lieutenant, 1926

When uniforms were authorized for the Lithuanian army after the war of liberation, French styles appear to have provided the model, despite the fact that the basic colour was khaki. The branch

H

241

could be identified by the colour of the piping on collar, sleeve and cap. The branch colour was orange for the infantry, black for artillery, and white for cavalry.

THE SECOND WORLD WAR 1939–1945

The Second World War was fought by the Axis Powers—Germany and Italy, supported by Japan, Finland (briefly), Bulgaria, Croatia, Rumania, Slovakia and Hungary—and the Allies—Great Britain and the Dominions, France, Poland, the Soviet Union, America, Belgium, Denmark, Greece, Holland, Jugoslavia, Norway, and others. The outcome was settled in Europe, but the war was fought on a global scale, except for the American mainland itself. The course of the conflict was complex. In 1939 Germany conquered Poland, which was divided with Russia. In 1940 she occupied Denmark, Norway, Holland and Belgium, and defeated France. In 1941 Germany conquered Jugoslavia and Greece, while the Axis was also supreme in North Africa. The same year, Germany attacked the Soviet Union, occupied the Ukraine and threatened Moscow and Leningrad. Finally, Japan came in the same year and conquered most of the Far East. In 1942, the Red Army halted the German advance in Russia while the Axis was also driven back in North Africa. In 1943 the Allies landed in Italy which withdrew from the war, though the Germans continued their struggle. In 1944 the German troops were virtually driven from the Soviet Union, and the same year the Allies landed in Normandy. With their troops in retreat on all fronts, the Germans were compelled to capitulate early in 1945. In the Far East, Japan capitulated late the same year. Territorial changes following the war left the world much as it is at the present time.

445. Germany: Air Force. Lieutenant (Flying Branch), 1939

The German Luftwaffe (Air Force) was formed in 1935. From the outset, to emphasize its independence and probably as a result of British influence, it adopted uniform of a special colour. Besides the flying tunic or blouse, worn on active service, an airman's jacket, like the army field-tunic but with lapels, was also standard. Later, during the war, the airman's tunic was replaced by a field-tunic like that of the army. N.C.O.s and other ranks wore collars and ties only when off duty. Besides the badges of rank on the shoulders, as in the army (very much as during the First World War), these were also worn on the collar patches in the form of wings and oak leaves. The patches were white for generals, bright red for the anti-aircraft branch, yellow-brown for anti-aircraft warning service, blue for stores and pink for aircraft maintenance/flight engineers. The piping of the collar and shoulder straps was of the same colour as the patch for the other ranks. The band on the sleeve cuff was worn by units carrying on the tradition of a famous squadron.

446. Germany: Infantry man, 1940

At the outbreak of war in 1939, the uniforms of the German army, in their main features, resembled those worn by the 1921 national army, which were in their turn based on the standard First World War uniforms. Braid, formerly the mark of special units, was now characteristic of the whole army. In 1930 a smaller version of the former steel helmet was introduced. When Hitler came to power in 1933 various details of the uniform were changed, though the main effect remained unchanged. The service emblem was moved to above the right-hand pocket, and was also worn as a shield on the left side of the helmet. The matt white belt buckle also bore this badge, with the inscription *Gott mit uns*. The edging of the shoulder tabs, and the narrow bar on the collar lace were in the branch colour. The latter system was introduced in full in the 1915 uniform. In 1939 the infantry wore white, the artillery red, the cavalry gold, pioneers black, signals yellow and supply branch pale blue.

447. Germany: The Navy. Commander, 1939

At the outbreak of war in 1939 the uniforms of the German navy were generally as they had been in the time of the Kaiser. The officer's dagger, following the example of the Russians, was introduced in 1901. In 1934 service emblems were introduced for tunic and cap, while in 1936, on the British pattern, gold braid was adopted for the peak of the cap. A dark blue field cap of the air force pattern was introduced during the war, for use in naval bases and on small ships.

448. Germany: Air Force. Parachute N.C.O., 1940

Formation and training of parachute troop units accompanied the expansion of the German Air Force (the Luftwaffe). When going into action they wore a special helmet and an outer garment later made of camouflage material. The wings on the sleeves of the outer garment are a mark of rank. On the left side of the helmet was the special Luftwaffe emblem without a shield. The Luftwaffe also used steel helmets of the army pattern. The parachute troops wore the yellow collar patch of the air force personnel, and a green band on the right arm with the badge of the unit.

449. Poland: Infantry. Captain, 1939

The main characteristics of the uniforms of the Polish army were established in 1919. The special Polish helmet was introduced in 1936, up to which time French type helmets were worn. The leather equipment worn by the ranks was brown, as were the laced boots worn with puttees. The zigzag stripe on the collar, the special badge of the army, originated with the Polish general's uniform of the Napoleonic period. The infantry wore blue collar patches, the artillery dark green, and the engineers black. The numerically predominant Polish cavalry wore collar patches shaped like small pennons, in a wide variety of colour combinations.

450. Denmark: Infantry man, 1940

In 1903 a grey-green uniform was introduced for the Danish army but in 1911 there was a return to the historic dark blue, with pale blue trousers, for the infantry. In 1915 a uniform of pale grey natural wool material with coloured piping was introduced, and in 1923 a 'yellow-brown', i.e. khaki, uniform. A steady reduction, however, of the allocation for defence had the result that in 1940 the Danish army wore completely obsolete types of uniform, while the newer patterns for economy's sake remained in storage. The oldest item of dress was the coat, which was much the same as in 1864 (339). Grey coats were produced between 1916 and 1923, but were still not in use. The long trousers of the 1915-type uniform had the characteristic turn-ups of the Danish army. Black leather equipment was so abundant that it was intended to be worn also with the 'yellow-brown' uniform when once this began to be used. The steel helmet, designed in 1923, had the army badge at the front in oxidized bronze. Gas-masks were introduced in 1926. The Danish infantry man's trenching tool was the oldest in use at this period, and had been introduced in 1870. The 'selvbek-laedere', i.e. those who provided their own uniforms—officers and others—wore the 1923-type 'yellow-brown' uniform and were thus sharply distinguished from the ranks.

451. Netherlands: Infantry man, 1940

The field-grey uniform introduced in the Netherlands in 1912 remained almost without alteration until 1940. The steel helmet had an oval shield at the front, with the arms of the Netherlands. Edging to collar and cuffs indicated the regiment and branch of the service, in combination with a bronze badge. The branch colour was red for grenadiers, green for light troops, dark blue for infantry and engineers and red for artillery and bridge-building troops. The officers wore badges of rank in the form of stars on their collars, while the N.C.O.s wore (angled) 'stripes' on the lower sleeve. Officers normally carried a short sword in a brown leather scabbard for field duties.

452. Belgium: Infantry. Colonel, 1940

Apart from the introduction in 1930 of tunics with lapels for officers, there had been no noteworthy changes in the Belgium uniforms since 1915. The officers wore badges of rank on their collar patches and the regimental numbers on their shoulder straps. The steel helmets had a lion's head on the front.

453. Norway: Infantry. Private, 1940

In 1912 a 'field-grey' standard uniform was introduced for the Norwegian army as a whole. Ski troops wore fabric skiing caps and fabric leggings. Leather equipment was in natural undyed leather. The adoption of rucksacks rather than packs was noteworthy. In 1935 there was a change, taking the form of the adoption of visible buttons and green edging for the tunic. Nevertheless, the earlier type of uniform remained in use in 1940. The steel helmet was of British type (497).

454. France: 37th Fortress Regiment. Corporal, 1940

Khaki was decreed for the French army in 1935, but with the style unchanged from the previous uniform. Construction of the great fortifications along the Franco-German frontier, the Maginot Line, during the 1930's, resulted in the creation of special garrison regiments, or the conversion of existing units for such duties. Under the regulations of 1937 the garrison regiments were uniformed like the infantry, but with berets with a special badge. In certain regiments the tunic was worn inside the trousers, with a sash worn outside. Under these same regulations the identification colour was madder red. The piping of the shoulder straps, cuffs and trousers was not included in the standard issue, but was provided by the individual regiment, and was worn only on parade. The regiment was decorated with the *Croix de Guerre* by virtue of which the men were permitted to wear a shoulder-loop with a

fouragère or knot in the colour of the decoration ribbon.

455. France: Army of the Air. Captain. 1940

Until 1935 the French air force wore 'horizon-blue' uniforms with orange collar patches. In that year khaki was introduced for the army and the air force adopted a special dark blue uniform. Blue or white collars could be worn with it and white cap covers. The 'number one' cap for parades carried bands of gold braid matching the number on the sleeves. For special ceremonial duties, plaited shoulder pieces in gold cord were worn, and dirks. The branch of the service was indicated by the ground colour of the cap badge, and that of the braid stripes indicated rank: dark-brown for administration, violet for technicians, and wine red for stores and medical personnel.

456. France: 24th Regiment of the Line. Infantry man, 1940

The active service wear of the French infantry man at this period was still the greatcoat. The steel helmet was an improved version of the 1915 design and carried, as did the former, a flaming grenade on the front. Although the garrison troops wore leather equipment of the old type (454) the infantry wore the system established in 1937.

457. Germany: 4th Armoured Regiment. N.C.O., 1940

With the expansion of the German panzer branch a special black uniform was introduced for use in armoured fighting vehicles. The black beret was theoretically only for parades, for wearing over the protective helmet, the latter being worn in the vehicle. For other duties, and for wearing on leave the infantry uniform was worn, but with the identification colour of pink.

458. Germany: Field-Marshal, 1940

The rank of general was distinguished from the ordinary officer's uniform by—in addition to indications of rank on the shoulders—gold buttons, special collar patches, gold lace and edging on the cap (instead of silver) and by wide red stripes on the trousers. The shoulder pieces were of plaited gold and silver lace. Gold on the cap was introduced in 1927. Embroidery on the collar, introduced in 1900, was in 1927 once more used on the red patches that had been done away with in 1915. Wide red trouser stripes had characterized the generals' uniform since 1832. For daily duty a special riding crop could be carried instead of the marshal's baton. Note among the decorations the Iron Cross, 1st Class, on the breast pocket, with the additional decoration to indicate that the Cross was won in both world wars.

459. Italy: Calabria Infantry Brigade. Corporal, 1940

In 1934, an entirely new uniform was introduced for the Italian army. The collar had patches in the traditional brigade colours, including the active-service stars. The shoulder straps carried the branch badge in gilt. Officers and N.C.O.s both wore marks of rank on the lower sleeve. Those for the officers consisted of short braids, the upper with a loop, while the N.C.O.s wore black chevrons. During the war the N.C.O.s' chevrons moved to the upper sleeve, and were worn in smaller form and with the point down. The 1935 model helmet was worn with the plume on the right-hand side in the Bersaglieri units.

460. Italy: Air Force. Captain, 1940

Uniforms with lapels were worn by the Italian air force by the 1920's. Cap and rank markings on the sleeve were similar to those worn by the army from 1934, except that the latter had a flattened loop in the upper stripe instead of a lozenge.

461. Great Britain: Royal Air Force. Sergeant, 1942

The uniform adopted by the Royal Air Force in 1918 was pale blue, with gilt buttons and with rank indicated by gold braid. In 1919, however, the grey-blue 'Air Force blue' which has since characterized this branch was adopted, and at the same time the rank markings became black with pale blue stripes. Originally the uniform of the other ranks was the same as that of the army, and so included a high collar, but in 1936 the ranks began to wear tunics with lapels, and shirt with collar and tie. On the outbreak of war in 1939, the lapelled tunic was regulation for all duties, but under army influence a uniform including a blouse, called 'battle dress' was introduced. In its original form the tunic had a collar that closed at the neck, but which was always worn open, since the other ranks were issued with neckwear. For the officers the working blouse had a proper lapel, like the ordinary tunic, and in this form became regulation after the war also. The sergeant is an air-gunner and wears a badge consisting of the letters 'AG' in a wreath with a single wing, embroidered over the left breast pocket.

462. Great Britain: Infantry, 1st Corps. Private, 1942

In the Second World War also the British came to dominate military fashion by means of the battledress introduced in 1938, which was copied throughout the world. Even in Germany this type of uniform was standard in 1945. A new type of webbing-pack system, characterized by the large 'universal knapsack' big enough to store clips for the light automatic weapons, was adopted. The British army puttees were replaced by webbing leggings, and steel helmets became deeper. When battledress was introduced it was decided that, in wartime, the uniform should carry no identification, so that troop movements should not be betrayed to possible spies. But such total anonymity also involved disadvantages so 'formation signs', as were used during the First World War, were introduced in 1940. They were made of fabric, and indicated brigade, division, corps, army, etc., and were worn under the 'shoulder title' or 'arm flash' which gave the name of the regiment. Below were one or more 'arm-of-service' stripes, indicating the branch. They could be in a single colour, such as red for the infantry, green for rifle regiments and crimson for medical units; or in two colours, such as red and blue for the artillery, blue and white for signals and yellow and red for armoured units. Pack systems of the earlier types were found side by side with the new; indeed, the home army wore exclusively the quite obsolete system in brown leather.

463. France: The Foreign Legion. Corporal, 1942

Since its formation in 1831 the Foreign Legion wore uniforms like the infantry's, modified for the special conditions under which it operated. It is startling to reflect that at one time the Legion wore great-coats in North Africa under campaign conditions. Under the French uniform orders of 1937 the Legion adopted linen uniforms. The tunic, according to long-standing custom in North Africa, was worn inside the trousers with the official sash worn outside. The green braid and lace were certainly inspired by the green epaulettes which were the badge of the Legion after 1855 and which were still worn for ceremonial purposes. White leather equipment of the earlier type was also worn with this dress. The white cap cover, also characteristic of the Legion, was worn always.

464. Great Britain: Infantry, 8th Army. Private, 1943

On the many fronts of the Second World War, troops wore uniforms appropriate to the conditions. The British army favoured shirt and shorts for the desert war. 'Formation badges' were worn on the shirts, either as a 'slip-on' for the shoulder strap or on a piece of material worn on the sleeve and attached at the shoulder.

465. Germany: Naval Artillery. Senior N.C.O., 1943

By the period of the First World War, the German naval units operating on

land wore army uniforms with various special identifications. Likewise during the Second World War, during which coastal artillery, in particular, wore the army grey-green, but with gilt anchor-buttons and two crossed anchors on the shoulder straps. Gold braid was also worn by N.C.O.s: that on the collar and shoulder straps indicating rank, and the sleeve braid the trade. Field caps resembling skiing caps (*bergmütze*) had earlier been for Alpine troops only but were more widely used during the war. There was also a certain standardization of uniforms during the war. For instance collars and shoulder straps were no longer made of dark green material, but, as with the former slate-grey trousers, were the same colour as the active-service tunic.

466. Germany: Air Reporting Service. Auxiliary, 1944

In 1940 the German forces began to enrol women for auxiliary and similar duties, the *blitzmädel* as they were called. In the Luftwaffe, for instance, many of the Air Operations personnel consisted of women. Their service uniform was an adaptation of the respective branch uniform. Originally they wore the service cap but ski-caps were also worn. In the Luftwaffe, the reporting service badge was worn on the sleeve and the badge of the Luftwaffe itself on the breast. Women did not wear the marks of rank of the armed services, but adopted a system of chevrons on the left upper sleeve.

467. Germany: Afrika Korps. Infantry man, 1943

A special dress was originally adopted by the Afrika Korps: service tunic and breeches in khaki linen. The tunic, worn open at the neck, had braid on the collar and dark green shoulder straps made of material, and edged in the branch colour. The footgear consisted of knee-length, laced boots, in brown. The leather equipment and helmet was as worn by the home forces. During the war the uniform was simplified.

468. Italy: African Rifles (Cacciatori d'Africa). Private, 1939

The 1934 pattern uniform for the Italian colonial troops was in khaki linen with detachable collar patches and cloth shoulder straps. The plaited white shoulder cord was for ceremonial and parade duty. The Italian askaris, also, wore khaki uniforms made of linen.

469. The Soviet Union: Field Artillery. 1st Lieutenant, 1940

The Soviet artillery adopted black edged with red as an identification colour in 1922. In 1924 rank markings were shifted from the sleeve to the collar, and the large star, formerly worn over them, was abandoned. The triangles and rectangles themselves were enamelled in red. A system of chevrons on the sleeve was added in 1935, and was revised in 1940. The greatcoat with visible buttons was adopted in 1935 for officers, and the same year the star belt-buckle was adopted for the 1932-pattern belt (of Sam Browne type). The pointed cap was entirely displaced as a winter garment by the fur cap in 1940.

470. The Soviet Union. Infantry man, 1943

In 1922 the Russian tunic had a turn-down shirt collar, and in 1924 the trimming on the chest was done away with, being replaced by front pockets. In 1943 a high collar was adopted, with shoulder straps edged in the branch colour. French type steel helmets, which were previously worn, were replaced in about 1940 with a special type. A special pack suspension system, a combination of leather and webbing, was also developed.

471. The Soviet Union: Administrative Service. Sergeant, 1943

Uniforms for women in the Red Army were adopted in 1941. Collar patches were discontinued in 1943, when shoulder straps became official. The rank markings for N.C.O.s consisted of lace bars across the shoulder straps. Irrespective of the branch colour, they were in red

braid for active service, and in gold braid in peacetime.

472. The Soviet Union: Air Marshal, 1943

About 1930 headgear in the traditional Russian peaked cap form began to oust the pointed cap in the Red Army. A winged badge was adopted on the crown of the peaked cap in the Red Air Force in 1940. In 1943 there was a considerable change in the entire uniform system. Collar and sleeve rank marks were replaced by shoulder boards like those of Czarist times. The turn-down collar was replaced by a high one, and parade or ceremonial uniforms were to a great extent adopted. The branch colours were located on the shoulder boards under the gold braid, and appeared on the cap and—on the parade uniform—on cuffs and collar. The wide stripes on the trousers had already been introduced for generals in 1940. Uniforms of marshals and generals were very Czarist in style. Thus collar and cuffs were adorned with gold braid very like that worn before 1914. Gold embroidery on the cap front was a novelty for marshals and generals. Gold-cord chinstraps came in in 1940. Parade uniforms for marshals and generals were grey, and those of air-marshals and air-force generals were distinguished by the blue branch colour. In 1945 a big step was taken, in that marshals and generals adopted the same green colour as had been used under the Czar, and with red edging, gold embroidery and gilt buttons. After tunics with lapels were introduced in 1949, these field-rank officers went on in 1955 to adopt uniforms in dark blue throughout, but with the latter details in pale blue and gold. The air marshal, like all officers of this rank, is wearing the marshal's star on his collar. The stars on his chest represent the Suvorov, Kutuzov, Alexander Nevsky and Red Star Orders. The red band contains the Order of Lenin and the Order of the Red Flag, while over these decorations is the Golden Star indicating that this officer is also an honorary Hero of the Soviet Union.

473. Germany: Waffen SS. Lieutenant, 1943

The special Waffen SS corps formed on the initiative of Hitler and attached to the German army in wartime, fighting side by side with it, was formed into divisions covering all branches. The latter were identified by roughly the same colours as in the army. The Waffen SS also wore army uniform, but with collar patches with marks of rank as in the political *Algemeine* SS. The right collar patch carried the SS emblems (runes). The shoulder straps were black, and the emblem was worn on the left sleeve. The peaked cap or *schirmmütze* had a black velvet band carrying a death's head under the emblem on the front of the crown. Besides the rank markings on the collar the Waffen SS also wore army indications of rank. The belt-buckle carried the emblem and the inscription *Meine Ehre heisst Treue*. Among the decorations note the Knight's Cross of the Iron Cross and First Class, as well as the German Cross in gold. Volunteers from the Scandinavian countries generally served in the ranks of the Waffen SS, while other volunteers served in special legions in the army.

474. Hungary: Hussar Regiment. Hussar, 1940

The uniform of the Hungarian army was established in 1922. A special characteristic of the army was the collar patch, surrounded by Hungarian and hussar-style frogging. Collar patch and shoulder straps were in the branch colours, green for infantry, red for artillery, dark blue for armoured troops and black for the medical branch. The entire Hungarian cavalry consisted of hussars. Both officers and N.C.O.s wore badges of rank on the collar patches. The steel helmets were German.

475. Rumania: Infantry man, 1940

Though there was no change in cut or identification colours, the uniforms of the Rumanian army became khaki in 1921 (424). In 1931 certain changes were introduced: for instance the steel helmet was adopted, of national type, with the crowned royal initials at the front.

476. Finland: Infantry man, 1940

Khaki was decided upon for the Finnish army in 1927, but in 1936 grey uniforms were again adopted. On the collar patches, which were in the branch colour, badges of rank were worn. The shoulder straps, edged in the branch colour, carried also the branch or regimental badge. As in the Norwegian army, rucksacks were worn. In summer, as illustrated, linen tunics were worn, and in winter garments of stouter material over which were worn white camouflage. The steel helmet was German in type.

477. Croatia: Bosnian Infantry. Corporal, 1943

As happened during the vast upheaval of the First World War, new states and governments in exile were set up during the Second World War, and their volunteer units fought on all fronts. While the troops of governments in exile tried to maintain their traditional uniform to the last, the armies of the new states generally wanted to break with an often-detested past. In the beginning the Croatian army was dressed in remnants from the Jugoslavian stores, sometimes dyed and fitted with new badges. The Bosnian infantry, wearing fezzes and peculiar trousers, was a special branch also represented in the old Austro-Hungarian army. The badges of rank were according to the old Austrian system, with the exception that the stars were replaced by a Croatian symbol, the trefoil.

478. Slovakia: Infantry man, 1942

During the Second World War the Slovakians generally wore Czech uniforms with certain national modifications. On the Czech 1934-type helmet was painted the special defence emblem, the Slovakian double-cross, above a blue line.

479. Italian Social Republic: Parachute Section. Private, 1944

The armed forces of the republic set up by Mussolini in Northern Italy in 1943, at first wore the earlier uniform, only with the active service star replaced by the defence badge, an antique dagger on a spray of leaves. When new uniforms were produced, the basic colour was reddish brown. A special design of uniform was adopted for the parachute unit of the Republican National Guard, which was included as part of the army. The tunic had no collar or lapels, the yoke formed the flaps of the chest pockets and the uniform fastened with a band at wrists and ankles. The patch in the collar position carried the parachute-unit badge, an antique dagger on a wing with a double 'M' monogram below. Black shirt and tie could also be worn. The dark blue beret was a sort of special indication of the defence forces.

480. Germany: Don Cossack Division. N.C.O., 1944

A number of Cossacks served in the Second World War as volunteers in the ranks of the German army. Although most volunteers generally had to be content with an armorial shield in their national colours on the sleeve of the normal *wehrmacht* uniform, the Cossacks managed to set their own stamp on the uniform. With the German tunic, they wore their characteristic fur caps and dark blue trousers with the traditional wide stripes. The cockade of the fur cap had the same colour as the shield on the sleeve, and the cap crown matched the trouser stripes. Siberian Cossacks had shields in yellow and blue. Caucasian Cossacks wore a special type of uniform (414).

481. Jugoslavia: Captain on General Staff, 1941

The Jugoslavian army maintained the Serbian tradition in uniforms. The officer's cap, a stiffer version of the service cap (416) originally had a somewhat more projecting peak. Collar patches and edging were in the branch colour— red for infantry, blue for cavalry, black for artillery and green for supply.

482. Greece: Infantry. Lance-corporal, 1940

Only small changes had taken place in the Greek army uniforms, since the introduction of khaki in 1912. The *evzones* adopted a khaki-coloured tunic, similar in design to the blue formerly the field uniform (392), but with a row of buttons and turn-down collar with red patch. Stockings, too, were khaki, but the fez remained red, and the shoes with the large pompons were retained. Shortly before the start of the war, steel helmets of Greek type replaced the British design hitherto worn. The collar patches were black for the artillery and green for cavalry.

483. Great Britain: Field-Marshal, 1944

Whereas ordinary officers had to wear battledress on active service, the higher echelons had more freedom of choice in uniforms. The 'bush-shirt' was worn in hot climates. The red collar patch, called a 'gorget-patch', combined with the red cap-band, was the mark of the general staff. Both details were adopted from the earlier dark blue service uniform. The cap shown here is of the light, linen-crowned type, lacking the gold embroidery on the peak normally worn by generals. Field-marshals were distinguished from generals by a special cap badge consisting of two crossed batons, in addition to the marks of rank.

484. Great Britain: The Parachute Regiment. Parachutist, 1944

In response to the German parachute troops, the formation of British airborne units commenced in 1940. Equipment and clothing were copied from captured German items and, as shown, the British parachutist wore a one-piece garment over his normal uniform like his German counterpart. The helmet, shown here in his hand, had special straps and was free of protruding edges. Following the example of the Tank Regiment, which wore black berets from the time of its formation, other special units adopted berets in various colours. The Glider Regiment wore red berets, like this one, but the best known is the Commandos' green beret. In 1943 a type of beret was prescribed for the whole army, but the issue for the other ranks was so unsightly and uncomfortable to wear that it never became popular.

485. U.S.A.: Parachute Infantry. Parachutist, 1944

In America an experimental formation of parachute troops was established in 1940. The success of the German parachute troops during the Second World War led to the formation of airborne divisions in 1942. The American paratroopers did not wear battledress tunics, but a form of windcheater made of proofed material. Both tunic and trousers were well supplied with pockets to carry the multifarious equipment needed.

486. U.S.A.: Infantry. Enlisted man, 1944

The American infantry man was, in all probability, the best-equipped soldier of the Second World War. The American-type steel helmet has since been worn all round the world. The American version of battledress before the end of the war was being displaced by a camp uniform consisting of tunic and trousers made of light, proofed material, which was to prove itself much superior to the former. The long leggings were replaced during the war by high laced boots. The large container was for the gas mask.

487. Great Britain: Infantry man in jungle dress, 1945

The very special conditions of jungle warfare resulted in the adoption by British troops of a linen uniform in special 'jungle green' during the Second World War. All webbing matched the uniform as closely as possible and all metal parts were blackened. The old-style bush-hat was widely worn once more. The regimental badges were worn on the shoulder straps and the formation badge on the brim of the hat or the arm.

488. Japan: Major of Cavalry and Infantry man, 1943

The Japanese army wore khaki after the Russo-Japanese War. Up to 1935 there was otherwise no great change in the uniforms, but subsequently various changes took place under the influence of wartime experience during the conflict with China in the late 1930's. The small peaked cap, which was to stand the test in the Pacific and jungle wars, and later to be copied all over the world, was introduced. The marks of rank on the shoulders, earlier taking the form of transverse blank shoulder strips, were moved to the collar after 1939. The system of braiding and stars was retained, while the basic colour was red in all cases. The branch could be identified by the colour of an approximately M-shaped fabric badge above the right breast pocket, and on the edge of the officers' cuffs. The colour was red for the infantry, yellow for the artillery, green for cavalry, brown for the engineers, dark blue for supply and pale blue for air-force personnel. Various officers still wore the old Japanese sword, which was usually an heirloom with religious associations. Linen uniforms were worn in hot weather, but for jungle warfare the Japanese often wore merely a loincloth and linen cap.

489. U.S.A.: Naval Aviation. Lieutenant, 1944

When the dark blue naval officer's uniform was found unsuitable for the Air Corps, the American naval airmen were supplied in 1917 with a khaki summer dress and green winter uniform. Both carried badges of rank on the shoulders. In 1922 these were changed to black stripes on the sleeve and at the same time the tunic was given lapels. The original breeches of the flying corps, worn with leather leggings in brown, were replaced in 1937 by ordinary long trousers.

490. Great Britain: Queen Alexandra's Imperial Military Nursing Service. Lieutenant, 1945

Today, *The Queen Alexandra's Royal Army Nursing Corps.* This corps was formed in 1902, to replace the 1881-established army nursing service. When on nursing duties, members of the corps wore blue or white uniforms, with white nurse's caps and red capes. Badges of rank, like army badges, were also worn on the cape. The tropical uniform included red shoulder straps with badges of rank.

491. U.S.A.: Infantry man in jungle uniform, 1944

Uniforms of camouflage material were not worn only in the jungle during the Second World War. They were worn on almost all fronts, usually in the form of special outer garments. Colours varied according to the terrain and the time of year. Equipment as well as uniforms were camouflaged. Special camouflage units were formed at the bases, responsible for ensuring that all equipment to be used in action was properly camouflaged. Leaves were worn in the helmet netting, to merge the outline of the helmet with its surroundings. The face-net was not so much for protection against mosquitoes as to provide further camouflage at a distance. When the net was not worn, special camouflage 'make-up' was used.

492. U.S.A.: U.S.M.C. Women Marines. Top Sergeant, 1944

Today, the *U.S. Marine Corps Women's Reserve*. This female corps was formed in 1918, and recalled to the colours in 1943. The usual uniform was green like that of the naval airmen (489). The white uniform was worn in summer. White gloves and shoes were prescribed for ceremonial occasions only. The badges of rank were as in the corps of marines. In 1952 the uniforms of the women's reserve was revised.

THE UNITED NATIONS TROOPS SINCE 1950

On several occasions since the Second World War, United Nations has requested members to contribute to 'peace-keeping forces', for instance in Korea, in 1950–1953, in Gaza, the Congo and in Cyprus.

493. Great Britain: The Argyll and Sutherland Highlanders. Officer of the Korea Force, 1950

Although the kilt was worn with a form of apron or outer skirt in khaki during the First World War, during the Second World War it disappeared from the active-service uniform. The Highlanders were thus only distinguishable by small details. One of these was the tam-o-shanter cap, and in fact a war version of the headgear of the 'no. 1' uniform worn by Highland regiments since 1947. Likewise the red garter flashes and the small knife in the stocking, the *sgian dhu*—both the final vestiges of the colourful Highland dress. They were inconspicuous enough to be worn in combination with the sober field-uniform required by the tough fighting in Korea (383 and 509).

494. U.S.A.: Light Artillery. Officer of Korea Force, 1950

Tough fighting conditions during the winter in Korea made considerable demands on the clothing of the troops. Experience from the Second World War was put to use, and field uniforms quite different from anything worn hitherto were developed. The Americans found that green shades were more effective than brown, and they replaced cloth with lightweight proofed material. Scarves in the branch colour were adopted at the end of the Second World War.

495. India: Military Police. Lance-corporal of Gaza Force, 1958

White, pipeclayed webbing equipment and anklets for military police spread from Britain all over the world. This lance-corporal suggests a member of the British forces in other ways also: his battledress tunic with the collar done up, and the well-pressed trousers, for instance. The latter hardly overlap the anklets, and the boots are a product of British spit-and-polish. The Indian Army has been unable to forget the *raj*. The

251

arm badge, and the blue turban indicate service under the U.N. The turban is fastened in a way that has become the fashion in the last few decades, namely with a stiffly protruding fan-shaped portion.

496. Ireland: Infantry. Sergeant bagpiper of the Cyprus Force, 1963

Whether the bagpipes as an instrument are of Scottish or Irish origin is uncertain. The Irish army nevertheless adopted bagpipers as representing an ancient Irish tradition, and dressed them in kilts of the old Gaelic saffron colour. The combination of green and saffron, as in the piper's stockings, is typically Irish. The large shoe-buckles are very ornamental. Similarly dressed pipers are also found in the Irish Guards, and in the Northern Ireland regiments in the British army.

497. Norway: Infantry man of Gaza Force, 1961

Service abroad, and under very different climatic conditions from those at home, required certain modifications in the dress of the Scandinavian troops. The Norwegians wore the summer-dress as prescribed in the uniform regulations of 1957. Immediately after the Second World War the Norwegian army adopted British-style khaki battledress. Under the regulations mentioned, however, an olive-green field dress and webbing equipment was prescribed for active service. The blue helmet was worn by all the U.N. forces. The strip over the shield on the left sleeve carries the word 'Norway'.

498. Denmark: Infantry man of Gaza Force, 1958

A lighter uniform, additional to the battledress worn at home, was also provided for the Danish forces serving under the U.N. Shorts were worn, with a shirt, and a light, comfortable off-duty uniform made of linen was prescribed. In 1958, a linen tunic with concealed buttons was adopted, with a pale blue peaked cap in addition to helmet and beret. The tunic carries on its collar the badge of the regiment of origin, with the company

indicated on the shoulder straps. The U.N. badge is worn on the right sleeve.

499. Sweden: Infantry man of Gaza Force, 1961

In 1962 Swedish uniform regulations included, probably for the first time, details concerning special tropical uniform, 1961-pattern. Long trousers were included, as well as shorts—likewise a tunic and peaked cap. While Denmark and Norway used their flags in a shield as nationality badge, the Swedes adopted the national 'three crowns' emblem. Above is the inscription 'Sverige'.

500. Nigeria: Infantry. Sergeant of Congo Force, 1963

Khaki has so far dominated the field uniforms of the new national states of Africa, but the jungle-green uniform is becoming popular. As in the British army, this sergeant is wearing a sash over the shoulder for normal duties and parades. The regimental plume is also worn with the U.N. cap.

CONTEMPORARY GUARD UNITS, ETC.

The need for convenience and functionalism in uniforms resulted in the exclusion of all colour and decoration. Certain countries, however, have retained their traditional and more colourful uniforms for use by military units which have a certain ceremonial function as well as a purely military one. More colourful uniforms are also beginning to be used by countries which once entirely did away with them, or where they never existed, in this instance for purely representative purposes.

501. Finland: The Cadet School. Army Cadet, 1965

For ceremonial purposes the Finnish cadets still wear the 1922 dark blue formal uniform. This uniform, in the Finnish national colours, blue and white, also bears signs of a certain Czarist Russian influence. For instance, the sash, which has no tassels, and which is fastened at the front with a transverse loop. The shoulder straps carry the badge of the cadet school, the Finnish lion against a rising sun.

502. Norway: His Majesty's Royal Guard. Guardsman, 1958

This unit was formed in 1856 as a Norwegian guards company for the king of Sweden and Norway. Until 1888 it was on garrison duty in Stockholm but in that year it was transferred to Christiania, i.e. Oslo. The uniform is the same as when it was specially introduced for the guard in 1860. The hat plume was replaced, from 1864 to 1868 by a wide, dark green cock's feather. The cockade at the front carries the king's crowned monogram, while the buttons are decorated with the Norwegian lion.

503. Denmark: Royal Life Guard. Guardsman, 1965

Formed in 1658, during the siege of Copenhagen, this unit has a guard-duty and ceremonial uniform that bears evidence of its long life. Its details stem from various periods and have been traditionally retained, but they nonetheless form a harmonious unity today. The bearskin was introduced in 1803, on the French and Austrian model. The sunburst with the national arms in front was introduced in 1842. From the commencement the cap was fitted with a retaining cord, which took its present shape in 1848. The red tunic was introduced in 1855, to commemorate the fact that the regiment had been entitled to wear red uniforms originally. The normal blue tunic was introduced in 1848. In 1842 the guard was permitted to wear the monogram of the reigning king on the shoulder straps. From 1713 the guardsmen have worn silver lace; the lace-trimmed cuffs originate in their present form from 1812; the collar lace from 1840. The white cross-belts were prescribed, in their present form, in 1788, and the silvered shield on the sword belt at the same time. The cartridge pouch on the shoulder belt has been worn from the time of the Scanian war, but its present

form was established in 1806. The sword, booty from the 1st Schleswig War, was prescribed for the guard in 1854. The origin of the sword knot is lost in the mists of antiquity, but this detail was a company badge in the time of Frederick VI at least. The pale blue trousers were prescribed in 1822, while the white stripes were a guards' privilege as early as this. On guard-duty, the unit has always carried the latest type of rifle. The white rifle sling was first used in 1955.

504. Sweden: Royal Life Guards Squadron. Captain, 1954

This unit was formed in 1949 from the Horse Guards Regiment (*Livregimentet til Hest*) which was itself formed by the amalgamation of the Horse Life Guards (*Livgarden til Hest*) formed 1770, with the Guards Dragoon Regiment (*Livregimentets Dragoner*) whose origin goes back to early in the sixteenth century. The squadron perpetuates the uniforms of its two regiments of origin. The helmet originated in the horse guards, whose nickel-plated helmet was introduced in 1879, and who adopted the same style as the Prussian cuirassier helmet in 1900. At the front it carries the Swedish 'three crowns' arms, flanked by lions. For officers the ground-colour is blue enamel. When the two regiments were amalgamated in 1928, the gilt laurel wreath, worn by the Guards Dragoons Regiment on the fronts of their helmets at the Battle of Lund (1676) (see 28), was adopted for the helmets of the horse guards. The white horsehair plume, worn by both regiments, was discontinued in 1932, but has been restored. The tunic, stemming from the horse guards, was introduced in 1895. The Guards Regiment Dragoons wore white collars without lace. In 1932 epaulettes were abolished, since when officers have worn shoulder badges of rank, with the royal initials. The gold sash, 1817 model, was originally the privilege of generals and field officers of the guards regiments, but is now worn by captains and captains-of-horse. The pale blue trousers with the broad stripe originated in the 1850's, but were replaced in 1881 by breeches worn with riding boots.

505. France: Republican Guard (Cavalry Section). Corporal, 1966

This unit was formed in 1802, as a *gendarmerie* unit, and called the Parisian Guard. Its present title and the uniform still worn were adopted in 1870. The helmet is like that of the cuirassiers in 1872, but carries on the front the arms of Paris on a brass plate. The plaited aiguillettes, and the shoulder knots are signs of the *gendarmerie*, to which the guards still belong. The long cuirassier boots, formerly worn, were replaced after the Second World War by ordinary riding boots. For escort duty on motorcycles the same uniform is worn, only with white crash-helmet instead of the cuirassier helmet, and without the sabre. For less important ceremonial duties, medium-blue breeches with wide black stripes are worn.

506. Italy: The Carabinieri. Man, 1961

The origin of the Italian *carabinieri* can be traced back to the Sardinian *carabinieri*, a *gendarmerie*-type corps whose uniforms have hardly changed. Still performing police duties, they now wear various contemporary uniforms, retaining the traditional dress only for ceremonial purposes. The bicorne hat originally considered just the thing for everyday wear, now has a highly ceremonial appearance. The Italian tricolour has been used for the cockade since 1860. The loop on the front of the hat carries a flaming grenade—one of the emblems of the force. The coatee has red turnbacks on the tails, with white grenades on them. Since 1871 the silver-braided collar has carried the active service star, indicating that the *carabinieri* serve with the army. The aiguillettes, as in France, are another mark of the *gendarmerie*. It has been customary since the Second World War to wear the shoulder belt buckle and fittings—normally worn at the back—at the front. The sabre still has a sword knot in Savoy blue. The Papal *gendarmerie*

wear very much the same uniform, except for all-red feathers and a Papal white and yellow cockade in the hat, plus silver braid at cuffs and medium blue trousers with black stripes.

507. West Germany: Artillery lieutenant, 1966

When the West German defence force was to be uniformed in the middle of the 1950's, understandably enough, a break was desired with memories of the Wehrmacht. The basic colour was grey, and the cut for the field uniform was a notable combination of a double-breasted tunic and a battledress blouse. For off-duty wear, a very civilian-looking double-breasted jacket was chosen. When, however, the People's Democratic Republic revived the Wehrmacht uniform traditions, West Germany ventured to smarten its uniforms somewhat. The service uniform once more had a tunic, but with lapels, collar patches in the branch colour, and silver lace. A social or formal uniform without external pockets, and with darker trousers has also been introduced. For special functions a ceremonial cord, popularly called the *abegyngen*, can be worn, resembling that introduced in 1927.

508. Netherlands: Guard Fusilier Regiment 'Prinses Irene'. Officer, 1966

This unit was formed in 1941 by the Netherlands government in Great Britain, and called the Prinses Irene Brigade. In 1948 the unit was promoted to the status of guards regiment, and the same year was allocated the parade or ceremonial uniform illustrated. In memory of the regiment's British associations it was decided to adopt a uniform closely resembling the former British infantry 'full-dress' (401). The helmet, however, was not quite unfamiliar in the Netherlands: such a design had been worn by the Colonial army and the Marines (372). The star at the front is five-pointed to commemorate the badge worn by the Allied invasion force, to which the original unit belonged in 1944. The buttons of the tunic carry the Netherlands lion in relief. Only the upper button on the cuff flap carries the lion, however, the middle one having two crossed cannon barrels and the lower an antique helmet, symbolizing respectively the infantry, artillery and engineers. (The original unit comprised these arms.) The lace on the collar is a mark of the guards in the Netherlands army, while the cuffs are shaped on the British guards model. The retaining cord has, since the 1860's, been a sign of commissioned rank as well as an indication of rank in the Netherlands army. The sash is edged in gold to contrast with the tunic. It has subsequently become more common for the Netherlands drummer or trumpeter corps to wear regimentals from an earlier, more colourful period.

509. Great Britain: Gordon Highlanders. Drum-major, 1958

The question of providing a more colourful uniform than khaki for the ranks in the British army was often considered in the period between the wars. Officers were allowed to wear the old 'full-dress' but not, however, on parade when the other ranks were present. The blue 'no. 1' dress, which was to be re-adopted in 1946, was introduced in 1937. The 'no. 1' was generally dark blue, but rifle regiments, light, and Highland regiments wore green, the latter in a shade called 'Piper green'. The Highlanders did not wear the tunic, but the 'coatee', a short jacket with bottom folds in the regimental colour, and better adapted for wearing with the kilt (which the Highlanders retained in peacetime). Bands and pipers still wore most of the traditional items of equipment. The drum-major is an example: the headdress with huge plume, or the blue tam-o-shanter with pompon worn by this regiment; the plaid on the shoulder, the drummer's sash with the regimental badge, the sword belt with the Highlander broadsword, the plaited bandsman's aiguillette and the gauntlets are all from the traditional uniform. In the new uniform the officer's gold lace-trimmed belt was discontinued, and the decorative ceremonial sporran was replaced by a simpler version. These details are worn by the regimental drum-major to commemorate earlier splendour. Hose and gaiters are retained without alteration.

510. U.S.A.: Military Academy, West Point. Cadet, 1965

The first uniform adopted by West Point at its establishment in 1802, was dark blue, but the now-renowned grey uniform was adopted in 1815. In past years this uniform has changed only slightly. However, in addition to a later dress uniform worn only for ceremonial purposes, the cadets have worn various forms of dress for working, daily use, field use, and summer and winter wear. All these, curiously enough, have been as far as possible in grey, with black distinctions. In 1899 the dress uniform was altered and made to a degree more old-fashioned. The present shako was introduced from earlier patterns, while the waist belt was retained simultaneously with the reintroduction of crossed shoulder belts. The shako carries in front the coat-of-arms established for the academy in 1898. The uniform is now worn only for ceremonial purposes, and the cartridge pouch on the bandoliers is a dummy. Grey trousers with wide black stripes can be worn as well as white trousers.

511. Congo-Brazzaville: Republican Guard. Corporal, 1963

The new African states almost all inherited a number of native regiments from the colonial period, and which have formed the nucleus of the new national armies. As regards uniforming them, each state has attempted to make them nationalistically expressive. Nevertheless, a complete break with the past has proved difficult, and the Republican Guard in Brazzaville has an unmistakeably French appearance. The Guard is mounted—on motor-cycles.

512. Thailand: Royal Palace Guard. Captain, 1965

Western modes of dress have merged with national tradition in a very delightful way in the uniforms of the Royal Palace Guard in Thailand. The black velvet cap is based on local models. On top is a pagoda-like metal point, and in front the crowned royal arms, the mythological 'Garuda' bird. The tunic, however, is clearly European. It fastens like an early buff coat and carries the royal cypher on the collar. The stars on the cuffs are marks of rank. The sash is trimmed with gold as a mark of distinction. The sword is gilded all over and based on ancient Thai examples. The trousers are certainly the most interesting item: in fact they are a loincloth, called a *panungh*, and folded from several metres of Thai silk, with a wide embroidered gold border.

MILITARY TERMINOLOGY

The following glossary deals with expressions and terms in the text which may not be readily understood by the non-specialist. In each case a short general explanation of the meaning is provided. The numbers in brackets refer to the relevant illustrations.

Adjutant. This is a title given to an officer of a regiment or staff who is appointed to assist superior officers mainly for the purpose of communicating orders.

Aiguillette. The aiguillette as worn today is a rich plaited cord of gold or silver ending in two solid metal points—the original 'aiglets' or needles. The first aiguillettes were much shorter and originated in the 'points' on the shoulder of the leather jerkin under the armour and were necessary to secure the metal plates. After the disappearance of armour the vestiges remained as an ornament although they may have been used as a form of knot to keep the sash in position on the shoulder. Later elaborate development produced a complex affair hanging from the shoulder and looping up on the chest (226). Originally a mark of a senior officer they were worn by others as in the case of N.C.O.s in the Household Cavalry. On the continent they are a sign of gendarmerie (506, 511).

Attila. The German word for a type of single breasted tunic worn by hussars (310, 442).

Badges. Badges had been worn on the garments of the retainers of knights and lords during the Middle Ages. Such examples were the Swan of Bohun and the ostrich feather of the Prince of Wales. The kings of England each had their distinctive badge and some may be seen today on the Colours of the Foot Guards. The early cloth caps of grenadiers were also embroidered with badges as well as other devices (42, 48, 82). When metal plates came in use the badge was also to be found and many regiments were granted badges as a special privilege (131). In modern times the regiment or corps to which a soldier belongs is usually indicated by the badge worn on his cap or his collar.

Badges of Rank. See **Rank**, etc.

Bagpipes. These musical instruments though of civil origin provide the martial music in Scottish and Irish regiments (83, 496). Indian and Gurkha regiments have also adopted the bagpipes. The bagpipes can be traced back to ancient Rome and other European nations carry them in their armed forces as in the case of Poland (58) where two different types of bagpipes are still played.

Bandolier. The bandolier of the seventeenth century was a leather belt which went over the left shoulder and was used by the musketeer for carrying the small wooden powder chargers (8, 9). There was also a bullet bag at the lowest point under the right arm. The term bandolier continued in use long after the wooden containers disappeared. The leather cartridge belt which carried cartridges in the Boer War had the same name (384). On the continent the term bandolier also applied to the shoulder-belt which supported the cartridge pouch or side arm (18).

Battledress. The 'battledress' was introduced into the British Army just before the outbreak of the Second World War. Experimental clothing inspired by the ski-suit finalized with a blouse-jacket and trousers which fitted closely round the ankle. At the end of the war the collar was worn open to show the collar and tie (461, 495).

Bearskin cap. This is the fur cap worn by British grenadiers from the eighteenth century onwards. The British Foot Guards still wear the bearskin cap in all regiments for full dress occasions. Many regiments on the continent also had and have their own pattern of cap (112, 149, 189, 236, 504).

Beret. This cloth cap originated in the Basque district of France and was adopted by the Royal Tank Regiment in 1925. In the Second World War a green beret was worn by commandos and a red beret by parachutists (484) and eventually a light blue beret was worn by airborne troops. The light blue beret is now a distinguishing feature of U.N.O. forces (499, 500).

Blitzkrieg. A modern German word meaning a 'lightning war' created to apply to modern warfare but also used for earlier times.

Braid. This is the woven material (also tape) used from the sixteenth century to strengthen edges, seams and button holes of a garment. For the common soldier the braid was woollen or cotton, with, later, a coloured stripe or elaborate pattern. The officers had a silver or gold flat 'lace' also known as 'braid'.

Breeches. These were the common nether garments worn by civilian and soldier alike. Coming up to the waist, they reached down to the knees buttoning at the sides or fastening with small buckles (128, 130, 131). See also 'overalls' and 'trousers'.

Buff coat. This body garment was made of buff leather, a process which made the skin soft and pliable (15). The colour 'buff' also derives from the light colour of the finished skin. This coat (or jerkin) was worn under the cuirass, leather being able to stand up to the hard metal better than cloth.

Bush hat. The broad-brimmed hat is similar in material to the old slouch hat of the Boer War period (384) but as it was used in the 'bush' of the Second World War it received a new name. It also had a characteristic dent on top and the brim turned up at the side where it was frequently ornamented with a cloth unit or formation sign.

Bush Shirt. This garment also was worn in warm climates during the Second World War. It was worn with the 'tails' either in or out of the trousers. It was cut like a tunic, buttoned down the front and had pockets on the hips, which did not make for comfort when worn inside the shorts (464).

Busseroon. The continental name for the sailor's blouse or shirt made of linen or drill (426).

Camisole. Continental word for undercoat or long waistcoat worn in the eighteenth century.

Camouflage. A French word originating in the First World War but now widely used to cover all methods for disguising or hiding.

Campaign hat. The American name for a broad-brimmed field hat, used in the Civil War (327) and later ordered for the whole army (436).

Cantinière. A woman who carried a canteen or a receptacle for holding spirits. In several continental armies (specially the French) women accompanied the troops to the battlefield to administer drink and give such help as was possible to wounded and distressed soldiers (203, 308, 333). The introduction of such a person was not part of a British regimental practice.

Carbine. A shortened musket originally carried by carabiniers on horseback but later the weapon was carried by infantry men.

Cartouche. A small pouch on the shoulder belt of cavalry and mounted officers.

Cartridge. This originally was a method to combine both the round musket ball and the gunpowder into a single charge by means of a piece of cartridge paper. In the twentieth century a brass cartridge case was used instead of the paper holder.

Casque. French word for helmet (9, 15, 430).

Casquet. A continental term to indicate a peaked shako.

Chaco. Chako, chakot. See **Shako.**

Chapka. Shapka, schapska, tschapka. See **Lance cap.**

Chevron. Originally an heraldic charge but in the early nineteenth century an angled mark was used to denote an N.C.O. See **Rank Markings**. Chevrons were also used in the British Army to denote long service.

Coat. The term 'coat' covers a wide variety of sleeved body garments and is not limited to one special type.

Cockade. In early days a bunch of ribbons was worn on the headdress, reminiscent of a cock's comb, in the national (or other distinguishing) colours. Later the cockade developed into an elaborate pleated affair or even a piece of pressed leather. Other nations had cockades of metal on the headdress, in the case of Germany, two, one for Prussia and the other for other state or kingdom.

Cocked hat. The brim of the original hat was liable to droop in rain and the hat to become misshapen in use. Thus it became the fashion to turn up the brim in a variety of ways, first on the side and then on both sides and finally on three sides making a tricorne. There were many varieties of 'cocking' over the years each having elaborate rules.

Couse. This was a type of *glaive* or ornamental blade (the edge of which curved backwards near the point) on a staff carried by certain house guards (109)—a relic of early fighting weapons.

Cravat. This was a cloth which went around the neck. Black was eventually accepted as the practical colour, and being worn over the shirt became the ancestor of the tie. It was replaced by the stock.

Cross. The cross being used by military forces since the Crusades frequently appears throughout the centuries on uniforms and flags of many countries. The white saltire of St. Andrew is not only seen in Scottish uniform but also in the old Russian Army. The white cross used in the French Army was not only borne on colours but on uniform (4).

Cuirass. Armour consisting of front and back plates (15) but sometimes only the front plate was worn (61). Worn today by the Life Guards and the Royal Horse Guards.

Dolman. This is the continental word for the body garment of hussars. In England the term 'jacket' sufficed. Whereas the British garment fastened in the normal way the continental pattern fastened on the left (85). The dolman was replaced by the attila in most continental armies after 1850 (q.v.).

Dress uniform. This normally means the full dress uniform as worn on parades and not adapted for fighting (see also **Undress**).

Elite troops. The introduction of special troops such as light companies and light infantry soon proved the use of specially trained men who carried out specialized tasks rather than be employed in the normal weight of a battle attack. To encourage such men they were named elite troops and given distinctive uniforms to encourage their performance in action.

Embellishment. The modern usage of this word covers the extra distinctions added to the normal issue uniform. This embraces coloured hackles, feathers, pompons etc. on the headdresses as well as embroidered patches.

Embroidery. Although the sewing of decoration on grenadiers caps and allied items was popular in the eighteenth century coloured silks and worsted was used and gold and silver thread was used later to distinguish and ornament the clothing of officers. This highly specialized craft was originally carried out by hand but in modern days some badges are embroidered by machinery.

Engineers. The engineer was at one time considered a civilian and was responsible for fortifications, field works and planning. The word is derived from the Latin and meant 'ingenious', thus indicating the cleverness of the individual.

Epaulette. The elaborate gold or silver ornament worn in full dress of the shoulders of officers had a long and complicated development with several influences from different European countries. The French soldier in the late seventeenth century had bunches of ribbon on the point of the shoulders, following the current fashion. These ribbons served to keep the wide sash or baldric on the shoulder. The ribbons or cords were then arranged in a stylized knot and the tasseled ends led to the fringed ends (129). The loose fringes were made rigid or 'boxed' (197) and the officers also had badges here which eventually indicated the rank (q.v.).

Infantry men, like those of the French Army, wore a pair of cotton epaulettes. In Napoleonic times, most grenadiers wore epaulettes usually in red. In modern times units like the French Foreign Legion wore epaulettes but the British infantry man discontinued them at the time of the Crimean War.

Espontoon. Pole-arm carried by officers in the eighteenth century as a sign of rank.

Esquavar. These leggings of continental hussars (85) consisted of a pair of cloth hose worn with short leather breeches. They were not worn in the British Army.

Facings. The military coats in the seventeenth century were faced or lined with a material different from the basic colour of the coat. Thus when the long sleeves were turned back to make cuffs, the different facing colour made a strong contrast as did collars when they appeared. The turnbacks of the skirts to give greater freedom to movement of legs allowed the facings to appear and when the chest opening was favoured the fronts or lapels soon reached a formalised shape. Eventually the collar and cuffs became separated from the lining. A modern version of facings occured in the Second World War when the front of the battle dress blouse was worn open and unofficially the inner lining was given a special facing.

Field cap (also field service cap). A lightweight soft cloth cap of widely varying shapes, mainly intended for undress use. Also known as a 'quarters' cap (355) to be worn in quarters or barracks but also worn elsewhere.

Field mark. To distinguish between opposing parties in the seventeenth century when a common dress was worn, a field mark was chosen. On the day of the battle a piece of white paper might be worn in the hat, a white arm band or a piece of foliage in the headdress. The loss of this mark either accidentally or intentionally could bring safety in anonymity or it may well bring death from one's own side. The oak leaves of the Hanoverian headdress no doubt arose from this practice.

Field officer. In the seventeenth century each company had its captain, lieutenant and ensign and could act as an independent unit. For better administration of regimented companies a senior staff was created consisting of a colonel, lieutenant-colonel and major. These minor staff officers were known as field officers.

Fifers. Although the Parliamentary Army considered the fife as a profane musical instrument and abolished it, Charles II brought the fife back to the British Army. It was usual for each company to have a fifer as well as a drummer. Grouped together these drummers and fifers made the first 'music' attached to a regiment.

Fireworker. This unusual title was given to gentlemen of the Ordnance who were responsible for the gunpowder and for the special fireworks in use in the early part of the eighteenth century. Shells, bombs and rockets all had specially made contents and the fireworks made for great occasions were also produced by the Artillery or Board of Ordnance.

Fleur de lys. The Lily of Ancient France which was borne in the Royal Arms of Britain up to 1801 still has the memory of this association indicated in the drummers' lace of the Foot Guards.

Flintlock. This was a type of musket of which the lock or cock had a flint which striking upon steel produced the spark which ignited the gunpowder.

Flügelmütze. See ***Mirliton.***

Forage cap. Originally an undress cap to be worn on forage or stable duties but in 1829 this name was given to the broad-brimmed peak cap which was worn by many branches of the British Army, including infantry. In the U.S.A. the term means a service cap (325).

Formation sign. Although a formation sign was used in the nineteenth century it was not until the First World War that the formation sign was extensively used more or less as a secret symbol to disguise the exact unit, brigade, division or corps. From vehicle signs the system developed into an elaborate complex of cloth signs to be worn on the clothing, which could indicate division, brigade, battalion and even company of the wearer. They were revived in the Second World War in the British Army and are still in being in many countries throughout the world.

Fouraschka. A Russian field cap (386).

Frock coat. In England, a long blue coat with skirts reaching the knees. In the U.S.A., a coat with shorter skirts (but not so short as the British tunic) is called a frock (327).

Full Dress. A term for the complete parade uniform.

Fusil. Another term for the flintlock of a better type, 'focile' indicates the fire from the flint.

Fustanella. The pleated skirts worn by the Greek Evzone made of white fustian which takes upwards of 40 hours to make the 400 pleats.

Gaiters. Leggings or spatterdashes were introduced at the end of the seventeenth century. With a strap under the instep, they were buttoned up the side to the knee. They were worn with breeches until trousers were introduced.
   Short gaiters had been worn by light infantry men in the eighteenth century and with overalls early in the following century. The Highland regiments which had adopted gaiters about the same time continue to wear these items today in full dress and No. 1 Dress.

Gauntlets. Gloves with stiffened tops worn by cavalry in the eighteenth century were named gauntlets. Drum-majors of infantry and some drummers wear gauntlets today as do French Sappers (509).

Gorget. This crescent-shaped piece of metal was the insignia of an officer on duty. It is the last relic of armour to be worn. The gorget is the neck-piece on which the cuirass rested. When the latter was discontinued the gorget was suspended around the neck by ribbons. From a practical piece of defensive armour the size dwindled down to a small gilt ornamental object. Regiments originally wore gilt or silver gorgets to match the regimental lace but in 1796 all officers were expected to wear a gilt cypher with the Royal Arms. The gorget was discontinued in 1830 in the British Army but certain nations continue the ancient distinction.

Gorget patches. These small cloth patches worn on either side of the collar of staff officers indicate the place where the buttons were fixed to take the ribbons suspending the gorget.

Grenadier. Although hand grenades had been used in the Civil War by Royalist troops, specially trained grenadiers were not attached to all regiments until 1678. As the duty of this new type of soldier was dangerous and called for special qualities it soon became the custom to call on the grenadier company to undertake special attacks and other adventurous tasks. The grenadiers were given distinctive clothing. The coats had special loops to the button holes and because of their more vigorous activities wore a different headdress. It has been said by some that the arm was swung over the head to throw the grenade and that the broad-brimmed hat was knocked off. Other experts say that the grenade was thrown under arm and that the cap was needed when the musket was slung over the head. Although hand grenade drill continued well into the Georgian period, the actual grenade dropped out of use. The term of grenadier continued in use as a special distinction and in fact the First Regiment of Foot Guards were named Grenadiers as an honour after Waterloo.

Grenadier cap. The reason for the grenadier's cap has been discussed above and this cloth cap enabled embroidery to be used (36, 37). In early days both cloth caps and fur-edged caps were worn but the cloth cap developed in England to become the well-known 'mitre cap' of the mid-eighteenth century. On the continent a low fur cap grew into a tall fur cap with a metal plate in front. This pattern was officially adopted into the British Army in 1768. The fur cap continued to develop and change shape until it reached the version worn today by the Foot Guards and the Royal Scots Greys in full dress. Continental patterns vary much from the British pattern (503).

Halberd. Also halbert, halbard. A long-shafted weapon with a large cutting head, axe shaped and also with a point for thrusting. Originating in the Middle Ages it later became a ceremonial weapon (as carried by halbardier guards). In the seventeenth and eighteenth centuries it was the sign of a sergeant of infantry. It was discontinued in 1792 and replaced by the spontoon (q.v.).

Hat. Originating as a civilian headdress with a crown and a brim all round, it developed into a military item. First made of materials varying from leather, coney and felt in a very simple shape it gradually changed into a three-cornered hat (the tricorne q.v.) and then into the bicorne. The round or top hat was the civilian hat of the late eighteenth century which was worn on foreign service. With a fur crest it was very popular with volunteers of the Napoleonic period.

Helmet. Normally considered a metal headdress worn in ancient times but also continued in use for the fighting man in a variety of shapes and latterly also in stiffened leather. The top was ornamented with a wide variety of crest, plumes and fur attachments. In the seventeen-fifties a helmet was introduced for the newly-formed light cavalry and light infantry. By 1812 the heavy cavalry had their own pattern and in 1879 the infantry were authorized a helmet for foreign service use. The helmet in the British Army continued as a ceremonial headdress but during the First World War the introduction of the steel helmet brought back its original protective purpose.

Hessian boots. These special hussar boots which reached just below the knee and had a 'V' notch in front were popular with light cavalry at the end of the eighteenth century and the beginning of the next. They were also worn by infantry officers, in particular rifle officers who copied many hussar points of fashion.

Hoheitsabzeichen. This German word indicates a special emblem of higher formations worn in the Nazi forces by land, sea and air forces. In the main it was a stylized eagle combined with the Swastika and varied in shape for the three services as well as the National Socialist party.

Holster. This was a receptacle for holding a pistol or firearm in front of the saddle. It was covered with a piece of fur or embroidered cloth known as the holster cap.

Hose. In the Middle Ages a pair of hose were virtually the lower garments. Whereas the modern tendency is to think of two separate pieces like stockings, hose on the continent could mean a pair of tight trousers.

Hunting shirt. This garment was popular in North America and although originally a civilian garment (with fringed sleeves, collar, etc.) it was a practical fighting garment (126) and was worn by the early American soldiers in the backwoods.

Hussar. This type of light cavalry man had his origin in the Hungarian soldier who is said to have derived his uniform from the men who guarded cattle. The eagle feather in the headdress was worn as a symbol of their bravery and the fur-lined pelisse had its origin in the wolf which preyed on the herds and when killed its skin was worn as a cloak.

Jacked leather. This was a leather made hard by a process. It was invaluable for the headdress of light infantry and cavalry as well as for the stiff-jacked boots.

Jacket. This term was used mainly for a short coat without any skirts or at the utmost with short tails behind. This short garment was popular with light troops when the normal infantry had long and heavy skirts. The short jacket heavily braided was worn by hussars and horse artillery.

Jerkin. A leather jerkin could be the defence of the common fighting man in the late Middle Ages. It was frequently laced with a leather thong. In Great Britain it was a fairly short garment and much lighter than the long leather coat which usually had deep skirts.

Kaftan **(caftan).** Originally a loose Persian garment but in Russia applied to an open coat of loose fit (100).

Kepi. This is a French headdress, being a low type of shako. In early days the body was soft (318) but later the whole kepi was of stiffened cloth with a patent leather peak (433).

Khaki. Originally a Persian word meaning dust-coloured. The original khaki of the Corps of Guides was a bluish grey but when service drab was introduced, it took over the name of khaki.

Kilt. This typical lower garment of the Scots is made of tartan (or of a saffron colour in the case of the Irish). Originally the whole plaid was belted round the middle so that the lower part wrapped round the legs and the upper part could act as a cloak (83). When separate the kilt was sewn on to a waist band with many pleats at the back and sides (383) and had a fly opening on the right side secured either with rosettes or a blanket pin.

Kittel. This is a type of lightweight tunic for summer wear in the Russian Army (415).

Kiwa **(kiver).** A special shape of shako favoured by the Russians brought back into use just before the First World War.

Koller. German word for a coat of simple form favoured by cavalry men, which fastened down the front with hooks. Usually trimmed with a border on the collar, cuffs and front.

Konfederatka. See **Lancer cap.**

Lace. The term lace in military usage covers braid and other forms of woven gold and silver thread, the manufacturers being known as lace-men.

Lancer cap. The four-sided lancer cap was based on the shapka worn by the Polish Lancers fighting for Napoleon. This cap had its origins in the ancient peasant cap worn by the men of the Cracow district and known as the *konfederatka* (12). Originally it had a soft body with a peak and a four-side flat top. This simple cap was stiffened and ornamented to achieve a most complicated headdress (182, 196).

Lancers. The success of the Polish Lancers in the Napoleonic wars led to the adoption of four Lancer Regiments in the British Army in 1816, the 9th, 12th, 16th, and 23rd. Other nations had lancers regiments before this time. In Germany the term *ulan* was used (q.v.).

Lapel. The turnbacks of the fronts of a coat are now revers or lapels in the material of the coat. In the eighteenth century the turnbacks were made of the facing or lining. They developed into stylized shapes and then into the plastron before being displaced by the simple double-breasted coat in the infantry. Lancers continued the plastron later.

Levee dress. This dress originally intended to be worn at a levee or presentation at palaces such as St. James's Palace, London, was a most elaborate dress. On the continent the gala dress was the equivalent.

Line regiment. These were the normal cavalry or infantry regiments (not guard regiments) which made up the line of battle.

Litewka Originally a garment resembling an overcoat (247) and later in Germany a lighter garment worn indoors as a tunic.

Matchlock. One of the earliest methods of firing a musket was by a piece of burning match (or cord) held in a cock. Pressure on the trigger brought the burning end in contact with the priming powder. The common soldier had his matchlock replaced by the flintlock (q.v.).

Mirliton (also *flügelmütze* or *schackelhue*). This headdress was worn by the hussars of the eighteenth century. It was a tapering cap made of black felt (92). Later it had a wing added, this tapering piece of cloth being lined on the inside with material of the facing colour. The wing was made to wind round the cap thus making it appear all black (85 and 99).

Musician. The first musicians in the army (drummer, trumpeter or fifer) were expected to make field calls or convey signals. The use of the instruments to produce rhythm on the march led to the introduction of simple tunes. The full band of music came about the middle of the eighteenth century, not as a government ruling but permitted at regimental expense.

Musket. A long firearm which covered a variety of locks and originally with a smooth bore barrel. The introduction of grooves to aid the projection of the bullet brought the term 'rifle' as the barrel was rifled.

Musketeer. The common soldier of the seventeenth and eighteenth centuries who carried a musket was known as a musketeer. The term later changed to private or sentinel in England but musketeer was used later abroad.

Net, for helmet. A camouflage net was a device for breaking up the outline of a regularly shaped steel helmet and the introduction of foliage or artificial material deflected or absorbed the light.

No. 1 Dress. Full dress uniform was not restored to the British Army after the First World War but a demand arose for a more ceremonial dress than the battle dress. The red coat did not return to line troops but experiments in blue and green brought about a suitable dress later called No. 1 Dress.

Opanker. This distinctive peasant footwear of Southern Europe was worn by the Slovakian troops in the Austrian Army (920). This footwear was worn in modern times by the Serbians in the First World War (416).

Overalls. These are the nether garments which went over the breeches and gaiters. These frequently buttoned down the sides. They were replaced by trousers.

Overseas cap. An American type of service cap (434).

Panzer. This German word originally referred to the armour of a person but now has become the word to indicate armoured fighting vehicles.

Papachka. Russian name for the fur cap of Cossack pattern. The early pattern (305) was not so practical as the later development (414) which is better known.

Partisan (partizan). This staved weapon had a sharp broad blade intended for thrusting. Later it became the weapon of an infantry officer.

Patrontache. A cartridge pouch.

Pelisse. This is the name given to the top garment once worn by hussars in full dress. The first hussars came from the Hungarian horsemen who wore a wolfskin over his shoulders. The fur skin or 'pelz' became known as the pelisse—now a short jacket edged with fur and heavily braided (62, 85). This was the hussars' 'overcoat'.

Percussion arm. The percussion lock replaced the flintlock. A small cap containing fulminate of mercury was struck by the cock and the resulting explosion through the touch-hole set off the main charge.

Peruke. A wig worn in the first quarter of the eighteenth century. It had a long tail behind.

Picker. A small pin or piece of wire suspended from the belt and used to clean the touch-hole of a firearm (78, 128).

Pigtail. The hair at the back of the head was bound into a tail with ribbons. To make a more imposing length, a false queue was sometimes added.

Pike. A long version of the spear. In the British Army the pike was to be 18 feet long, the better to repel charges of cavalry or infantry. For easy handling it was common for the pikeman to cut the length down with his sword. As a fighting weapon it was discontinued in the reign of Queen Anne.

Pioneer. In the eighteenth century each company of infantry had a pioneer who was expected to march at the head of the regiment and clear the way for those who followed. These men carried axes and wore stout aprons. Later they became qualified carpenters. In the German army the title was *zimmerman*. The French used the word *pionier*, said to have come from *pion*, *pedone* or *pedis* meaning 'foot'. The Spanish word *peon* not only indicated a foot soldier but also a labourer which is closer to their duties. Pioneers were also permitted to wear beards, as in warfare their task was considered more arduous.

Plastron. The name given to the broad piece of cloth worn on the front of a lancers' coat or on that of an infantry officer. This segment developed from the lining turned back as lapels (317, 373).

Pogoni. This is the Russian term for the shoulder markings of an officer (414, 472).

Polrock. This long-skirted frock coat had hussar braiding on the chest and sleeves (258). Derived from *pol*, Polish and *rock*, German for coat.

Pompon. French word for the woollen tuft on the headdress, in a variety of shapes.

Port-epée. French for sword-knot, to carry the sword from the wrist.

Powder charger. The small wooden bottle containing powder hanging from the bandolier of early musketeers.

Priming horn. A small horn containing gunpowder to prime the touch-hole of a firearm.

Putties (puttees). A leg wrapping which originated in India (369, 384). In Denmark known as *viklers*.

Queue. Name given to long tail tied behind hair in the eighteenth century. Frequently an artificial tube covered in black ribbon with a tuft of hair at the end was added to give the impression of long hair.

Rank badges. In the early days of uniforms, rank was not clearly defined by the clothing. In fact badges of rank did not develop until the end of the eighteenth century when a star and later a crown was added to the strap of the epaulette in Indian and British armies. Combinations of the Crown and Star served to distinguish the grade of regimental officers, while the badge of a sword and baton served to note the various General Officers. British N.C.O.s were granted chevrons in 1806 and other special distinctions developed in the nineteenth century.

Rank markings. Officers' uniforms had no special badges in the early days of development but the richness of the cloth and ornamentation served to mark the distinction. Gold or silver lace and embroidery on the seams and elsewhere distinguished the officer in the early part of the eighteenth century. The introduction of the epaulette allowed the officer a place for his badges of rank (q.v.) but after the Crimean War the badges of rank were placed on the collar. In 1881 the rank badges went back to the shoulder this time of gold or silver cords, or even directly on to the service drab or khaki. Continental armies had different methods of distinguishing the rank of their officers, and N.C.O.s.

Ranker. This is the term for a junior soldier. The common soldier paraded in a company consisting of ranks and files—the ranks going from left to right and the files going from front to rear. Officers were not lined up with the rank and file but took post outside of the fighting mass, thus making a distinction from the ranker.

Reamer. This boring tool carried by the artillery man was used to clear the touch-hole of a cannon.

Regiment. In the sixteenth century infantry were formed into companies or bands of men. When several companies were grouped together they were said to be regimented and extra officers were added to act as a staff.

Rifle. When the barrel of the musket was made with grooves to add a twist to the bullet the barrel was said to have been 'rifled' as opposed to 'smooth-bore'. The twisting movement of the bullet helped to steady the bullet on its flight.

Rosette. This ornament on a hat was held down by a loop and a button. At first it was silk or fabric but later was moulded in black leather. Abroad the cockade served to indicate the national colours but not in Great Britain.

Round hat. This was practically the civilian version of the hat with a narrow brim which was used abroad or on expeditions. It was favoured by volunteers in Napoleonic times. Hats with a large turned up side piece were called Corsican hats.

Sabretache. The Hungarian hussar wore tight trousers which did not permit the use of pockets. Thus he had an attached 'tache' (German for pocket) a kind of bag which hung from the same belt that carried his sabre (90). The flap of this item served as a useful place to display the Royal Cypher or regimental device. It was discontinued in the British Army at the end of Queen Victoria's reign.

Saddlecloth. The aim of this cloth was to prevent the saddle galling the horse's back but it developed into an ornamental trapping. See also **Shabraque**.

Sam Browne belt. This belt of world-wide fame was invented by General Sir Sam Browne who as an Indian cavalry officer lost an arm in battle. He devised a series of straps to secure the sword to the body so that it could be drawn with one arm only, not needing a second hand to hold the scabbard. The shoulder strap supported the waist belt and the slings of the sword were made very short. The same belt was also made to carry the pistol holster.

Sapper. This type of labourer attached to the army was expected to undertake arduous semi-engineering tasks. To 'sap' was to dig a trench towards a besieged place. See also **Pioneer.**

Sash. This was the development of the scarf (q.v.). It was worn by officers but was not so full as the scarf. It was also worn by sergeants, made of cotton or worsted instead of silk and was tied on the left side for infantry.

Scarf. In the days of the seventeenth century uniform had not developed and normal civilian dress was worn. Field marks were worn but a more permanent recognition sign was a scarf in the national colours, French officers wore white scarves and the English wore red, a colour inspired by the red Cross of St. George.

Schapka. See **Lancer cap.**

Shabraque. This is the name given to the original Hungarian saddle cloth. The British hussars who adopted it in the early nineteenth century had a pattern with squared or rounded ends in front and long points at the rear. Embroidered devices indicated both the sovereign and the regiment. Heavy cavalry had a pattern with shorter rear points. The shabraque was discontinued at the end of the nineteenth century except in the case of the Household Cavalry and Staff officers.

Shako. This type of cap developed by the Austrians was taken into wear by the British infantry in the last years of the eighteenth century. Originally of 'stovepipe' pattern, it later developed into many shapes before it was rendered obsolete by the helmet in 1879.

Shoulder cords. When officers' badges of rank were moved from the collar to shoulder in 1881 they were placed on gold (or silver) shoulder cords. These cords worn in full dress are still used with No. 1 Dress.

Shoulder knot. The British cavalry of the mid-eighteenth century had a large shoulder knot behind the shoulder, no doubt indicating a loop to keep a shoulder belt in place but eventually no more than an ornament.

Shoulder straps. These straps were originally added to coats of infantry men in the eighteenth century with the purpose of keeping the shoulder belt in position (27). Later a second strap was added and the colour which had been the same as the coat was changed to the colour of the facing and piped white. In the last full dress the initials, title or badges of the regiment might be placed on the shoulder straps.

Side arms. These were the arms for personal use of the soldier which were carried on belts and hung at the side of the wearer, like a sword, sabre or bayonet.

Spatterdashes. Another name for gaiters. A buttoned protection to keep the lower leg clean from mud and dirt.

Spencer. The name occasionally used to indicate the short jacket worn by the lancer or ulhan.

Spontoon. A spear-like pole-arm carried by company-grade officers of infantry: in the British Army it was carried by infantry sergeants from 1792 to 1830.

Sporran. The name for the Highland purse carried in front of the kilt (which has no pocket).

Stock. The name given to the cloth which went round the soldier's neck in the eighteenth century. It became stiffer and served to keep the soldier's head upright. Later it was made of leather but was very unpopular. Eventually it dwindled in size until it was a small tab inside the collar.

Supervest (or *soubrevest*). A loose over-garment without sleeves which became an ornamental vest rather than a practical garment. It was worn by honour guards.

Surcoat. This was also a loose garment or coat which went over armour and was very popular in the Crusades as a protection against the heat of the sun. It continued in use throughout the Middle Ages and became a coat on which armourial bearings could be displayed—hence *coat-of-arms*.

Swallow's nest (*schwabelnesten*). The pieces of cloth worn on the point of the shoulder by musicians developed into a curved and barred piece of cloth. They were called *schwabelnesten* by the Germans or wings by the British.

Tape. A flat braid used on buttonholes and seams of coats in the eighteenth century. Also worn on the edges of hats (31) for the purpose of strengthening.

Tête du colonne. French for head of the column and referred to the special soldiers (mainly musicians) which led cavalry or infantry in Napoleonic times.

Tjerkeska. Caucasian cossack dress which had distinctive cartridge holders on both sides of the chest (414).

Trabant. These men of a Trabanter Guard were ceremonial troops. The German word *trabant* means 'satellite', the hench man or member of retinue which revolved around a great man.

Tricorne. When the brim of the common hat was turned up on three sides, three corners were made. Although tricorne is of foreign extraction it is now part of the English language (117).

Trousers. These nether garments reached to the ankles (not to the knee as with breeches) and could be worn loose or tight.

Tunic. Originally a long tube-like garment. When it was adopted into the British Army in 1855 it was a coat of medium length with skirts all round the body wrapping over in front, thus affording greater protection than the short waisted cutaway coatees.

U-bot. The German term for 'undersea boat' *(unterseebot)*, in other words a sub-marine.

Ulan. German word for lancer, originating in *oghlani,* the Tatar word for a young nobleman.

Ulanka. A military coat of special cut worn by lancers. It was a tunic with a wide front or plastron.

Undergarments. Usually meaning the waistcoat and breeches. Another word was *smallclothes.*

Undress. An informal dress used by soldiers instead of a parade or review dress. Normally with few trimmings and more comfortably cut garments.

Undress cap. A cap to be worn with undress uniform, varying much in form but usually of cloth.

Vivandière. A woman attached to French troops mainly for the purpose of selling drink and food. See also **Cantinière.**

Waistbelt. The waistbelt served in the seventeenth century to suspend the sword of the common soldier. When the bayonet was introduced it was on the same belt. At the time of the American War the belt was worn over the shoulder and only officers (mainly mounted officers) continued to wear the waistbelt for the sword.

Webbing. Equipment which had been of leather was stiff and difficult to maintain. The strong webbing equipment introduced in 1908 continued to develop and replaced leather.

Wings. These pieces of cloth on the shoulder served to cover the joint when the sleeve-less jacket was worn in the eighteenth century. They became the mark of flank companies like grenadiers (104) and light infantry. Musicians also wore them (509).

INDEX

This is arranged under countries and units, and in date order under those headings. The reference number is that of the illustration and description.